From Struggle to Strength Part-I

A Memoir of Overcoming Crisis

May 5, 2026

To Jackie

May all your struggles become strengths

Thank you for being kind!

Silvia Planas

Silvia Planas Prats

From Struggle to Strength:

A Memoir of Overcoming Crisis

by Silvia Planas Prats

Copyright © 2024 by Silvia Planas Prats

All rights reserved.

ISBN: E-Book: 978-1-966556-02-2
Paperback: 978-1-966556-03-9
Hardcover: 978-1-966556-04-6

Librabry of Congress Reg. # 2024925858

Cover Design by Gerard Feu Planas

Illustrated by Felip Planas Prats

For more information about the author, please visit:
https://kindnessinspectrum.com/author/

Table of Contents

Dedication

To my son, Marc, and to anyone who has a loved one with autism.

I want to share the light that my son and all the people I've met with autism have shown me. I like to call it the *Spectrum Light*.

THANK YOU, MARC.

Thank you for teaching me to speak without words.

Thank you for being so authentic, never lying, never faking.

Thank you for loving your brother Gerard since the day he was born.

Thank you for your giggles with Dad.

Thank you for the challenges.

Thank you for awakening empathy and kindness in me.

Thank you for building my resilience.

Thank you for the many places our family has lived because of you.

Thank you for secretly giving us a life out of the ordinary.

Thank you for the diverse people I've met along the way.

Thank you for the tough times that made me stronger.

Thank you for the suffering that made me feel vulnerable and a work in progress.

Thank you for reducing my ego to humility.

Thank you for the runaways that kept me fit and healthier.

Thank you for pushing us to dismiss some conventional ways.

Thank you for bringing out the best in us.

Thank you for helping us understand that nobody is perfect and that perfection is not something to be pursued.

Thank you for moving me from doubtful to assertive, from planning to doing, from judging to accepting, from crying to fighting, from thinking to speaking up.

Thank you for that permanent smile that lives in you, and that same smile also lives in me.

Above all else, thank you for being you.

Acknowledgment

Throughout these twenty-one years of my life after Marc, I had always entertained the idea of writing a memoir. In my life after Marc, so many events have impacted me so profoundly that, each time, I've had the urge to share them with the people around me at the particular moment—about the people whose paths I've crossed. I'm not talking about friends and family, but about the other group of people who are around us, yet whom we don't consider close. What happened was that, more often than not, after these interactions, we became closer and started sharing a deeper connection.

Being an extroverted person and having the need to connect with others for support and understanding, especially when confronted with crises, I shared my experiences many times with very diverse people.

What struck me was that regardless of the person or the particular challenge I was sharing, there was something common about everyone's reactions: my life stories always stirred some raw emotion in them.

Sometimes, I saw tears in strangers' eyes. Sometimes, they felt sorry for me, or Marc, or for both of us. Other times, the tears came from empathy or emotion. If I shared a small success story, then perhaps the tears were of joy. Sometimes, the tears reflected admiration or wonder. I also experienced faces of total shock, as if I was sharing situations or challenges; they didn't really understand or hadn't known about it's existence.

Some people didn't react right away. Some of them later described how they got shivers or how they shared my story with others once they had processed it. Others immediately related to me because they had also been touched by autism or they knew families who were. Some of these people later reached out to me for support. They understood that I was deeply involved and that Marc's case was one of autism with severe needs, likely more demanding than others who have milder forms of autism.

For one reason or another, most of the people wanted to hear more about autism and my constant struggles, and so the idea of writing a memoir began to take shape.

In 2014, when I founded the MIAMI IS KIND Foundation (now KINDNESS IN SPECTRUM Foundation), I became a more public figure in the autism and disabilities world in Miami. Many moms reached out to me for advice, and the idea of writing a memoir to touch and inspire more people became more compelling by the day.

Writing is something I've always enjoyed, and helping others is my passion, so why not help others through words? I told myself. I read many books on autism and decided there was a niche for this memoir. My approach isn't medical; it's from a mom's perspective—a mom who has researched, sought advice from the best professionals, and has her own credentials and experience as an autism entrepreneur, coach, consultant, speaker, and long-time business executive. With a positive attitude toward life and some successes under my belt, I thought this memoir could inspire others and give them hope. It's not limited to autism but also addresses how to overcome crises of any kind.

For me, fun is a basic ingredient in life, and my son helped me with that because many of the anecdotes we've lived together are entertaining.

This memoir is meant to inspire and entertain a wide audience—from those who are curious to those who enjoy stories of personal growth, perseverance, and overcoming adversity. The idea of having a positive impact on lives across the world was very exciting.

However, I still needed to find that inspirational moment in my life to gather the courage and determination to say, *"Yes! Now, this is a priority! I'm doing it because I believe I can contribute my life, experience, and vision toward something positive and of moral worth."*

Thank you to **Rosa Termes**, without whom this memoir would have never been written. Rosa, my childhood friend, is the person who made it all happen. She, and only she, persevered through three consecutive summers and moved me from the exciting idea of writing a memoir to opening a blank page on my laptop and actually starting to write. Despite being nine hours apart, Rosa has been steadily present at every step of this memoir. She cheered me up when I fell and was the voice urging me forward: "Yes, Silvia, yes. Stop questioning if you should do this or that—just write, write, write, let your story flow, and you will see."

Rosa was and is convinced that this memoir will turn into a movie and touch lives on a bigger scale. I will try to make your vision come true, and if there is a movie, you will be my muse on opening night.

Thank you to **Michelle Adams** for being pivotal in this project. Once I had the first drafts, your extensive knowledge of the publishing industry was key in bringing this memoir to market. Most importantly, thank you for always being supportive, even when I've been demanding or particular about my choices, and for challenging me when your experience told you that some of my first ideas weren't the best. You've earned my trust, and I'll count on you for any future endeavors. Your team has been invaluable, too. Special thanks to **Hosanna Flores**, who made the book shine brighter with her edits, to **Hannah Zechariah**, who backed you up when life was throwing things your way, and to **Claire Winslet**, who has been so sweet and a solid project manager, among many others.

Thank you to **Dr. Amaia Hervás**, Marc's psychiatrist in Terrassa, Barcelona, from the **Mental Health head at Hospital Universitari Mútua de Terrassa**, a pioneer for ASD in Spain and abroad with a long history in research and clinical approaches to this disorder. Only when I met Amaia did I begin to make sense of Marc's condition and how to start helping my son. Amaia, count on me for any contribution I can make to improve the well-being of those with autism in Spain.

Thank you to **Dr Michael Alessandri,** Executive Director **at UM NSU CARD, Center for Autism and related disabilities at the University of Miami**, for your crucial impact on our lives, even before we landed in Miami. As those who live in South Florida know, he is "the man" for autism in that community. Beyond that, he is a uniquely kind person who has always helped Marc. His level of commitment and support to the families is unprecedented.

Seriously, who does have conference calls with an autism mom on the other side of the ocean you have never met when you have so much on your plate already? Yes, a special kind of person, a genuine person with very strong values and ethics.

Michael, count on me for any contribution I can possibly make to improve the well-being of those with autism in South Florida.

Thank you to **Dr. Susan Folstein**, a pioneer in genetic studies of autism and 2010 recipient of the Ming Tsuang Lifetime Achievement Award by the International Society of Psychiatric Genetics and the late founder of the University of Miami Autism Clinic. I will always be grateful to you because your new medication regime and diagnostic recovered Marc from the most severe crisis he ever had. Only a very extraordinary person can accomplish what you did for Marc with an open heart, humility, and kindness out of this world.

Thank you to **Isabel García, former CEO of Parent to Parent of Miami**. Your teachings were invaluable when I was Treasurer at Parent to Parent; you were the best mentor, and your self-made resilience was truly inspiring. Later, as a friend, you helped me come to terms with my reality, and it takes an authentic person to take a parent who is struggling as I was then to accept the excruciating truth, no matter what. I'm in debt with you, so name your wish, and I will be there for you. Thanks to your exceptional Parent organization, a jewel in Miami, I met **Nicole Robinette.** Thank you, **Nicole,** former Education Specialist at Parent to Parent of Miami, for being an angel to Marc and me; with your ongoing support, we achieved all the achievable in our first three months in Miami. Nicole, count on me forever.

Thank you to all of Marc's teachers, like **Olga Carretero, Silvia Torredemer, Miss Acebedo, and Miss Marvis**... and to all the many brave teachers I've been blessed to encounter for giving Marc so much understanding and opportunity. I always advocate for Special Needs teachers. Count on me. You are my heroes.

Thank you to all of Marc's psychologists, therapists, and scientists... from various backgrounds—all exceptionally generous persons who support our children with autism. Thank you to **Ana Miralles, Noemí Balmanya, Laila Raiss, Silvia Rodriguez, Chris Webber, Priscilla Yaniz, Dustin Moraczewski, Carlos Uz**... I will not name you all because the list is so long, I'm in debt to all of you.

Thank you to all **Miami Is Kind** volunteers: **Jacky Acosta, Peggy Slott, Sue, Magaly and "Antman" Hurtado, Flor Kaplan, Begoña Escondrillas, Helga Dienes, Ana Narberhaus, Nuria, Abril and Lola Guerrero, Johana Bonanno, Kathy Valladares, Barbara Diaz, Hannah Brown, Ivahna Gil, Elsa Dominguez, Joseph Paz, Elia Gressin, Maria Bestard...** and every one of you that helped, the list is too long to fit this section. You are the most courageous people, the one who made it all possible at Miami Is Kind Foundation, now Kindness in Spectrum Foundation. You helped put persons with autism to work. We will do it again!

Thank you to all **Miami Is Kind donors**, and a very special thanks to **Tom Whitehurst,** Senior VP of Investments **at Raymond James, and Marie-Ilene Whitehurst,** who were the first to believe in me when I shared my project with them. Marie-Ilene, thank you for the comment you made when we met for the first time I brought some macaroons, still a very basic first homemade version of the pastries. "Silvia, you already did something. You have just arrived in Miami, and you already did something for autism." You empowered me with that comment and the honesty written all over your face when pronouncing those words. I felt valued and welcomed in the community, and that propelled me forward. I'm in awe of your affordable housing communities' work with **Casa Familia**. Count on me in any way I can contribute to your mission.

Thank you to **Shelly Baer** and **Bethany Sands,** my two professors on the **Emerging Transformation Leadership Program at Mailman Center,** for educating me on the history of Disabilities in the U.S. and much more, but especially for giving me the opportunity to connect with great leaders in the Miami disabilities community in my cohort with whom we created the **Miami Employability Movement**. Thank you to **Sandra Ampudia**, Director of Professional Development at **The Discovery Source** and professor at some **Miami-Dade County Universities.**

Sandy has been one of my angels, present in any relevant events in my life since we met. Above everything, Sandy has always been there for Marc, and for that, only I owe her the moon.

Thank you to **Dr. Lydea Ocasio-Stoutenburg**, professor of Special Education at **Penn State University** and author. Lydia, your authenticity made me shiver when I first met you. You have profoundly impacted the way I perceive humanity. Count on me for any advocacy effort you lead. Thank you to **Erin Kozlowski**, Vice President of Development at **Special Olympics Florida**. Erin, you are one of the most assertive women I met. Meeting you helped me develop that wonderful skill; collaborating with Special Olympics is a great pleasure; what a great organization!

Thank you to **Lili de Moya and the de Moya Foundation board for believing in and supporting the Miami Is Kind Foundation. Your mission is my mission, so I am** always ready to collaborate.

Thank you to **Peggy Slot,** a Special Education teacher at **Ruth Owens Kruse.** Your hedgehog attitude to life is inspiring. You found the first kitchen for Miami. Kind, what can I say? You are my hero.

Thank you to **Robbin Matusow and Pedro Diaz**, who led the **JRE Baking Program of the Florida Department of Education**. Thank you both for making it an exceptional program and for your invaluable support at the beginning of Miami Is Kind. It was a privilege to meet and employ many of the young adults who graduated from your program.

Thank you to all Miami Is Kind employees for sharing your light with me. You are all amazing and unique. **Alessandro, Anthony, Catherine, David, Guillermo, Jared, Lauren, Lexus, Markus, Michael, Noel, Yordi...**and all the young adults who stayed with us to all the young adults who did an internship in Miami Is Kind, mainly coming from the Baking Program of the **Dan Marino Foundation.**

Thank you to the **national and international media.**

CNN, CBS, FOX, The Miami Herald, France 24, Ivanhoe, PBS 4, Huffington Post, Telemundo, Univision,WPT, and all the others that I will probably miss. Everytime that the media shares about autism employment, about the abilities of the persons that have autism and about the support that families touched by autism need it's a win for us all, so thank you for picking up our story.

Thank you to the **HistoryMiami Museum a Smithsonian Affiliate** for the partnership with Miami Girls Make History Campaign, led by **Ekaterian Jukowski** Miami Girls Foundation CEO, where my life's mission to fight against Autism Unemployment was showcased.

Thank you to **Hilda Mitrani**, who sadly is no longer with us, for helping me improve my first grant writing. I will never forget Hilda's kind smile.

Thank you to **Frank** and **Lisa Valdivieso** for embracing us in Palmetto Bay and opening many doors so that together, we could make that community more inclusive to persons with autism.

Thank you to all the stores and schools in Miami, like **Joanna's Marketplace, Westminster Christian School, Graciano's, Whole Food Market, Milam's Market** …and all the others, that helped Miami Is Kind in so many different and critical ways. A very special thanks to **Chef Francisco** at **Westminster Christian School** for being an angel to Miami Is Kind bakers, offering them lunch every day and nurturing their hearts with his smile.

Thank you to **Alejo Chouela** at **Biscayne Point Capital** and **Carlos Ramirez, Business Consultant,** for all the energy and good actions you took as part of our Advisory Board for Miami Is Kind.

Thank you to **Debbie Dietz**, Executive Director at **Disability Independence Group**. Debbie, thank you for your support of Marc and so many with autism. Also, thank you for being the first organization to order Miami Is Kind macaroons. I am ready to collaborate whenever I can be of use.

Thank you, **Orfa de Armas,** for being the first person to subscribe to Miami Is Kind's monthly macaroon deliveries. Your enthusiasm unforgettably touched me. You can count on me for anything.

Thank you, **Gerardo Viera,** for your support with our website. You are full of humanity, empathy and kindness for those in the spectrum. I'm in debt to you.

Thank you, **Mike Moran,** at **Moran Capital Partners,** for your generous donation of some baking equipment.

Thank you, **Evita Francuz,** for your support to our Foundation and to **Syed Zafar** and **Greg Francuz** at **Zafar Francuz & Company** for your exceptional support in the first years of our Foundation.

Thank you to my best employer, **DuPont,** for embracing this memoir, but mostly for the values that you instilled in me while working for this very fair corporation that walks the talk. These values have proven very useful in navigating corporate life and my personal life. A company doesn't exist for more than 200 years for no reason. I will not name anyone because, again, the list would be too long.

Thank you to all the trailblazers who inspired me to create Miami Is Kind. **Cristóbal Colón,** Founder of **La Fageda,** we have not yet met, but there's not a single Catalan who doesn't know about La Fageda's story, which has long been **Harvard's** business study case for a social enterprise model. You were an inspiration to me even before my son Marc was born.

Thank you to **LaFACT Fupar** for existing in Terrassa since I was born and for giving me a chance to meet persons with disabilities washing my car when my dad was taking me there to clean his. I could not have guessed then that you'd inspire me years later. In fact, I had not noticed any disability among your employees but their many abilities, so I only learned of your social value and importance when my dad shared that with me.

Also, thank you to **Tom d'Eri and his family** at **Rising Tide Car Wash**. I'm in awe of what you have contributed to the employment of persons with autism in Florida. You certainly instilled in me the mindset that the idea to kick off Miami Is Kind was a very realistic and feasible endeavor—I will never say easy.

Thank you, **Rubit, Maria, and the entire team,** for giving Marc exactly what he needs: feeling loved and surrounded by honest people with the highest values. You have me forever.

Thank you to my brother **Felip** for illustrating this memoir with his wonderful drawing of Terrassa, that industrial city close to Barcelona that has so many pearls of the past and that his magic fingers have captured so beautifully. Love you, Pip.

Thank you to **Nuri Ricart**, my mother-in-law. Her foot on the ground and assertive attitude make her a unique grandmother. Marc is so lucky to have you, as are Gerard, Bernat, and Gemma. I'm in debt to you.

Thank you to **Nuria Boada**, my cherished childhood friend, who had the brilliant idea to make this memoir "more me" by structuring it around my passion for the ocean. She suggested that each part of our lives should be represented by the body of water that was next to us at that particular time and place—all those paradises we've been blessed to live in, mostly thanks to Marc. You are a great communicator and an extremely funny comedian, so if there's a movie, you will have a role in it.

Thank you to **Titin**, my childhood friend, for being my go-to person when I'm feeling down. Your ever-realistic approach to life has always lifted me, especially during the eight months I've spent immersed in writing this memoir. Without you, I would be broke! Imagine all the therapy sessions I'd have had to pay for. I love you. Count on me for whatever you need.

Thank you to **Jesica**, my friend in La Jolla. You were my first friend when I moved to La Jolla, California, and we will always be friends. It's not a coincidence that you support so many children with autism to thrive at school; you have a great heart. Your desires are orders to me.

Thank you to **Xavi**, my husband, for trying to be the best version of yourself. Also, thank you for loving Marc and Gerard the way you do—in your own way. I know you sacrificed so much to raise Marc, and I do not take it for granted. We are a great team.

Thank you to **Gerard**, my second child, for all your numerous daily sweet interruptions when you find me writing after coming back from high school. I can't forget one of the latest interruptions, this time with **Stella**—one of our two sister cats, the other one named **Nala**—I can still hear the little sounds she made when you touched her mouth. "Look at her, Mom! Look at her! Oh no, now you missed it," you'd urge, but I was finishing a sentence. "It's okay; I didn't want to show it to you anyway," you'd say, pretending to be mad.

And what about our laughs about the CNN reporter? The guy holding his cap during Milton's hurricane coverage, getting closer to the waves. "Mom, why is he doing this? Who does this help?" you'd ask, intrigued by the weirdness of the situation.

"It's TV, Gerard, it's all for the show!" And we'd crack up, commenting on all the bizarre images of reporters getting wet for no reason. Those were the best breaks—filled with affection and connection—that inspired me to continue writing the memoir. Gerard, you are my sunshine, so witty and creative, I will always root for you.

I'm sure I've forgotten many names of invaluable persons, so thank you to everyone who has supported this memoir, Marc, or supported Miami Is Kind in its mission.

Thank you to the **national and international media**—I will not add names because it would be too long—for sharing my story and the Miami is Kind and Kindness in Spectrum Foundation story, which encouraged our communities to take action for persons with autism.

Thank you to the city of **Miami, FL.** This city was home to our story and gave name to our powerful program, Miami Is Kind, because I felt the need to give back to the city that opened its doors to Marc and our family. The disabilities community in Miami is amazing, but also all the stakeholders. Thank you to **Francis Suarez**, Miami Major, for the Salute I received from your constituents. I will always be at the city service to improve the lives of persons with autism in Miami.

Lastly, a patriotic thank you to the **land of the free and the home of the brave**. If it hadn't been for all the systems and laws that empower parents in this great nation to provide a future for their children with autism, our story would have been a different one, and this memoir might never have been written. My promise is to make it my life's mission to continue giving back to this nation by fostering understanding, support, and kindness in the autism community.

Disclaimer

This memoir is intended to entertain, and if any part of it resonates with you or helps you, then my main reason for publishing this memoir has been fulfilled.

I am not a doctor. Among other things, I am an expert in autism and offer services related to it. You can find my credentials in the [credentials section]. However, as the author, I'm writing this memoir from the perspective of Marc's mom, and it relates specifically to Marc, my eldest son with autism. That said, it's true that some of the challenges described and some of the learnings and strategies I used may be useful to help other individuals in the spectrum or with any neurodiversity. Take what is useful for you and let go of the rest.

It is absolutely not the purpose of this memoir to define how a person with autism is, behaves, or feels. Honestly, I believe nobody should attempt to do that. This book is about Marc and only him. In fact, having autism does not define a person at all; we are much more than our diagnoses. Every person is special and unique, whether they have autism or not. Additionally, individuals on the autism spectrum are diverse from a medical perspective in terms of how autism impacts their lives.

What I write about Marc is based on what I observe with my "neurotypical" eyes. I am in awe of and deeply support all individuals on the autism spectrum who can speak up and advocate for themselves in their voices. In Marc's case, as with many caregivers of individuals with high support needs, I had to advocate on his behalf.

This is not a "how-to" book. It's a memoir that may inspire you to take action in your own life. If you choose to use any of the strategies mentioned in this memoir to help a loved one, always consider your specific circumstances and those of the person you're trying to help. Based on my experience, I recommend seeking advice from top professionals in each relevant field you struggle with, or you want to see improvements in.

Throughout the memoir, you may come across terms like "person with autism," "developmental disabilities," or "intellectual disabilities," or even just "person with disabilities" or "person struggling with mental health." I believe that, regardless of diagnosis, some strategies may work across the board. Again, always consider your unique circumstances and consult with professionals.

I am an autism coach for caregivers, so if you'd like personalized advice, I'm here to help. All consultations are out of pocket, with 20% of the fees donated to the **KINDNESS IN SPECTRUM** foundation's **Families at Risk** program, which supports parents or caregivers of persons with autism, with high support needs, and who cannot afford autism coaching.

Introduction:
One, two, three Immersion

I must have been around ten years old that Autumn day. I had just picked up Nuria, my childhood best friend, and together, we were wandering the streets, leaving the creaking sound of the fallen leaves that were piling up on the sidewalks behind us. The deciduous trees ran the full length of the block, each planted in a cube of dirt. It was All Saints season, and we loved getting hot chestnuts in La Rambla, one of the main streets in Terrassa, our beloved city next to the world's admired Barcelona in Catalunya, what many Catalans consider a little European country that Spain swallowed up.

La Castanyada is a traditional Catalan festival in the All Saint season, pagan in its roots, resisting over time despite the competition Halloween gives it. Terrassa, like all Catalan cities, smells of roasted chestnuts, panellets, and sweet potatoes.

Panellets, a delicious pastry similar to the macaroons, that some years later inspired me to do something kind, but let's cross that bridge when we get to it. The Castanyeres are scattered with their stalls throughout Catalan cities, and despite their sometimes scary look, everyone adores them, especially children.

We were always vividly loud, joking and giggling around. When crossing Firefighter's Street, all of a sudden, a vision changes it all forever...

A mother was holding hands with her son; she was helping him drink from his water bottle as he was dripping all the water when he first tried doing it for himself.

The kid could have been six years old. He was walking with some difficulty; he was cute, but somehow he wasn't. The features on his face were perfect but lacked expression, and his eyes were not those of the other children's eyes. I wasn't certain what it was. They probably didn't express enough intention to be just like any other kid. He seemed lacking in energy, and his eyes were not saying enough. *"Here I am with my mom, drinking my water, and I'm thinking about what a great afternoon I'm going to have with friends in the park."*

He was there, but, in a way, he was not fully there. That kid's look seemed lost in even knowing who he was, where he was going, or even where his little fingers ended and the street air began.

All of a sudden, I don't know what happened, I was his mom. I stopped breathing as if the ocean had engulfed me and water was filling my lungs. I felt such an unbearable weight that I could have lost balance and fallen to the pavement. This weight has been stored as a very vivid memory throughout my life. A second later, I was Silvia again, and I took the deepest of breaths. What a relief it was.

"How does this mom live with such an overbearing weight in her lungs?" I whispered to the air. "I would never be capable of raising a child like him. I would drown!" I added, looking down, completely ashamed of my endless cowardice while still vividly noticing the feeling of that tsunami leaving my lungs. It all felt so real. I do not remember anything of what my friend Nuria said or the funny jokes that brought us so much laughter just one minute ago. What I do recall is that later, all my bubbly conversation mode with my best friend vanished, and I was tongue-tied for the rest of the afternoon. My hands were deadly cold. Something changed inside me so deep that the rest of the day, right after that vision, I could not experience warmth again, not even when Nuria and I reached Las Ramblas, and I extended my hands to the embers where the chestnuts were made.

Thirty-five years later, I was living in Miami with my family. We lived in Miami-Dade, a county full of different neighborhoods that, like Venice, in Italy, Europe is embroidered with canals that lead to the vast Atlantic ocean.

Xavi, my husband, was working at the bank. Gerard, my sunshine, my love, was at the nursery, the wonderful Montessori School by Palmetto Bay, and I was home with my eldest son, Marc, my love, my life, who had just turned ten, the age I was when I saw that mom with a child who had a developmental disability which I now consider a vision of what life had in store for me.

Marc and I were playing with a stuffed Barça soccer player that every Barça fan admires, the beloved Messi! Marc loved his Messi;

he would not stop pressing his nose, an important nose because it would play the Barça anthem. *"Tot el camp, cha cha cha, es un clamp, cha cha cha···"* Marc's smile transformed when hearing those notes. Marc was such a handsome and cute kid. His dance moves have always filled my heart with joy. Loving to dance myself, I took Messi and danced with him and Marc. Every time the anthem was reaching the end, Marc would open his brown eyes so determined that his long, dramatically thick, and perfect eyelashes seemed to reach the ceiling of his bedroom in their delicate curve, and he would press Messi's nose again.

Marc learned to sing it when he was two but would never sing along. Marc never sings along. The confirmation that he would never sing along came when he did his first End of School Festival in L'Espígol school in our city, Terrassa. We had practiced at home, and he knew the catalán song perfectly well. *"Soc com soc i es igual ser com soc i descobrir-ho tot."* In English, it would be, "I am how I am, and it doesn't matter how I am; I just want to discover it all." The first time I heard Marc sing this song, my lungs expanded to let later go of the deepest, longest breath they had exhaled for years. The melody was just like any other children's song, but the lyrics sounded like a powerful early childhood self-advocacy cry. I knew that Marc didn't understand abstract concepts, so he could not grasp the meaning of the lyrics, but still hearing him sing those words out loud was a memorable ray of sunshine amidst the long thunderstorm. On the End of School Festival Day, he appeared on the stage with his cute jeans, a white t-shirt, and some angel wings made of wonderfully soft white feathers. The whole school sang the powerful song, a core of angels speaking out their truth. Marc was there on one side moving his body and head softly with the music and watching everyone singing while he was silent.

When I picked him up from the stage, I asked: "Marc, why didn't you sing?"

Marc didn't answer, but by that time, I already knew the way I'd learned most of Marc's preferences, by his smile and his mysterious eyes. He was smiling all the time up there, and his brown eyes were touching all the other kids graciously up on stage; his movements were freely caressing the music, and they came from deep inside like those of a real angel. He was in the groove; he was Marc and only Marc. I told him, "You prefer to watch the kids and listen, right?"

The angel smiled again.

Back to Messi, our stuffed Messi, I wanted that play never to end. A few little plays produced so many smiles in Marc, so I simply didn't want to stop the delight, the fun. Fun to me is the name of the game, and finding those little moments of pure connection and fun with Marc was absolute gold. Life with Marc can be extreme and painful and scary, but I always find the moment to have fun and laugh. It's my way; without fun, life defeats the purpose. At this point, I had the urge to pee; yes, I could not hold it any longer, so I woke up and was about to take Marc with me, as I had done for ten years now, but I saw Marc totally focused and immersed with the music so I felt inclined to respect his magic moment and I thought, *"I'll go fast. I've learned fast, and I'll be back with no time left for Marc to misbehave."*

Marc's entire bed came from Terrassa in a container with everything we had to Miami.

When we moved, I said to Xavi, "We will take everything so that at least when we live in Miami, Marc feels at home in the new home."

I bought Marc's bed when Gerard was born. My dream had always been that they would grow up as brothers sharing their room. One of the beds had a useful drawer under it to stick any toy the kids had, and the other bed had a pull-out bed to be used in case any of their friends were staying home for a sleepover. As a matter of fact, Marc and Gerard could never sleep in the same room for multiple reasons, and the sleepover was never even something we would consider, not for a day. It was impossible to have a friend over, especially for a sleepover. In fact we had never invited anyone home, except for that one day when Sandy came over, my dear friend Sandy, an angel that crossed paths into my life and never left me. However, I never moved the bed out of the room. I'm not giving up on dreams easily. Another way to put it is that I'm really stubborn.

I went to the bathroom and left the door open. Marc's bathroom was between his room and the home entrance, and in the other direction was the living room and all the day rooms of the house. I went straight back to Marc's room and he was not there. I mentally reviewed all the options, and he could be located. I had been gone for about two minutes. I heard the anthem for about one minute. And with the bathroom door open, I had been looking towards the corridor the whole time. So, I would have seen Marc leave his room if he had and I had not seen him. I had not heard the main door open or close or his footsteps moving around.

I looked for Marc everywhere in his bedroom, behind the curtains, under the bed, in the huge drawer under the other bed, in the closet ···Marc was not there.

I guess I started sweating when I came back to Marc's bedroom because I noticed deep, cold sweat under my clothes, as if all of a sudden, Miami, Florida, had become Finland, Europe.

While shivering, I started searching for him everywhere possible in the house: in the kitchen cabinets, under the little table in the living room, in the backyard, under the bushes and trees. Marc was ten years old, so he did not fit in that many spots, so Marc must not have been in the house.

At that point, I began to feel like I was suffocating, like thirty-five years ago, when I was ten and had the vision of that mom with that kid. Again, as it happened to me then, I stopped breathing as if I had been swollen from an ocean, with water enveloping my lungs. I felt such an unbearable weight that I could have lost balance and fallen to the pavement. This time, however, the tsunami did not subside. It didn't allow a breath, a mere survival breath. My mind went blank, and my instinct took control of the situation.

I opened the main door and looked back at the house from outside on the rare chance that Marc was inside and I had not seen him. I went to the neighbor's house and asked for help. Only a short sentence from a desperate mom was needed to start a chain of neighbors asking neighbors to look for Marc. The children looked on bikes, the adults in cars, and everyone stopped doing what they were doing and joined Marc's search.

My first destination was the canals. Images of Marc's clothes hanging on the bushes around the channels appeared like a horror movie in my unstoppable mind. His socks, his sports pants, here one Croc, the other floating in the water.

In addition to my shivering body and my suffocating breath, I had now developed a heartbeat so loud as if I had swallowed a bomb that could explode at any time. I wasn't Silvia anymore. I searched for Marc frantically, first one canal, then the other, all the ones we used to go to one after the other. I would get close to each canal fence and look around for Marc's clothes. Then, because I was aware of how little air I was getting with each breath, I would try to get a little more energy by lowering my head to look in the water. While looking through the last possible canal, I saw Marc's cap hanging off a eucalyptus branch, and my whole body was about to fall to the ground. Seconds later, I realized that it was a cap that Marc had thrown a few weeks ago, for no apparent reason, while going on one of the countless walks that we had around our neighborhood. Marc often exhibited behaviors that did not have an easily identifiable cause. When there was no obvious cause, I became adept at deducing the reason because I had learned that there was always a cause triggering his behaviors. Thus, my theories were elaborated.

On the one hand, I thought that Marc was attracted to those canals full of water; who wouldn't be? And especially my son. I'm also passionate about water. And on the other hand, I knew that he deeply enjoyed seeing my face when he was being naughty.

Realizing that it was Marc's old cap, I felt relieved. At least he had not thrown himself into a canal. The relief indeed lasted only seconds because Marc was still missing. I looked at my phone and realized that fifteen minutes had passed since Marc was missing, so I figured it was time to call the police, and so I did. The policeman told me that he would be at my house in thirty minutes. I resolved to visit Publix, a South Florida supermarket chain that Marc has always been fond of visiting. I went directly to the Customer Service area, and as soon as I got there, I heard on the loudspeaker, "Marc Feu, Marc Feu, if you are in the store, please come to the Customer Service area. Your mom is here looking for you." I waited, but Marc never came.

I went home as the police would arrive soon. I opened the door, and it was all quiet. I went to Marc's room and repeated all the searches I conducted in the beginning and found nothing. At this point, the shivering intensified, the tsunami hit maximum intensity, and the bomb was about to explode in seconds. I had returned to the beginning; my instinct had taken me to all the places Marc would go, and I had not found him; something was terribly wrong. At this stage of the game, I started throwing Marc's pillows in the air, grabbing Marc's games in the big drawer, and spilling them to the floor. I removed the pull-out bed completely and looked under the left space; illogical because the pull-out bed was filling that space, but I was desperate, and I was doing desperate things. There, in an impossible place, sleeping horizontally and sideways, completely straight like a stick, like a mummy, against the wall from head to toe, was Marc, hidden in a pose and place like one of those ladies who magicians make "disappear" in their shows.

Seconds later, the police arrived. I left Marc where he was. I did not even consider waking him up; I could not handle Marc and a policeman at the same time, so he continued "comfortably" sleeping.

I pretended to be a typical mom with a typical kid. I didn't find the energy in me to explain to the policeman the situation as it really was: Marc's autism, Marc's unsafe behavior, my deep anxiety… I assumed he wouldn't get it; who would? So I shared the facts as if I was a typical mom and Marc was a typical kid; I acted completely "normal," average, a version of the story that I thought the policeman would understand better than our very real atypical lives and with a bit of luck would keep us out of trouble. Hiding it all, I started explaining to the police as formally and serenely as my acting skills would allow me. "Well, sir, the thing is that I found him. Yes, he was home all this time. He likes to joke, and be silly, you know, so he hid himself behind the pull-out bed under his bed just to give me a scare later. What happened is that he was tired because he was back from a tough day at school, and fell asleep, so when I entered the room, he didn't respond to me, and I could not find him because I would have never guessed that my ten-year-old son would fit in there, but Marc is very flexible and sneaky and always finds ways to surprise me! Sorry for wasting your time."

The policeman left, nodding his head, and I could finally wake Marc up, give him a big hug, and breathe and breathe again.

The day Marc was born marked the beginning of a new life, one characterized by perpetual crisis. For the next ten years, and many more after that, my existence became a constant battle. There was never a moment to breathe, to act unscripted, to be myself. Each day and night was a relentless struggle. Chaos, danger, and frustration became the permanent ingredients of our daily life. My world revolved around strategies to keep Marc safe—strategies that involved anticipating, limiting, or redirecting his behaviors.

Marc's life, too, has been a constant struggle since birth. Imagine being perpetually asked to change the way you do things, trying to live your life while constantly failing to meet others' expectations. Now, imagine not understanding what you are doing wrong or how to do things differently. Marc uses few words to express his immediate needs, and that's the extent of his verbal communication. We could never find a way to help him communicate beyond that, to share his struggles and feelings. Acquiring those skills is likely not in Marc's nature. However, I've learned to understand him through less conventional means—no words or gestures needed.

It wasn't always this way. It took years of challenges and countless setbacks for me to understand Marc, to grasp why he was so incredibly difficult, and to find ways to ease his anxiety and contain him, to nurture him, and to keep him and those around him safe.

Before Marc, I had a career in the corporate world; I was particularly good at crisis management. Naturally, I began applying my professional strategies to our home crisis, combined with advice from autism and behavioral sciences experts. Trying to make these strategies work consumed me physically and mentally because my success rate at home was significantly lower than what I was accustomed to in my business life. Planning and strategy have been part of my functioning since childhood, and they have always worked well for me. But Marc's behaviors were so intense and frequent that just surviving our extremely adapted family life was a daily challenge that exceeded all my abilities, energy, and resources.

I failed every day, multiple times, and Marc, my family, or the community often ended up in compromised situations. For years, it was incredibly hard to see the light at the end of the tunnel. At home, it was tough because Marc couldn't stop moving, throwing, and breaking things. I started taking him outdoors, but it was even tougher because the community wasn't prepared for Marc's behaviors, which only multiplied the dangers and failures.

When I was forty-five and living in Miami, with Marc at ten years old, I fully understood why I was so deeply moved by that mother and her son back when I was just a child of ten in my hometown of Terrassa, living with my parents.

Why? Every single person intuitively knows that families touched by these conditions—no labels needed, no explanations given—have it extremely difficult in life. Walking the streets with Marc, I've seen many people move, just as I was that day as a child. I've seen their sorrow as they observed the two of us.

Only those who have been parents or caregivers of a child with Autism or an Intellectual Developmental Disability (IDD) can fully grasp what this is like. It took me ten years to reach this deep understanding, and in the following decade, I delved even further into what it truly means to be a parent or caregiver of a person with Autism or IDD.

However, any kind person with moral values and empathy knows that raising a child with such a condition is an extremely challenging job. You don't need to know that the condition is called Autism, Autism Spectrum Disorder, Developmental Disability (DD), or Intellectual Developmental Disability (IDD) to understand this. I understood it in the tenth year of Marc, with no experience or knowledge of these conditions. I believe most people would agree that both the person with a condition and their family—the parents or caregivers—need extensive support in the form of resources, capacity, empathy, and kindness from their community.

If we agree that we all know and feel the need to provide support, the next question is: What can I do to support people with Autism or DD and their families?

Returning to my story, when I was ten, I met that mother and her "different" child. At that age, I had encountered many types of people, but never anyone who was not typical. Deep down, I probably viewed people with Autism or DD as almost extraterrestrial—unknown and alien. I may have crossed paths with atypical individuals on the street, but I hadn't paid attention. There was a very functional girl with Down Syndrome in the neighborhood who was cheerful and socially adept, so I never considered her atypical. I also had a classmate in a wheelchair with macrocephaly. Being curious, I once asked him why he was in a wheelchair. He explained his multiple head surgeries plainly, without drama. I felt empathy and appreciated his openness. Friends always surrounded him, so I never saw a barrier to being close to him.

I've learned that social atypicality has a huge impact on others. When someone behaves in ways that aren't considered appropriate or mainstream, it creates a barrier. That unpredictability in behavior can block connection, at least it did for me. I honestly thought that the mother in my vision was the least fortunate person in the world. I saw the immense effort she was making and felt the weight she carried.

As a child, I assumed the world was made up of typical people—individuals who behaved more or less like I did. I knew some people weren't as smart, like a classmate treated poorly by our teacher, but I connected with him, so he seemed typical to me. I had no clue some people communicate and behave so differently. Without Marc, I might still be living with that false assumption.

When I encountered a person with Autism, I didn't know what to do or think. I froze, panicked, and felt completely out of my comfort zone. It was like being transported to another universe. That day, I felt the burden on that mom, but I also saw her skills, tenderness, kindness, and devotion. Despite the lack of verbal communication, they were in sync. What struck me most was that, unlike me, she, the mother I saw in childhood, didn't seem scared; she was fully dedicated to her child' s wellbeing, much like my mom, but with a much heavier weight to bear.

I wondered if she had learned through experience, through countless trials and errors, when her initial attempts didn't work. Maybe she had guidance, a coach, or a mentor—if she had the courage, time, energy, ability, and resources to find such help. Or perhaps she had to learn the hard way. Regardless, I respected her immensely. She became a part of me forever, her strength, effort, and unconditional love for her child etched in my memory. She was the most courageous mom I had ever met.

I felt sorrow for both the mom and the son. However, I was disgusted by my own pettiness and the pain I felt in my heart. I intuitively knew I was misjudging something. The mom was just doing what my mom was doing with me, loving and helping him with whatever he needed and, of course, helping him with his individual needs. Those needs that my son had where never my needs as a child; I had other, more typical needs. That's why the term 'special needs' kids exist. Also, the son was definitely cute. He was adorable, again not the typical pretty, because there was an expression and some features on his face that stood out to my not educated eyes that blocked my ability to see him, to see beyond the differences. His awkwardness was a barrier to me. I was disturbed, and for that, I felt guilt all over. My emotions were deeply troubled and didn't accompany the thoughts that were somehow signaling that I could be a better person and that I could try to connect with him or his mom. Why could I not silence my judging mind? Why did that scene seem so tragic to me? Why did I feel pettiness? Why did I find myself wishing with all my heart that this would not happen to me as a mom? But back then, I didn't have the answers to all my agitated thoughts.

Today, the kind of questions that I wish had crossed my mind that day would have been …

"What if a mother with a child is just a mother with a child, regardless if the child is typical or not? What if the only difference is that the mother with the atypical child needs lots of support from humanity, from the community around her, from all of us, starting with me?"

"Maybe I could have said something nice to the boy or have turned my scary face into a genuine smile when crossing them, giving them both a sign that I see you, I acknowledge you, and I'm here with you?"

"What if I had seen the differences and identified he was an atypical child and that, yes, he was socially awkward, but immediately after, I had focused on finding his similarities with me?"

"If nobody chooses to be atypical and we can all bring typical or atypical children to this world, shouldn't we all be educated at a young age to replace our fears with the right education? Shouldn't we all, starting as kids, be encouraged to support and help flourish the persons and the person's families and caregivers who, for no choice of their own, have it tougher in life to achieve what we humans mostly need: to be loved, to fulfill our wishes, to feel we belong, to have wings to fly as high as possible?"

It is obvious to me now because of Marc and because of the life I have had the opportunity to live, but it doesn't come naturally to most of us.

When you come across families or individuals touched by Autism or DD, be certain that you can help them tremendously just by being kind and acknowledging every person as someone valuable to you and to the community. Remember that feeling petty doesn't help anybody. Act normal, find your bridges to communicate when communication is different and experience the connection with no fear. Look for the things that might connect you with the person or the family, and make a conscious effort not to look at the differences anymore. It's a transformative process. You will soon start feeling that you are receiving more than you are giving; it has happened every time to so many people I met on the way. It is applicable to all ages and avenues of life. It's my personal experience with so many people during my life and that of many others. It's a priceless process that changes you and your perspectives forever. If you've been there, you know what I'm talking about. If not, I encourage you to try. You might be fearful the first time, the second maybe, but once you learn to do that, you are a much better version of yourself because you've started changing others' lives, and others will appreciate your support. My experience is that life works like a boomerang-when we support one another, life gives back to us.

Each of us are unique, and in the same way that being typical does not define a person, being atypical does not define a person either. Looking beyond the disability and appreciating the person as such and all the abilities doesn't come naturally to typical persons, but once you learn the drill, you realize how beautiful it is to connect with each person where they are and with their uniqueness. We all have our strengths and weaknesses and our different interests and personalities, and some of us behave differently socially, and some extremely differently. No matter how insurmountable differences might appear at first glance, the essence of who we are as people doesn't have anything to do with a condition or a developmental disability. Each person we encounter along the way, regardless of whether that person has a developmental disability or not, or if the person communicates and is social or not, should read in our lips, "You are you, and I see you. I see your abilities, your strengths, your interests. I respect your likes and dislikes, your preferences. You belong. I want to connect with you because you are worth it. After all, you make this world a better place for all that I'll find a way to connect with you. It doesn't come to me intuitively, but I do have the ability to put myself in your shoes, to be kind, to be patient. And I want to learn from you because you are a lovable, unique person with so much to offer."

Part I
By the Mediterranean
My life before Marc

"You may say I'm a dreamer, but I'm not the only one. I hope someday you'll join us. And the world will live as one."

—John Lennon

Chapter One
My little island where I felt safe and happy

*"Success is not final; failure is not fatal: it is the
courage to continue that count."*

−*Winston S. Churchill*

Life is like the ocean. We all experience times when we ride the
crest of a wave, effortlessly steering toward our desired direction as
favorable currents buoy us and the sun illuminates our path. During
these joyful periods, feeling appreciated and loved seems as natural
as a gentle breeze on a hot summer day. Yet, amid these golden
years, I forgot that storms are also inherent to the ocean. At twenty-
six, the surf carried me to a small island, exactly like the one I had
often dreamed of—a place where I felt safe and happy.

A permanent smile seemed to live within me. My long, semi-curled blonde hair would frequently fall across my face, and I'd brush it aside with a practiced flick, a nervous tick reflecting my ever-anxious mind. At the time, I was preparing to present a benchmarking project at the German company I worked for at the time. I had devoured five books on benchmarking in the previous week and reviewed my questionnaire intended for leadership at least ten times. I was confident it would be a success. I still remember the director's words when he saw the first draft: "Silvia, I'm absolutely impressed by your project. I didn't realize you had so much potential."

"Ha," I thought immediately, *"if only he knew."* I was stuck in an office where my suggestion to use clear folders, rejected for being "too slippery," symbolized deeper issues. Instead of employing an IT system for document storage—a simple solution in 1997—I was forced to manually transcribe information onto colorful folders, a daily chore that was both time-consuming and wasteful. Frustrated, I often worked on necessary cost-reduction projects at home during the weekends because I cared.

I was deep in these thoughts, lamenting poor leadership, when he added, "It's so damned good... did you write it, or did your husband?"

Internally, I scoffed. *"Really? In this day and age, he still thinks women are less capable."* It was a stark reminder of the outdated attitudes still prevalent, even among those who should know better.

Struggling to suppress a laugh and flatten my smile, I managed to say in the most professional and composed voice I could muster, "This was entirely thought out and prepared by me. My husband, as intelligent as he is, specializes in finance rather than in the Theory of Constraints, Benchmarking, or Operational Excellence."

Despite his preposterous remarks, I felt a surge of optimism that day while reviewing the project. It felt like the beginning of a new phase of personal achievements. My smile, a signature trait featuring prominently curved lips, a notable gap between my top middle teeth, and always uniquely mine, comfortably settled on my face. I continued working on the project in my home office—a beautiful space with solid blue desks, my favorite color, and a texture that made work even more enjoyable. In our new apartment, life seemed perfect.

Xavi, my husband and the love of my life, whom I had recently married, sat at the other desk—yes, we had two, one for each of us. I was so delighted that a giggle almost escaped my perpetual smile. Xavi, interrupting his work on stock exchange charts, looked up to ask, "What's so funny?"

In his logical world, laughter results from humor, and he hadn't noticed anything amusing. While I knew the deeper reasons for my joy, I simply answered, "I'm happy," and then observed Xavi's slightly puzzled expression. Unlike me, who revels in the abstract world of emotions Xavi lives in a realm of facts, grounded firmly in reality. His typically stoic face often made my friends think he was upset with them; some even found him intimidating, suspecting he might be untrustworthy. Ironically, he is the most reliable and honest person I know. To me, Xavi is an enduring mystery, endlessly fascinating—like an unsolvable puzzle. And because he rarely smiles, when he does, it feels like witnessing a rare, magical event. I've seen how people are drawn to him despite his seemingly indifferent attitude; he has a unique way of winning people over.

We chose to buy our apartment in Terrassa, the city where I grew up because we felt real estate in Barcelona was overpriced. It was a sensible choice, not just for financial reasons but also because Terrassa is only twenty minutes from Barcelona, where Xavi was born and raised. Nestled east of Barcelona, towards the majestic Sant Llorenç del Munt mountain, Terrassa's beautiful pedestrian old town was perfect for my childhood explorations, allowing me to roam the city center alone when I was just six years old.

At twenty-six, I was convinced that everything happening in my life was not coincidental but the culmination of my choices, values, and actions from the ages of six to twenty-six. During those early years, I watched the waves from a distance, not yet venturing beyond the shallow waters as the adults around me doubted my capabilities. My childhood ocean was filled with currents that unpredictably changed direction and breezes that were sometimes pleasant and sometimes harsh. Experiencing life's tougher moments early on, I lost my naivety young and was changed forever. It was perhaps why, at the tender age of nine, I began planning my future in an attempt to control it. I was sure of what I wanted—and especially of what I didn't like—for the rest of my life. I approached my life with a vision of "future history," determined to ensure that my story would not be one of regret. It was at nine years old that I meticulously planned my entire perfect life and resolved to steer my destiny.

That day during school recess, I had traded so many of my cards for the Mazinger Z album that I was left too short on cards to deal the next day. I reached into my pocket and, finding a 25-peseta coin, I grinned and said to my best friend, Nuria, "Yes! I have 25 pesetas." That meant I had enough of the old Spanish currency to buy more cards for my collection at the bookstore. "Wait for me here, okay? I'll grab some cards, and then we can go dance at my place," I continued.

"Sure, we'll wait for you here," Nuria replied.

Living just across from my elementary school in a modern building in the city center, I cherished my dancing moments. My parents had recently gifted me a "comediscos" for my ninth birthday—a portable record player affectionately called a "disc eater" in Spanish. Shaped like a car CD player, it had a slot in the middle where you would insert a vinyl single. Mine was bright orange with a shiny metal handle that retracted for playing and extended for easy portability, resembling the handle of a cute purse.

I walked into the bookstore located on the same pedestrian street as my home and El Pi Elementary school, eager to expand my Mazinger Z collection. While browsing, I overheard a conversation between two middle-aged men that left a deep impression on me. One, a burly blue-collar worker with a slightly overweight build, and the other, a leaner white-collar worker, were deep in conversation just ahead of me. The bookstore clerk was attending to a third person.

"How's it going?" the leaner man asked.

"The usual crap..." the larger man responded with a nod. "They always run out of paper at my office, and I have to rush out to buy more reams. At least it gives me a chance to stretch my legs. I'm so tired of this administrative job. It's incredibly boring!" He sighed heavily. "The hours drag on endlessly. Sometimes I feel like my desk is stuck in a time loop, where the hours just stretch out to torment me."

The conversation shifted as the larger man continued, "It's no better at the warehouse, man! They make me work overtime without pay, and dealing with the truck drivers and their constant delays is a nightmare. Then, I have to unload quickly, which isn't safe, and still my boss yells, 'Chop, chop, chop! This is urgent, don't you know that?' It's exhausting." His worn blue pullovers and an old, dust-covered white helmet, now more gray than white, seemed to echo his fatigue.

"I hear you. It's life..." the leaner man replied, nodding. "But at least we've got the bar for a few drinks, right?" He was dressed in a suit that looked like a cheaper version of what my dad wore daily.

"Yeah, I guess we just have to hang in there. We'll keep meeting for wine and tapas after work, and someday, we'll retire," the chubby man murmured, his left hand on a torn pocket of his baggy blue pants, cigarette in his right hand.

At nine years old, I suddenly realized not everyone had engaging careers like my parents. The thought of possibly ending up with a mundane job and unfulfilling lifestyle like these two men—whom I dubbed Mr. Skinny and Mr. Fat—terrified me. I was always the one initiating new games to play during school recess, inventing them alone in my bedroom. I also loved writing short plays at my sturdy white laminated pine desk, a unique piece designed specifically for my room in our new apartment. I would spend hours crafting stories there, which I then shared with my classmates. After some practice, our teacher even let us perform these plays during class.

As I listened to the conversation in the bookstore, a wave of panic washed over me at the thought of being trapped in a repetitive, unchallenging job like those men described. I yearned for a dynamic and engaging career, one where I would continually learn new things and be surrounded by interesting, cheerful people. I needed to find a workplace that not only fostered my learning but also allowed me to share my knowledge with others later. *"I need to start planning for my future job now,"* I thought determinedly. *"I must love my job, and it needs to be a place where I can innovate and never feel isolated."* Inspired by my ideas, I believed I could make the world a better place. Freedom was also essential—I wouldn't say I liked the thought of anyone bossing me around. My passion for languages, fueled by hours spent listening to Speak Up magazine cassettes during lonely summer days, meant my career had to be international, filled with interactions with people from diverse cultures. This wasn't about ambition; it was driven by fear, a profound understanding of what I didn't want in life. Given my fragility and insecurities, a well-laid plan felt like a steadfast ally.

From then on, planning my professional life became my priority. *"Yes, my mind is made up. Like my mother, I will put all I have into becoming an entrepreneur. This is my plan!"*

My mother was the lifeblood of the family business she started as a teenager, which had provided us with a stable European middle-class lifestyle.

Education was given, and small luxuries like dining out or trendy boots were commonplace. She exemplified that any dream could be achieved.

"Understood... I will not deviate from my secret plan. My hard work, attitude, and, hopefully, the genes I've inherited from my mom will guide me," I thought, looking up to a God I didn't quite believe in. Raised nominally Catholic, as was customary in Spain at the time, my mother wisely chose a non-Catholic school for me "so I could choose." It was later revealed that she did so because the Catholic school had not supported my younger brother's life decisions well.

"I'm invincible," I often thought, mixed with, *"Who would believe that a nine-year-old can control her life into adulthood?"* The idea filled me with a mix of determination and dread.

At fourteen, I was writing in my diary—my second one since I started at thirteen. *"I wish I could sit next to him during recess and talk. All the other boys and girls from class sit with him and just chat. I talk to other guys and too many people, but I can't speak to him; I'm too shy, and it's so frustrating!"*

Years passed, and I completed my bachelor's in business administration and later my master's in international business. I learned English, French, and German, completing one internship in my hometown and another in Germany, where I lived for a year in Holzminden, near Hanover.

"I'll put everything I have into building a professional career that makes me proud and happy. I won't stop fighting for that. If it doesn't happen, it will be because others stopped me, not because I

didn't work as hard as my mom." That was my philosophy, and I lived by it.

Back when I was nine, I was deep in thought, planning my entire future at a pace that would make one dizzy. The store attendant's voice pulled me back to the present. "How can I help you?" he said, but I didn't hear him. "Hello, how can I help you?" he insisted.

"Yes, sorry—I was lost in thought," I said, slightly embarrassed at being caught in my deep reflections once again. "I need five packets of Mazinger Z cards. They're 5 pesetas each, right?" I asked, ensuring that my 25-pesetas coin would cover the cost.

"Yes," he confirmed, handing me the cards.

I grabbed the cards and ran to meet my friends, not wanting to miss a second with them—they were my adrenaline. Within two minutes, I found them playing dangerously at a construction site where old houses in the city center had been demolished to make way for a modern building similar to the one I lived in.

"Magda! Are you nuts?" I shouted when I saw Magda, one of my friends who was also my cousin, balancing on top of a stack of wooden panels that jutted out from the third floor. Below her feet was only wood, then air.

"Come on, Silvia, come up here! Let's see if you dare..." she called down. She thrived in such situations! I would never risk my life with all my secret plans, but Magda could handle it—she was extremely skilled and lived on the edge every moment of her life. I admired her for her unconventional confidence and her unapologetic defiance of typical girlish behavior.

"Magda and everyone, please come down; we're going to my place to dance," I shouted impatiently. Dancing was my forte. Amid jokes and giggles, with more balancing, jumping, and the handling of dangerous construction materials like bricks and mortar on that deserted third floor, supported only by massive gray pillars and no walls, it was the perfect playground for my daring friends. I was just an entertained spectator, providing the background soundtrack of gasps and cautions: "OMG! Careful! Watch out! Please, not again... please, noooo."

Suddenly, we heard a stern voice command, "Get out of here. This is private property, and it's not safe!" It was Pedro, the supervisor, whom everyone called "El Blanco" due to his white hair—a feature quite unusual and intriguing to us as nine-year-olds. I always addressed him as Pedro, believing he deserved that respect. I felt a kinship with him; like me, he wanted everyone to be safe. That day, I was particularly grateful to Pedro for his effectiveness in persuading my friends to leave the site, which finally allowed us to head to my home to dance.

Once we reached my apartment on the third floor, I hurried to my room to grab the disc eater while my friends gathered in the living room. I eagerly began teaching them the dance I had planned. This time, it was to Boney M's "Daddy Cool," a super hit in Europe. "First, you raise your right hand, then the left, move the right to the middle, and then the left to the middle, and repeat," I instructed. At that moment, I relished being both the director and the dancing queen. After practicing my choreography, we shifted to freestyle dancing, letting loose in a burst of pure friendship and fun. With my parents at work and my brother, Toni, elsewhere, our house transformed into our private club.

I cherished my friends immensely. When I was with them, I felt secure and relaxed; I belonged. We constantly planned fun activities, and our time together was always intense and joyful.

Nuria and I often delved into deep conversations; she was very mature and always had interesting points of view. Nuria, who almost played the role of a sister to me, an only child, was remarkably brave. Her determination and courage were awe-inspiring. Next to her, I felt like a complete coward. My fragile bones and muscles were in stark contrast to hers. Not only did I think little and insignificant, but I also like a total wimp and scaredy-cat. Nuria always defended the wimp, making one feel safe next to super-Nuria, my superhero. She was pure fun, so unapologetic, she would have made a great standup comedian. However, what I admired the most about her was how gentle and considerate she was with everyone. Everyone adored her, and I felt grateful to have her as my friend.

Isabel was the quintessential straight-A student, always with glasses and her hair in a long ponytail, ready to absorb new knowledge. So balanced, organized, and put together, her ability to focus astounded me. How could she take such neat notes in class? Her notebook was a marvel—unit titles in capital letters, subtitles neatly underlined, and key takeaways highlighted in different colored boxes. Was she from another world? Why were my notes a mess, with my sloppy handwriting and colors changing only when I lost my blue pen and continued with black? At home, when I tried to study, I couldn't grasp a single point because half the explanations were missing.

"Far too much on my plate to be able to focus just on class. My friends, my efforts to understand how life works, the secret recipe to accomplish my secret plan, my hobbies, and my family pull me in so many directions that I can't focus on notes and grades." were my excuses.

Then there was Magda, a bundle of unstoppable energy and daring. Raised in a progressive, well-educated family that owned La Atenea, a bookstore in the city center, she devoured novels one after another. Her father also owned several clubs in Ibiza. She spoke her mind without filters and shared unbelievable things. "In Ibiza, we go to a nudist beach with mom and dad." Today, that's not unusual in Spain, where toplessness is common on many beaches, but in the 80s, some of the older generations would say that nudism was a practice for a bunch of hippies." She was daring and naughty despite being skinny and cute.

Titin was arguably the smartest among us, but, as is often the case, her grades did not reflect her intelligence. "What's wrong with the system?" She exuded pure confidence, unlike anyone else I knew, and embraced her individuality without care for fitting in. "I do what I want and when I want to do it" was her mantra. Her priorities were clear: live in the moment, have fun, and let everything else fall into place. Always ready for anything, she was empathetic and a dependable friend, ever-present in both my happiest and darkest moments. Even now, when I find myself lost in the complexities of my life, I turn to her for guidance. She simplifies things, leaving me with practical takeaways. She has been my lifesaver before, and I hope she continues to be in future turbulent times.

Rosa was the creative and naive one, kind, sweet, and incredibly intuitive. She navigated life with a positivity that was contagious and a beauty that was simple yet profound. Once, curious about her ambitions, I asked, "What do you want to be when you grow up?"

She replied, "I want to have a flower store and sell flowers."

Her reply stunned me with its clarity and simplicity. *"How could she be so assertive and concrete about her future while the same question would trigger in me a half-hour speech filled with complex ideas, possibilities, dreams, and fears? "*

A few years ago, during a summer visit to my hometown, Terrassa, Rosa suggested, "Write a book. Your story has to be shared. It's like the American dream."

I don't even remember my response, likely a string of doubts and maybes, barely acknowledging her advice. The following year, she insisted, "Have you started the book?"

My response was equally non-committal, perhaps a vague "I'll consider it..."

Next year, Rosa approached me more assertively. She took my arm, sat next to me, and looked directly into my eyes, her face only three inches away. Startled, I wondered if something tragic had happened. She continued, slowly and with conviction, never breaking eye contact, "Silvia," she paused, "write that book, I had a vision. Write that book, and do not delay it."

We were all true friends, part of the middle to upper class in our city. Each of our families had their businesses and their share of drama, from parental separation in a time when divorce was not legal (before 1981) to challenges with family businesses or sibling rivalries. Soon, I would face my drama, but knowing about their imperfect lives allowed me to share my struggles openly. I've always been grateful for their support. I never needed a psychologist; among my friends, I could speak freely, confident that we respected each other and would keep our secrets.

It was a cold February day, just outside my apartment, where we often gathered to plan events. Boada Riera was a refined Renaissance-style bookstore owned by Antonia Boada, a true lady in every sense of the word. Located on Sant Pere Street—the bustling commercial heart of downtown Terrassa that blended the charm of old and modern stores—Boada Riera served as our tribe's meeting point. Antonia, Nuria's mother, was like a mother to all of us, especially since our mothers were often busy with their businesses.

Other friends in our close-knit group included Montse, Adela, Laura, Olga, and Silvia, as well as my first love from elementary school, Ramon, and his best friend Santi, whom we tragically lost in a motorbike accident after an elementary school reunion. Santi's memory especially lingers with me, recalling a moment when he playfully stole Ramon's lunch, holding it like Gollum with his ring, and darted around the classroom tables during a class transition. I vividly remember watching the chase and, from the window, seeing Mireia, the next period's teacher, approaching. As if on cue, when Mireia entered, everyone was serenely seated at their desks, though Ramon and Santi were barely containing their giggles, still catching their breath. These friends, each teaching me something valuable, have shaped who I am today. It was a cold February day, just outside

15

my apartment, where we often gathered to plan events. "What are we doing this year for Carnival?" Titin asked. Carnival here is akin to Mardi Gras, a time of festive tradition.

"We could be a puzzle," suggested Nuria.

"Yes, that's a great idea! How do you imagine it?" I asked, my eyes filled with enthusiasm.

"We could use cardboard boxes and paint all the pieces," Nuria explained, motioning with her arms to show how the boxes would fit around our bodies, from just under the neck to above our knees.

"It would look better if the pieces were made of fabric, don't you think?" I mused, glancing sideways at the group.

"Fabric would definitely look better, more professional than just coloring boxes," Magda agreed.

"But how are we going to do that?" Titin asked, her lips pursed in thought.

"I think I know someone who can help..." I said, flashing a knowing smile that revealed my two front teeth.

That evening, as my mom prepared dinner, I shared our idea with her. Without hesitation, she responded warmly, "Sure, Silvia, I will make those puzzle costumes for the four of you." Her gaze, coming from large brown eyes and accompanied by a gentle smile that tugged at her thin lips, always made her seem like a star to me.

"One day, you all come to the shop and pick the fabric and the print you like; what do you think?" she continued, her hands cradling the base of my neck. It felt incredibly safe between her magical hands— hands that never rested from creating yet were always tender and caring. She never played the piano, but many complimented her on having the fingers of a pianist. Her fingers were long and elegant, each topped with perfectly shaped fingernails always painted a matte garnet color—a shade so constant it seemed natural to her. Her hands were perpetually immaculate, a testament to her meticulous care.

After our conversation, I hugged her tightly, kissed her, and told her, "You are the best mom, always the best mom!"

On Carnival day, my tribe attended a costume event at a fancy club in Barcelona, where we won the award for best group costume. Each of us received a voucher to spend at upscale stores in Barcelona. I had a blast shopping for my prizes. I bought some fashionable yellow shoes that made me proud every time I wore them. I'd always think, *"These are special, less functional than all my other shoes, just a treat. I would never have them because my mom would have said they weren't practical, but these were the yellow shoes I had earned, and just putting them on made me feel incredibly happy and special."* My friends and I were overjoyed—a day we will never forget.

I've always been passionate about costumes. I loved every aspect of it—the planning, the creativity involved in inventing something new, the making of the costume, and the experience of doing it with others. I had won several competitions, thanks to my mom and my confidence when wearing my costumes. The first competition I won was when I had just turned four years old; I dressed and danced as a "sevillana," a traditional Spanish dancer from Seville. It was during

17

a Mediterranean cruise with my family—the only time we did something together with both my parents and my two brothers. I remember every detail vividly, feeling part of my complete family. When the music started, the lights, the audience, and the huge amphitheater where I was supposed to dance became part of my superstar dream. I wasn't nervous at all. I thought, *"This is going to be so much fun; I'll give it my all!"* And I did. I remember the applause that erupted as my feet didn't stop stomping the ground. I convinced myself I was a true "sevillana," even though no one had ever taught me the dance; I had simply mimicked what I'd seen on TV. But my lack of formal training was the least of my concerns—my confidence soared. When they announced, "And the winner is Silvia," applause thundered from the crowd, which felt as grand as if the entire Wembley Stadium were cheering for me. At the end of the competition, they called me up to receive my trophy—a ceramic chimney from the ship "Enrique C," painted yellow with a navy blue 'C.' It served as a pencil holder, and I've kept it all my life as a reminder of the joy and passion I can feel.

By 1996, at twenty-six, I had become exactly what I envisioned as a girl—I was safe. I was married to the love of my life, and we shared a relationship grounded in absolute respect and trust, much like my parents. Additionally, I was finding success in my career path; I was on the verge of being promoted to my first supervisory role at a thriving German company where I felt valued. As the Warehouse and Distribution Manager of a manufacturing company, I was accomplishing my secret plans. The waves of life's ocean were always present, but my feeling of accomplishment was so overpowering that I scarcely noticed them. I was living the dream and felt unstoppable, enveloped in a never-ending sense of completeness and rightness.

"From now on, I can relax. I've built my little island, and I'm so happy in it," I thought. I concluded the Benchmarking project and suggested to Xavi, "Let's go out for dinner?"

He closed his laptop, looked at me with an assertive gaze, and agreed, "Enough work. Let's have some fun!"

"Yeah!" I exclaimed, leaping from my office chair and throwing my hands in the air in a playful dance. His refined English style always balanced my passionate reactions. *"We are so in sync,"* I thought to myself, *"everything is just so right in our world."* And a permanent smile seemed to live within me. Little did I know how soon and how dramatically everything would change, including myself, and how my smile would often flicker.

Chapter Two
Endless Pool Time
Satin Nightgowns, a Mother and a Cousin's Love

"The sea, once it casts its spell, holds one in its net
of wonder forever."

— *Jacques Yves Cousteau*

MNACTEC National Museum of Science and Industry of Catalonia. It specialises in the textile industry. Housed in the "Vapor Aymerich" building in Terrassa, designed by Lluís Muncunill, Terrassa's most celebrated architect.

March 1970 was a tumultuous time in the United States. The country was immersed in the Vietnam War while iconic bands like Pink Floyd and the Rolling Stones rocked the world. The microprocessor was introduced, and VCRs began to invade homes across the First World. Amid this progressive and creative atmosphere, Barcelona stood out in a culturally restrained Spain, which only held free elections in 1977, after forty years of Franco's dictatorship.

My mother, aged forty, had two children, Toni, twelve, and Felip, sixteen. Having another child was not in my parents' plans, yet on March 9th, I was born. My family often told me how fortunate my parents felt to have me, their first girl, bringing them a renewed sense of youth. Throughout my childhood, they took me everywhere, making it feel like a family of three. I enjoyed all the perks of an only child in the First World.

Always surrounded by adults or alone, that morning, I had just turned seven. *"How wonderful it would be to have brothers and sisters of my age,"* I mused, especially a sister. I imagined sharing everything with her, but then I stopped myself. *"That's not my life, so why waste time on a dead-end dream?"* I moved on to playtime in my room, never feeling bored. Alone play was my thing, and it was so fun! I had lots of Nancies, the dolls that were very popular in Spain during the 70s and the 80s. They looked like Barbies, but they were more like an early teenager, with smaller boobs, beautiful but more innocent, not as sexy as the Glamorous American Barby. Maybe they somehow resemble the old Madame Alexander dolls but much more modern. All those lovely dolls, but I had no one to play with, so I spent hours describing each one's character. *"Her name is Rose; she's athletic and doesn't care about boys. She finds them boring and is an independent woman. Her friend is the African American Nancy...*" My descriptions were extensive, detailing everything my Nancies loved, hated, and fought for, even their traumas. When they were on their stands, each one had a stack of stapled papers next to her—life scripts. Updating those papers was my way of playing with the dolls that never moved from their stands.

In retrospect, I see myself playing with my mind and feelings. Sometimes, when I was five and we still lived in our old house, I imagined I was dead. Later in my forties, when I started practicing yoga, I realized that back then, lying completely stretched out on the old parquet flooring, I could meditate for long periods, reaching states I couldn't as an adult. No one had instructed me in Buddhist teachings or meditation, but I could control my mind easily.

At seven, I had a special closet in the new, gleaming white kitchen of our modern apartment. I often opened the lengthy white doors and stared at the back wall of the pale wood interior, imagining it as a portal to the afterworld. This became a ritual for me, standing there and visualizing an alternate dimension. On the surface, my mom was cooking in the kitchen, and I was beside the closet, but deeper down, I was a free, immortal soul. The intensity of these moments sometimes made me feel as if the closet would pull me in. Yet, I returned week after week for that sensation of being more than just a child.

During the day, while doing chores, I made mental checklists to distinguish the 90% that was extra from the 10% that was essential. Watching the news with my parents and learning about global conflicts made my breath shallow with anxiety, imagining it could be us. This was often followed by a serene breath of gratitude that our family was unaffected and then by a steady breath, as constant as my thoughts: *"I'm ready for war if that's our destiny."* In those moments of euphoria and passion, which have been a constant in my life, I would think, *"I'd survive even on my own. I'd imagine nice things and eat whatever was available. I know the essence of life and need no adult or good fortune to save me."* Yet, a moment later, I'd snuggle with my mom on the couch, where she held hands with my dad, completely in love with him.

There was nothing compared to the joy of being with my friends! After so much alone time, friends were what I'd have died for. I was a silly extrovert with my close friends, but I struggled with an overwhelming shyness that prevented me from goofing around with everyone I wanted to. This shyness tormented me, making me feel trapped in a cage, unable to express all I had to give or grow into my full potential. I longed for more adventures, more people, more fun. I desperately wanted to break free from this frustrating character flaw.

As a child, I always sought out the paths with the greatest obstacles, unable to refrain from getting involved in the face of injustices, regardless of the consequences. My impulse control was nonexistent. Like my mother, I couldn't abandon the people I loved; it was something I simply couldn't do.

I always lived with high aspirations of doing something great, though I didn't know exactly what. Sometimes, I dreamed of being a dancer, a singer, an inventor, or a successful entrepreneur. *"I want to leave a legacy; I was born to make an impact on humanity"* was a constant, almost obsessive thought in my mind. However, I never shared those thoughts with my friends. I felt embarrassed to even think about that; they felt far too arrogant. Reflecting on this now, I realize that choosing obstacles was my way of preparing for the journey I had decided I would undertake. *"Yes, I'll choose math as an elective,"* my confident of seventeen-year-old self-decided. But in reality, I was barely passing; numbers held no meaning to me, and I spent all my math classes daydreaming.

My parents were entrepreneurs. They had built Datzira, a thriving textile and fashion design company specializing in nightwear and sleepwear, which was successful across Spain in the 70s. They worked all day long, and dinner table discussions were always about politics or business. By the age of six, I had become somewhat opinionated on these topics.

Mom was a very active woman. Her bright brown eyes sparkled, and her well-defined cheeks and perfectly styled hair, thanks to her weekly salon appointments, added to her elegance. Despite dedicating very little time to shopping, she always looked beautiful because she was authentic. Her lips were permanently curved upward in a kind smile. I'd proudly tell my friends, "My mom is so creative and imaginative. She solves problems at work, at home, and with friends. She's unstoppable and accomplishes everything with effort, never complaining and always being kind and accommodating. My mom is unique!"

Nuria and Titin, my best friends, would nod in agreement. She was definitely my idol.

My dad was a serious businessman, driven by numbers. I was in awe of his ability to separate emotions from business. "Numbers, speak up," he would say when my mom tried to convince him to pursue a creative idea that might not contribute to the bottom line. They balanced each other perfectly, making an ideal couple. I loved them so much. Although I didn't spend much time with them, the time we shared was precious and intense because of who they were, making it feel like a win.

The designs at our family business, Datzira, were sophisticated and romantic, making many Spanish women feel special and daring. They were classy yet sexy, allowing women to express themselves freely in the 70s when democracy was just arriving in Spain. These pieces of new expression could be found in prestigious department stores all over Spain, including Galerías Preciados (as featured in the Netflix series *Velvet*) and El Corte Inglés, a thriving department store even today.

The sound of the family workshop is etched in my memory; more than fifty Singer sewing machines working through delicate textiles like a powerful army marching for fashion. Climbing the fabric aisles and lying on the enormous bins full of rolls of silky textiles was one of my favorite things to do. The smell of batiste intertwined with satin, silk, and rayon filled my nostrils. This scent, combined with the dusty remnants from the fabric cutters shaping garments, might have been suffocating to a newcomer, but to me, it was a comforting home smell. Downstairs, I spent hours removing lace from their cabinets, delighting in their vibrant colors and textures.

My favorite place was the pattern makers' oversized tables. I'd ask them to turn up the volume on their little radios so I could dance and dance. I've never found a better dance floor than those wooden tables at Datzira. My brother Felip recently told me a story that struck me as inappropriate yet funny. I was five, dancing gracefully with cutters, pattern makers, and sewers cheering me on. Suddenly, I stopped and commanded, "Stop the music right now, you lazy people! Chop, chop, go to work!" For a moment, I must have realized that my playing around was interfering with my mom's commitments to deliver to the stores and my dad's focus on profit and loss. Feeling like a traitor, I stopped the madness. I apologize today for my "dictatorial" way of resolving my inner conflict.

My cousin Maite was another very special person in my life. Being younger than my mom, Maite was someone with whom I could share things I felt uncomfortable discussing with my mother, who was forty years older than me and from a distant generation. Maite was the perfect blend of fun and love, the most playful person I ever met. I spent many weekends at her house, especially after Elena and later Carlos were born. It was wonderful to have children to play with in the family finally.

Maite would organize all sorts of games for us. One sunny day at our villa in the mountains, Maite cheered, "Today, we will pick blackberries and make the best marmalade ever!" Like magic, she would effortlessly prepare the marmalade and then bake a cake, filling it with berries from the woods. No pastry ever tasted as good as Maite's.

Sometimes, after dinner, I would call my mom and ask, "Mom, can I stay until tomorrow and have a sleepover at Maite's?" While Carlos, Maite's husband, watched the Saturday night movie, Maite would rub my back. When my mom rubbed my back, it was always brief, and I had to say, "A bit longer, please, right here, yes, yes, here, please." She was always in a rush to do the next thing. With Maite, everything came in longer portions, and the back rubs lasted forever. She was present with me, and it felt wonderful. Maite loved me from the moment I was born; we were so close that I thought of her as a second mom and Elena and Carlos as my little sister and brother. Like my mom, Maite was a creative soul. She was my mom's right-hand designer, and the two of them were not only close colleagues but also dear friends, eternally optimistic and supportive of each other.

My family was part of the Catalan entrepreneurs of the 70s. Catalans are known to be very hardworking and good businessmen. In fact, a Catalan is saying very dear to me: *"els catalans de les pedres en fan pans,"* meaning Catalans make bread out of stones. My hometown, Terrassa, has a long industrial tradition dating back to the 19th century. In 1856, the train was built in the city, which allowed the textile business to grow as coal and other raw materials could be brought into the city and finished products distributed. In the 1830s, the steam engine, the spinning jenny, and the Jacquard loom in 1845 were inventions that boosted the economy so significantly that in 1876, the city walls had to be brought down to accommodate the growing population. That textile industry was the prelude to the fashion industry that opened so many doors for my family.

My mom was a self-made entrepreneur; her childhood experiences set her on that path and determined her future. She truly had the skills to thrive. From 1936 to 1939, Spain was in a civil war, and there's nothing less civil than a civil war when your enemy is your neighbor. My grandfather was on a list of people to be assassinated by the anarchists, the left party. He was not affiliated with any party and definitely not fighting for Franco, but he was treated as if he belonged to the Franco regime, a Falangist or a far-right extremist. His "mistake" was being the CEO of a company and generating employment, which made him a capitalist and thus a target. That was sufficient reason to kill you in the Barcelona of the Civil War.

Antoni Prats Font was declared missing on October 31st, 1936. My mother and her sister were at home when he was taken at knifepoint in the middle of the night. That was the last time they saw him. My grandfather could never be buried, and his family never had the opportunity to say goodbye. Teresa, my grandmother, found herself alone with two young daughters and no income. She was skilled at sewing, so she started doing repairs for the community to provide for her family. Soon enough, my mother, who was the youngest but very determined, mastered the art of sewing. The business grew from repairs to fashion design.

Later, my mother met my father. He was ambitious, with a business degree and solid experience from a sock manufacturing company. When they married, he transformed my mom's home business into an enterprise. Her talent, combined with my dad's organizational skills and marketing drive, made Datzira a thriving company from the '60s until the '80s. However, from the 80s to the 90s, Asian competition forced prices down. This pressure was too much for Datzira, which, like many competitors, saw its business slow. My dad dared to make the right decision, shutting down the company to protect the family. He was confident but slightly pessimistic, with a flat mouth that contrasted with my mom's upward curve. A man of few words and an ironic sense of humor, he filled my childhood with hilarious moments. He was born elegant, always looking and acting like a gentleman without much effort. My parents had robust values and conservative and capitalist beliefs and were the best role models I could have wished for.

During autumn and winter, we lived in the city center of Terrassa with my two brothers, Felip and Toni. Initially, we lived in a beautiful English-style house with a romantic backyard, where I stayed until I was five. I spent long hours in the nursery, making friends, and with a nanny at home while my parents worked and my brothers were often absent. Toni's whereabouts were often unknown, and Felip would isolate himself in the house, painting, playing instruments, or playing tennis with a beautiful girl named Carme. Felip has always been a very talented multifaceted artist. and then this other sentence Today he represents our city in the Sketchers Global Movement with sketches slike the ones he's including in this memoir. When I turned eight, my parents decided to move to an apartment. "Much more practical," my mom boomed. "Finally, everything on one floor! Goodbye, stairs! I'm tired of going up and down!" She waved her arms dismissively at the stairs, her face beaming with a wonderful smile and high cheeks, revealing her excitement about the move. It was a newly constructed, spacious apartment filled with custom-made solid wood furniture, engraved doors, and marble tables, all in a very contemporary, timeless, and elegant design. Felip didn't stay long in our new apartment; he married Carme, and they decided to live in our first house.

When spring arrived, the weather in Terrassa became too warm, and the school year was nearly over; we packed our suitcases and moved to our villa in Les Pedritxes, a community near the Sant Llorenç del Munt Natural Park next to Matadepera village. Our villa was only twenty minutes from Terrassa city center, but despite the proximity, it was a radical change in temperature, landscape, and lifestyle. It was a privilege to live there, surrounded by huge pines and oak trees in our gardens, all under the majestic view of Sant Llorenç Mountain and its refreshing breeze.

One vivid memory from my solitary times in the garden comes from when I was about twelve. With my eyes shut and my arms wrapped around my favorite of the three tall pine trees in the highest part of the garden, I hummed softly to myself. I pressed against the tree as if to keep it from vanishing. My inner voice spoke, *"This moment will become my past, a part of a life cycle, but it will never leave me."* With intention, I fixed this moment in my memory forever. I stared at the cypress tree where, for the first time years ago, I had seen a mother bird feeding succulent worms to her freshly hatched chicks. I imagined the earthy ground back then, now covered by a carpet of dried pine needles. I pictured my tiny, bare hands massaging the ground until I found similar worms to feed the newborn birds. My pulse quickened when I saw the first worm, and I thought, *"If the mother bird can find these worms, so can I!"* This was one of the many discoveries in what seemed like a vast garden to a girl like me. I was certain this was just one of my life's many cycles, and I so enjoyed that peaceful moment of true freedom.

The only downside was the solitude. Occasionally, I'd invite Nuria over, and those days were extraordinary but rare. I spent countless hours alone in our swimming pool, where I began to fall in love with water. I could swim and dive for hours, losing track of time as I crossed the thin line separating water from air. This was my magical barrier, and when most of me was underwater, I believed time ceased to exist. Sometimes, a girl my age, also named Silvia, from a nearby villa, would come and swim with me, becoming my summer friend. Later, my aunt, my mother's sister, built a villa on some land next to ours, and Maite's family moved there. I played with Maite's children, Elena and Carlos, whom I considered my "brother and sister." They were my rays of sunshine in a family filled with boring grown-ups, at least to a little girl. When Elena and Carlos were old enough, they were allowed to be alone with me in the pool while all the adults worked during our long school vacations. Those times were a blast!

The water in Les Pedritxes was rarely warm, so sometimes, my friend and I looked for alternative things to do. I invented a song with corresponding steps to prepare us for the cold water. "When the song goes 'Yay,' we put our right leg in, then keep singing and move to the stairs. When the song goes 'Whoop,' we go down three steps into the water." It was like a warm-up exercise and song to get into the freezing pool. With that trick, she was always willing to join me, and we played together, splashing in the water. "Now we touch the bottom and do a headstand, okay? One, two, three, go!"

August in Spain is the month of vacation. My parents closed the lingerie manufacturing workshop for four weeks, and it was time to pack for our annual beach holiday. We had an apartment in Calafell, in La Costa Dorada, just an hour away from Terrassa in the Tarragona province of Catalonia. Despite its proximity, Calafell felt wonderfully different. The white sandy beaches, the ever-reliable sun, and the warm Mediterranean waters were a refreshing change. The town had a unique vibe, with its old fishermen's quarter and a tourist area brimming with restaurants, bars, and hippie stores. While Calafell may be crowded today, in the 70s, it was a paradise for Catalans and tourists alike.

I didn't have many friends. My parents, older than most, didn't have friends with children my age, and I was burdened by extreme shyness, making it hard to approach potential friends. Thankfully, my aunt saved me once again by buying an apartment next to ours. Maite, Elena, and Carlos were my lifelines.

I would swim endlessly. The Mediterranean Sea, with its perfect temperature, invited me to dive into a world of play and discovery through my goggles, which I wore constantly. Though there wasn't much marine life on that beach, the tiny crabs walking backward and the small, pale fishes were enough to fascinate my young eyes. The taste of salt on my tongue and the tickling sensation it left on my skin when it dried under the sun were delightful. My restless mind would think, *"The water and sun temperatures are suspiciously perfect... There must be a beach god watching over Calafell."* A wry smile would cross my face as I remembered my thoughts in church, *"I don't believe it, I don't believe it!"* It was my way of resisting stories I didn't need in my life. The sea had cast a spell on me, or perhaps it was all part of the beach god's plan.

The shoreline was full of small, tasty clams called "tallarines" in Catalan, which I would collect. "Mom, I have a bag full of tallarines!" I'd shout to my mom, who was always sunbathing and chatting with her friend or my aunt.

"Wonderful, Silvia! They'll be part of our vermut today," she'd reply.

At our beach apartment, she cooked them to perfection. The intense ocean aroma of seafood mixed with garlic, olive oil, and parsley made my mouth water. My mom was the best cook; she excelled at everything. I wished I could be like her, hoping, as I had done a thousand times before, that some of her extraordinary genes were in me.

Afterward, we'd have a vermut or aperitiu, the Catalan version of an apéritif. It involved enjoying tapas, chips, and olives to stimulate the appetite before lunch, accompanied by a drink or liquor. For Catalans, Spaniards, and many Mediterraneans, it was a time to savor life, share moments with friends or family, discuss various topics, and relax. It wasn't just about the food; it was about the luxury of time, a collective luxury far more valuable than material wealth.

Mari became my mother in her forties in 1970, during a time when Spain was still under the rule of dictator Francisco Franco. Women were expected to be good wives and mothers, with their careers severely restricted. During those silent years, spanning four decades of Spanish history, women needed their husbands' permission to engage in any economic activity, own property, or travel abroad. A strict code of morality marked these years of dictatorship, imposing rigid standards of sexual conduct on women. Divorce, birth control, and abortion were illegal and deemed immoral.

Franco's death in 1975 coincided with the United Nations' recognition of women's rights. Over the next decade, the marital permit was abolished, laws against adultery were repealed, divorce became legal, and abortion was allowed under specific circumstances.

My mother's daily routines when I was six are etched in my memory. Though deeply asleep, I knew she had risen early, as I often over-heard her evening conversations with my dad at dinner around nine p.m. The conversation usually went something like this:

"Today, I arrived at the factory at six as usual, but I barely made progress on the winter 1983 collection. I'm very late, and the display has to be ready by the end of the month for presentation to El Corte Inglés and Galerías Preciados."

"You're always late with the collection. I still remember the chaos it caused last year…"

"I know," Mom would say with a shrug.

"But Maria needed my help with the overlock. She's covering for Emilia, who's still at home coughing. Emilia's delicate fingers are perfect for the satin robes, and Maria doesn't have that experience yet. Then, Teresa didn't know how to finish the embroidery cor-rectly. She's good with courtelle pajamas but not with satin…"

"Your designs are always overcomplicated, and then you have these issues with the stitchers," my father would interrupt, rolling his eyes.

"I know, I know," Mom would admit. Yet, she was aware that her collection stood out from other Spanish brands and could compete with French lingerie precisely because her designs were daring and groundbreaking. She had personally trained each stitcher, who ad-mired her as if she were an oracle.

As soon as my alarm clock urged me to wake up for school, I would hear the door open. It was Mom. She would rush into my room, singing, "Good morning, Silvia! It's time for school." Her voice was warm, and she always looked at everyone with gentle eyes and a joyful, open-mouthed smile. She was always formally dressed in a jacket, skirt, and blouse. Her neck and ears were adorned with modest, plain yet beautiful jewelry made by her jeweler, featuring exotic stones she had bought on her favorite trip to Brazil with my dad. I would turn over in bed, stretch my arms, and pull the blanket over my head, trembling.

"It's so cold, Mom. I wish I could stay in bed longer."

"I know, sweetie, but look, I just washed your corduroy pants with the wool jersey that has matching socks. You'll be so warm and beautiful in those."

Her voice was so caring, and I knew she had more important things to do later, so I got ready and dressed quickly. She waited for me at the kitchen table, where a bowl of hot milk with Colacao—the beloved Spanish chocolate powder—awaited, accompanied by traditional Maria biscuits for dipping. After breakfast, she gave me a huge hug, helped me with my backpack, and said, "Have a good day at school, Silvia!" Her tender voice warmed my heart.

By nine a.m., I was at school. Thanks to the dinner chat, I knew that at nine a.m., she was starting her meeting with the zipper supplier. "These zippers come from China, and the container was delayed. Unless the vendor provides a clear timeline, I'll be forced to change the zipper model," she would explain, her words quick and urgent. "I don't want to, though; this zipper is perfect for our collection. It's soft and thin and won't rub against a woman's skin when she zips it up. It's also the exact color of the pearl satin nightgown needs." Her tone would fluctuate, reflecting her anxiety. "But the delay is already impacting the winter collection production, damaging Datzira's reputation," she'd add, her voice rising and falling like a malfunctioning roller coaster.

Later in the day, she resolved two labor conflicts, attended a cost analysis meeting, and addressed material price questions. Finally, at four p.m., she could continue working on the spring collection designs. She left the workshop around six p.m. to do the groceries, stopping at the fishery for fresh cod, then the supermarket, and finally arriving home at seven p.m.

It was time to prepare her delicious cod with potatoes and tomato sauce, all from scratch. She would boil the tomatoes, peel them, and then mash them to prepare a tasty sauce with virgin olive oil and fresh oregano. She would pour the sauce over boiled potatoes and marinated fish, then bake it all in the oven. She served it at a well-set table with checkered tablecloths and sashes. We would all sit down, awaiting my dad's comment on the dish.

"Today, Mari, I find that the dish lacks a little salt, and the cod isn't as crunchy as the other day," he would mutter, his face showing the same level of disgust as if he had just seen a roach walking on my mom's cod. Mom would hug him and say, "You're right, I'm so sorry. I left it in the oven a little too long and forgot to correct the salt in a hurry. Let me add a bit right now."

In Catalonia, gender roles were still very traditional. My mother was a trailblazer in Catalan society. What was so fascinating about her was how she embraced and merged all her roles with grace. She excelled at being a traditional fifty-year-old mom and housewife of the 80s while also being a very successful entrepreneur. She built a business from nothing with her instinct, creative mind, fast-paced decision-making, and many other natural gifts that always filled those around her with wonder.

"But how do I sew that?" one of the women at the family stitching center would ask.

"You turn the fabric over, grab it from the bottom, and then give it three rows," Mom would reply.

The employee gasped, her confidence shaken. "Mrs. Mari, you always come up with the right answer," she said, her arms falling in admiration.

What made my mom unique was that she was excellent but humble in business and, at home, a traditional mom, always lovely and sweet to me.

"She is a very special woman indeed," my friends would tell me. "She is always so kind to us and so determined, achieving everything with a sweet smile, being feminine but also super-efficient."

I felt grateful and privileged to have her in my life.

That afternoon, as usual, she was running errands after work in her red Mini Cooper, dressed in high heels and a stylish two-piece suit. While loading the car with supplies, a pickpocket snatched her purse. Without hesitation, she removed her left shoe and struck him on the forehead with its pointy heel. The pickpocket, stunned by the blow, dropped the purse and ran away as fast as he could. A wonderful cocktail of kindness, creativity, and kick-butt— that was my mom!

Chapter Three
Turbulent Waters
I Could Not Save Toni

"Imagine trying to live without air. Now imagine

something worse."

— Amy Reed (American Author)

Being a teenager, mixing puberty hormones with the constant confrontation of my brother's addiction turned me into a bit of a rebel. I swapped my well-coordinated outfits for jeans, t-shirts, leather cowboy boots, and a leather jacket. Though still shy when not with my clique, I masked my insecurity with an *"I don't care—I kick ass,"*

attitude, a convenient shell for all my fears. Despite the facade, my core personality remained unchanged. I knew exactly what I wanted and feared nothing but my social anxieties. I never fit into the world of flirting or the meaningless chatter of young adults. For me, going out meant having fun with my friends, laughing, and basking in the comfort of our inside jokes. Sarcasm and irony were my shields outside this inner circle, helping me cover my lack of casual, cool conversation. I wouldn't say I liked drugs and tobacco, which set boundaries in my relationships. When clubbing, I'd have a few drinks to fight my shyness, just enough to push me past my social awkwardness. We danced and jammed all night long.

I have always admired my family's entrepreneurial spirit, especially my mother's strong values. Despite the constant battle to support my brother, she managed her demanding business, paying the salaries of around 50 skilled women who brought life to Datzira's luxurious designs and employed many family members.

From as early as I can remember, I felt lonely and acutely aware of my body's fragility. Yet, I never listened to my body, determined to live a life of strength and bravery. My mind was always the decision-maker, and my aching body simply followed. I was strong because I decided to be. From ages nine to twelve, I suffered from a gluten allergy that caused painful sores, almost splitting my tongue in two. With no wheat or milk, my arms were like feeble branches. *"One day, I'll wake up to find a nest on my arm,"* I'd think, picturing myself holding a worm to feed the bird already on the nest.

I was intentional with my friendships, ensuring I belonged to a group that loved me, fulfilling my utmost necessity. Despite my frail appearance, with long hair and deep brown eyes shadowed by dark circles, I was loud and funny. My positive attitude and eagerness to experience the world helped me hide my conflicts and make friends easily. I missed having siblings of my age, which made me lonely and insecure. My true sisters were my friends; they taught me everything and made me feel strong and successful. Luckily, I spent my days at school, a world where I found solace.

That day, I went to school from nine a.m. to five p.m., played with my friends in the construction area across the street, and then attended ballet class at the prestigious Marta Mos Ballet Academy with Titin and Magda, just a block away from school. Nuria lived on Sant Pere Street, where her mother owned Boada Riera, the most classy paper store in the city. It was the perfect place to buy unique gifts, an impressive pen, or a leather business portfolio. For me, it was where I purchased my diaries, each with different designs and delicate silk-like laces to keep my secrets safe. I wrote in them secretly in my room.

Nuria's paper store was right across from the ballet academy. I started ballet when I was five; Marta Moss was like my mom: a trailblazer, passionate about her business, and beloved by the community. Dancing was my thing, so year after year, I practiced my moves around the class, preparing passionately for the yearly festival. In my teenage years, though, not even the love for dance could stop my adolescent rebel spirit, and I was not alone. The ballet room, surrounded by large mirrors, had one special feature: if you looked carefully, you could see Nuria's face reflected in the mirror, tiny but

42

visible from her living room. As usual, I couldn't focus on ballet because I couldn't stop watching Nuria.

"Look at Nuria now!" Titin would whisper while it was my turn to practice my "Pas de Bourree" from fifth to second position. As I began my series of linking steps, I knew I shouldn't look—losing my balance was a real risk—but I couldn't resist. There she was, like a miniature superhero, alive and animated. One moment, she was a witch laughing madly; the next, a serious figure; then a joker making funny faces. Magda, Titin, and I were in stitches, and my "Pas de Bourree" ended with me on the floor, laughing uncontrollably.

Marta, our ballet teacher, who had put so many expectations on us, was furious. "Shhh," she hissed, giving us that stern look teachers give when they've had enough. We tried to behave for the rest of the class, but with Nuria's antics, it was nearly impossible. Finally, Marta guessed what was happening and pulled the curtain assertively, hiding Nuria from view. Ballet class dragged on, but the fun continued after it ended.

Around seven p.m., we played on Sant Pere Street, interviewing busy citizens for fun. For us, it was all a joke. Titin was supposed to buy bread from the bakery but always forgot, distracted by our antics. Her mom scolded her daily. "Titin, you leave home at nine a.m. and come back at eight p.m. Can't you do a simple errand for your family?"

Titin would reply, "You can't understand it, Mom."

When I got home, my parents had just arrived and were discussing something in the kitchen. Their faces looked disappointed and worried. Instead of saying hello, I went straight to my room to change into my home clothes and prepare for dinner. In Spain, having dinner at nine p.m. is normal. I had a window in my room that my mom had left open for ventilation. The window led to the laundry room, which connected to the kitchen through an open door. I overheard my parents' conversation.

"What can we do to stop him?" my dad asked, his voice tinged with desperation.

"We can't go after him. He's an adult. He's twenty-one," my mom replied, her voice was heavy with despair.

"I will not tolerate this. How can he be so reckless?" My dad was clearly infuriated. "All his friends knew when to stop. What's wrong with him? We've given him everything—a job at the company, a supportive family—and this is how he repays us?" His voice rose, cracking with pain.

"He must have his reasons. He doesn't tell me much. He says he's going to stop," Mom defended Toni, my brother who was twelve years older than me.

"Weed was bad, but this... I've heard heroin is much worse. It takes away your freedom and makes you physically and mentally dependent. It's nearly impossible to quit." Mom was out of words, and she started sobbing. She wouldn't stop until dinner time.

At nine years old, in my room, I learned that my brother was on drugs. I finally understood the tears that rolled down my mom's cheeks every evening as she prepared dinner. I understood why my dad rarely smiled and seemed rooted to the brown striped sofa, escaping into newspapers, looking distant and troubled. His mind seemed to be in a dimension where drugs didn't exist, a place full of other worries. He only seemed to wake up to eat dinner; then, he would return to his spot on the sofa. I never shared with my family that I knew about Toni's addiction, not until years later. I wanted to make my mom's life a bit less sad, assuming she wouldn't want me to know about my brother's struggles.

I was dressed for dinner, but instead of going to the kitchen, I lay on my bed, reminiscing. I recalled a day in Les Pedritxes, our house in the countryside next to the stunning Sant Llorenç Mountain. My parents had been relaxed all week. They weren't discussing the family company's challenges but behaving differently, younger and more joyful. They talked about hotels, reviewed the weather, and joked while packing their suitcases for an upcoming trip to Mexico with friends. The air was filled with unprecedented excitement and the scent of freshly cut flowers, and I loved it.

That evening, however, they looked troubled. Dad was especially silent, his mouth set in a flat line. It was around ten p.m., and we were on the couch watching TV when we heard the main door open. It was Toni. As he entered the living room, Dad stood up and, without a word, slapped him. Toni, more surprised than hurt, lost his balance and fell onto the couch. My world fell apart. I had never experienced violence before. This wasn't my family. Mom and Dad were kind people; they didn't even raise their voices, let alone their hands.

Later, my mom explained, "Toni did something terrible. Dad couldn't contain his anger and frustration. He's ashamed of what he did, Silvia. It won't happen again. "

That was much too intriguing for me to ignore. *"What could be so terrible?"* I wondered. Seizing a moment, I asked Toni.

"What did you do, Toni?"

"I smoke pot," he muttered.

I was furious. "Stop it!" I paused, fighting back my emotions. "It damages your brain. Live your wonderful life... please," I begged him.

"You don't understand. All my friends do it, and it's not so bad," he replied, walking to his room.

"This is bad for you! Stop it!" I yelled, but he didn't seem to listen. If anything, I felt I was putting Toni in an awkward position, and he tried to distance himself from the conversation.

"Good night, Silvia. It's hard to understand," Toni said in a condescending voice, the kind of voice I hated as a girl. The voice adults used me as an excuse not to recognize that I was right. At that moment, I started writing stories about drug dealers, tales that might have been deemed age-inappropriate, but my imagination knew no limits. My reality was what it was, and nobody ever read them. They were my private stories about the bad guys who had lured my brother into the underworld of drugs.

A second later, I snapped back to the present, realizing I was living chapter two of the same story. Only now, Toni was not a teenager dabbling in the fashionable drugs of the 70s. He was twenty-four years old and hooked on the killer—heroin. Still on my bed, I told myself, *"This time, I'm going to talk to him and convince him to stop. Now I can help him. This time, he has to listen to me because I'm nine."*

Toni came home just for dinner. It was dinner as usual, with the TV on, the Catalan anchor reminding us how Madrid was siphoning Catalan taxes and how Barça players were fighting for the Spanish La Liga. Schuster, with his long blonde hair, was the star striker. It seems unlikely now, but in the 70s and 80s, Barcelona rarely won La Liga. The Basque teams, or Real Madrid, usually claimed the title. Amid the transition from Franco's regime to democracy and with ETA terrorist attacks, watching the news was depressing, but we did it religiously every night.

Toni seemed particularly happy and had a great sense of humor. I scanned him, as I did every evening, trying to detect the drugs in his eyes, and I did. Tin foil in our shared bathroom was the only confirmation I needed to know that nothing had changed, that my efforts were useless. Each confrontation left me feeling a deep, painful impotence. I cried for hours alone in my bed, realizing I had absolutely no influence. Toni loved me; his eyes said that. He felt guilty for not being able to listen to me, tolerated all my demands, and my tears made him cry. But heroin was the queen, ruling his actions and thoughts. Everything and everyone else was insignificant before the hateful heroin that possessed him.

I tried one more time to reach out to him, but he was avoiding me. He was a shell of the person he once was, which meant I didn't know him anymore. I lived with a brother who didn't exist and who had withdrawn from all his loved ones.

I have another flashback of the day I planned to help Toni. I picture myself listening to Pink Floyd with Toni in our music room next to the entrance hall. I was fourteen, and he was twenty-six. He was already in the music room, and I entered with a clear plan. I was determined to talk to him, to see if I could somehow help. We both loved Pink Floyd, especially *The Dark Side of the Moon* album, so it was the perfect excuse to join him.

Nothing had changed at home. The tin foil and the little square papers, creased at the corners, kept showing up in the bathroom. By then, I had asked my parents for permission to use their main bedroom bathroom instead; I couldn't stand the sight of our bathroom anymore. The signs of burns and the tin foil floating in the toilet water felt like electroshocks through my body, leaving me unable to smile. My mom kept crying among the pots and pans in the kitchen, oblivious to my constant watch. My dad continued his escape, cross-legged on the sofa, his eyes either distant or laser-focused on the daily news.

"Why did you start?" I finally dared to ask.

"This doesn't happen overnight. I started with pot and soft drugs," he answered, eyes fixed on the floor in shame.

"But why heroin?" I urged him.

"That girl left me. I loved her, and she left me," he murmured. "Then one thing led to another. My best friend tried it, so I thought I had nothing to lose."

"What happens if you don't do it?" I asked, too embarrassed to look at him and too scared of the answer.

"I'll always find it. If someone told me that under this floor, 600 feet down, I could find it, I would start digging with my fingers until I found it." He was brutally honest.

I imagined Toni's hands bleeding, his nails torn from his fingers as he dug relentlessly. The pain would be excruciating, all his nerves screaming, yet his face would show no sign of it, focused solely on reaching the drug. The agony of withdrawal was worse than any physical pain.

Toni's raw honesty and vivid imagination made me grasp the magnitude of his annihilating addiction.

It was Saturday night, and I was dressing up in my black leather mini-skirt for a fun night with friends. I had recently gotten my driver's license and was sharing a black Seat Ibiza with my mom. I headed to the garage to take the car, only to find Toni in his vehicle. As I approached, I saw that he was about to inject himself. A wave of shock slammed into my chest, knocking the breath out of me. I had never imagined I would actually witness Toni doing this.

Fear paralyzed me as the image of Toni's fifteen-year addiction became overwhelmingly real. Then, my fear dissipated, replaced by labored breaths and an overpowering disgust. I decided to stop it—I had to. Breathing heavily, eyes wide open, I walked determinedly towards him. Without hesitation, I flicked the syringe from his right hand.

His look was dreadful, filled with desperation. For a moment, I wondered if he would hurt me, but I knew he wouldn't. I wasn't scared. I stared at him, searching for a sign of gratitude, a sign that only existed in my dreams. Holding the syringe with the hateful venom high above my head, I waited.

"Silvia, please, give it back to me," he begged, his voice desperate and shameful.

"No!" I yelled, my voice echoing through the garage. He made a vague attempt to reach for it but stopped, looking at me with hollow eyes.

I wanted to smash the syringe to the ground and crush it under my foot, spilling its contents all over the parking floor, lost forever. For a few seconds, my hand stayed raised as if pulled by an invisible string. Then, swallowing all my rage, I handed it back to him. There was no way out. I knew that love and reason could never compete with heroin.

I walked back to the elevator and returned to our apartment. In my room, I cried for hours. It was now a fact: I could not save Toni.

My parents tried many times to admit Toni to the city center hospital as an inpatient. Each time, he escaped, rendering our efforts and suffering useless. Once, my mom decided to take matters into her own hands. When Toni was in withdrawal, she locked him in his bedroom. We were in this together, and I was tasked with guarding his door.

"Mom, he hasn't come out, but I don't hear any noise in his room. Please come; this is weird," I shouted to her while she was housekeeping and I was studying on the floor next to Toni's bedroom.

"Let's open the door," she murmured. She had rigged the door to lock from the outside and now was reversing it.

The door swung open to reveal a wide-open window. Attached to the bed next to the window was a rope made from Toni's sheets, extending down the building. It reached from our third-floor apartment to the first floor. "From the first floor, he had to jump," Mom sighed, her eyes scanning the space for any sign of him. I nodded, stunned. I couldn't believe what had happened. Once again, heroin had prevailed.

These experiences were like meteorites crashing into my life, creating a dimension of existence as real as my nurtured, pleasant life with my parents and friends. Sometimes, I could forget about Toni's addiction for a while, and I'm grateful for those moments. But it was never completely ignored; it hung in the air I breathed, always coming back to remind me that life is not a free ticket—we must endure whatever comes our way.

I did not take my good times for granted. That's why I built deep bonds with my friends and cherished them. I wrote about everything in my diaries. I knew Toni's terrible experiences wouldn't just disappear, and I couldn't look away because that's not who I was or who I wanted to be. Helping out was not optional for me; it was rooted in my being. I was so stubborn that I would never allow myself to compromise my values.

There were indeed periods when I lived my easy life, but afterward, I felt remorseful. The times when I was committed to helping Toni were frustrating; I felt powerless, and it ate away at me. It's a trauma that I have only recently begun to overcome. I believe I have learned to distance any image of drugs from my personal life, and I can now talk about it with a certain stability.

Toni was so fun and spontaneous before his addiction. It hurts to think I never really got to know him. My cousin Elena, who was the same age as Toni, often recounted stories of his adventurous spirit as a child. He was daring and brave, more so than the older kids, despite being all skin and bones and significantly shorter than his peers. On a recent family hike to my beloved Sant Llorenç Mountain, Elena reminisced about how six-year-old Toni would jump from an Olympic-sized trampoline at one of the first public pools in Catalonia. "Everyone in that pool applauded him for his courage," Elena said. I had heard this story before; it was one of my mom's favorites to tell during BBQs at our round table in Les Pedritxes. How I loved that round table.

My dad was a BBQ expert. In Catalonia, barbecued lamb and sausages are more traditional than steak. Dad, a true foodie, believed the lamb tasted best when cooked over real pine wood, shunning chemical fire starters as a sign of poor taste.

"Silvia, get some mid-sized pine branches," he'd order.

"Right now!" I'd mutter, then proudly ask, "Do you need pinecones and dry foliage too?"

"No, I have those over there," Dad would whisper, his eyes focused on the brick barbecue, expertly fanning the initial flames. Sometimes, I thought of our BBQ as a family altar. These meals, prepared with intention, were clear evidence that our family was special.

Mom silently prepared the aioli sauce in the kitchen. Though more practical, she often added an egg to the mortar, a ceramic bowl used for making sauces in Spain. This was considered cheating in our family code. Traditionally, aioli is made with breadcrumbs, minced garlic, and a steady stream of olive oil, ground with a steady hand until it becomes creamy. The egg shortcut made the process quicker and more convenient.

Finally, Mom, Dad, Toni, and I would sit at the table, savoring our lamb BBQ with fresh salad and perfectly toasted homemade French fries. Toni would make us laugh with his jokes and sharp irony. What wasn't there to love about him?

Reflecting on Toni's story, I sometimes thought that his bravery and eagerness to win might explain why he struggled with addiction later in life. Perhaps he believed he could conquer anything, even drugs. He might have seen drugs as a temporary refuge during life's storms, not realizing that this refuge would suffocate him. Additionally, I'm sure he felt alone, possibly didn't fit in, and maybe inherited a tendency toward depression from Dad. In 1980s Spain, depression was only treated if severe, and early signs were often overlooked. There must have been a combination of powerful reasons that led Toni to waste his precious life.

My ever-fighting mom soon found a rehabilitation center for Toni near the sacred mountain of Montserrat, a multi-peaked mountain range made of sedimentary rock. It is well-known as the site of the Benedictine Abbey, Santa Maria de Montserrat, which hosts the Virgin of Montserrat sanctuary. Catalans call her 'La Moreneta,' or the Black Madonna, and she is the patron saint of Catalonia, a symbol cherished by all, whether Catholic or not. La Moreneta represents the Virgin Mary with the infant Jesus on her knees.

In that rehab center, patients learned countryside skills like farming, agriculture, carpentry, and pottery. It was a bright new concept, and my mom was so hopeful. Toni thrived there, gaining weight that filled his sunken eyes and cheeks. He shone with a renewed spirit. He recovered, and for a while, I had the chance to see my brother as he was meant to be. I remember picking him up from the center and having lunch together at my dad's friend's restaurant, Mr. Pastallé, a charismatic cook with a TV show on Catalan television. Toni laughed hard at Mr. Pastallé's stories, making him our private stand-up comedian.

The irony of life struck when, just as Toni was recovering and re-gaining his life, another huge beast haunted him. He contracted AIDS, a disease that people live with today, but in the nineties, it was often a death sentence. Toni died at the age of thirty-six, the same age Jesus Christ died. It rarely rains in Catalonia, but on the day we buried my brother, a frightening thunderstorm raged throughout the ceremony. In my mind, I imagined it was the cosmos condemning all drug cartels as the assassins they are, taking my brother and so many others who couldn't complete their journeys on Earth.

I was often tired, and to do all the things I wanted, I took long naps to gather enough energy. I was very fortunate that my parents gave me what I needed most: love and safety. I'd listen to music, dance, write a memoir, and study foreign languages, all with myself and my best company—my imagination and plans. In the background, I'd hear my mother's cries and my dad's stillness as he read the paper, so motionless that I sometimes wondered if he was a wax figure from Madame Tussauds. Most of the time, I heard only the sound of silence because my parents worked long hours.

Despite the challenges, the essentials were there: safety, warmth, love, and appreciation. My parents were great role models and became an indelible part of who I am. Even in moments of anger or extreme happiness, I was always in control, ready to lead my destiny and kick ass like my mom and dad. That's why I studied Business Administration.

Learning languages was my passion. I listened to old cassettes of Oxford British English lessons and "Speak Up Magazine," which introduced me to the cultures of the English-speaking world. Fascinated by English, I advanced quickly in formal classes and was invited to jump to the top levels. After mastering English, I learned French and German. I pursued a master's in international business, driven by my curiosity about other lands and cultures, and excited to put my language skills into practice.

Chapter Four:
Go with the Flow
I Find "The One," I Lose My Mom.

"The best way to observe a fish is to become a fish."

–Jackes Yves Cousteau

"What do you want me to say? I don't like him. Not happening. Tell him I'm not interested." I scoffed, raising my palms and shaking my head.

"But he is a good guy, and he truly cares for you," Titin insisted, her voice rising a bit.

"And he keeps asking me to tell you he wants to meet you," she continued, waving her hand dismissively. Titin could be persuasive, and I trusted her instincts, but at that point in my life, I wanted to fly solo—or with a very, very bad guy. I wanted to stay the rebel, to keep telling myself I was strong and could lead my destiny, deviating from the plans I had traced out for myself in childhood. I was hurt and wanted to live on my terms. Now, I dared. I had found my voice beyond my inner circle, and that made me feel powerful. Only now do I see how much I was struggling to find balance, how my aggressiveness was masking my wounds, and how much life I had yet to live to be myself truly?

The day I met Xavi in that club, all my preconceptions were confirmed. *"He's just a spoiled rich kid,"* I instantly judged. He was cute, but his approach was *"the worst."*

"You shine like a star…"

Eww. I still don't know how it happened, but despite it all, I agreed to go with him to another club and got into his red VW Golf GTI, a cool car back then. Trying to be romantic, he played Julio Iglesias for me.

"Ugh!" Another red flag. Everything about him screamed corny. At the time, I was into ACDC and Pink Floyd—my favorite band of all time. So hearing "Julito" as I stepped into his car, music my mom and aunt played when I was five, was jarring. Somehow, though, those things turned out to be irrelevant distractions, an outside facade. What matters in a person lies much deeper within. The inside of a person isn't visible at first glance; it speaks only if you're patient, quiet, and willing to listen. Back then, I was anything but patient. I was probably talking too much, but I've always been a good listener. Maybe it was my listening style that allowed me to connect with Xavi, to get to know him, and to love him.

So many remarkable things have happened in my life, no matter how much I tried to avoid them... Xavi is one of those things. At the end of that night, I was both disgusted and intrigued, but one thing was certain: I wanted more. I'm a Pisces, and so is Xavi. I once read that when two Pisces come together, it's like a bubbling witch's cauldron, where frog legs mix with snake skins, and once the spell is cast, anything is possible. Our relationship was unexpected and has always been unpredictable. After our first dinner, I knew I'd never be bored with him: he made me laugh, he surprised me, and most importantly, he didn't agree with everything I said. In fact, he often did the opposite, which I found much more fun. Xavi was different from anyone I had met before, unconventional. We shared values and lifestyles. Marrying him was easy.

Being a passionate woman, I often found myself drained, like those TV images of skyscrapers collapsing to the ground. But it only took a sentence from Xavi to lift me, to retake my flight into my world of emotion, imagination, and passion. He completes me. His confident posture, his dark humor paired with his sarcastic laugh—it can be quite annoying but always makes me smile—his grounded attitude and his few but honest words keep me intrigued and in love. Even in 2024, after more than 25 years of marriage and 30 years together, I'm still in love with him.

I met Xavi during my university years. I was studying Business Management, and he was pursuing Economics. Those years we spent together were precious. I left behind my need to be defensive, to kick ass, and to be in your face. We understood each other so well, not just in words but in a deep, almost synchronized connection. He gave me what I needed most: peace.

I was twenty-two, when my gynecologist found a lump in my left ovary. Fortune smiled at me; it wasn't cancer, but it had to be removed because of its size and growth. A few days later, I was in surgery. When I woke, they told me my left ovary was gone. The tumor had entwined itself so deeply with the ovary that the doctor had to remove it all.

Xavi and I had been together for about nine months. He showed up at the hospital. I must have lit up when I saw him, but fear gripped me, afraid I might lose him. I felt an urgent need to share my deepest fears. "Xavi, I might not be able to have children," I told him, looking him squarely in the eyes.

"I don't care," he replied, his face expressionless, unmoved. "It doesn't matter. I want you; that's all I want. There are too many kids in the world; we can adopt one." He made it sound so easy, so logical, so obvious that I believed him. I loved him deeply for those words, especially because I knew his nature; I knew he spoke his truth. Xavi doesn't lie. He says things people don't like, things I don't like, but he never lies.

Those words stay with me. Whenever I'm angry with him, I remember those words, probably the most beautiful he's ever said to me. As I said, Xavi is a man of few words, and I mean it—few words, few.

The first two years of our marriage were sweet and easy. We worked hard, focusing on our careers, but we also found time to relax, enjoy fine dining, and have fun with friends. During the summer holidays, we loved to travel. Drawn to the ideas of free trade and capitalism, our first international trip was to New York City, a place that captivated us so much it was hard to leave. On our honeymoon, we explored the West Coast, visiting San Francisco. Vesuvio on Columbus Ave. and City Lights Bookstore reminded me of similar spots in Vienna and Barcelona.

The first year, we also explored the East Coast. In addition to returning to New York City, we visited Boston, with its charming Boston Market where I tasted the most extraordinary ribs.

In Chicago, we jammed the night away with a black jazz band. The emotion in that room was so tangible; it felt as if the saxophones and trumpets were stealing my soul, taking me on a journey through the sacred origins and raw lives of the musicians. The French Quarter in New Orleans, with its cast iron balconies, added a romantic touch to our trip. Strolling through its streets, breathing in the timeless appeal and the intense smells of onions, peppers, and garlic from Creole cuisine confirmed their rich heritage.

Lastly, we visited New England. In Maine, we indulged in endless lobster. My dad would have argued that Mediterranean lobster is more complex and flavorful. Being his daughter and well-schooled in culinary art—not in cooking but in seeking out the best seafood restaurants—I had to admit, *"Dad, wherever you are, you're right."* But I'd add, *"For me, the experience is not just about the food, but the atmosphere and the company. That lobster served at the pier in an old-fashioned restaurant with a red-painted wooden table tasted almost as good as the ones we shared at Old Casa Jacinto."* And I'd imagine my dad's playful retort, *"Nah, not good,"* making me laugh.

In our second year of marriage, we sought a change and opted for a nature and wildlife adventure. We booked an international safari in Zimbabwe and Botswana, where we slept in tents near the parks. Our guide, Ian, a young Englishman who had lived there since his teens, felt more like a new friend than a tourist guide. He introduced us to his community, his places, and everything he loved about Africa.

At night, we'd hear lions roaring in the distance. *"How nice,"* I thought. One day, I literally felt a warthog's head against our tent. *"Not so nice,"* was my next thought. One of those huge heads was pressing against the tent wall, probably digging for bulbs and roots. A moment later, the whole animal was rubbing against the tent and, therefore, against me. *"Not nice at all!"* I assumed while Xavi, inexplicably unaware of the shaking tent and the loud oinking, checked his cell phone.

"Xavi, quiet! Switch off the cell phone light now!" I whispered urgently, petrified with fear and holding my breath to stay silent. I envisioned a news headline: *"Two Catalan Tourists Disappear in Zimbabwe,"* and imagined Catalans back home saying, "What were they thinking? Who goes camping in the savanna?"

Despite the incident, Africa had captured our souls. The laughter of its children, the silences of the Okavango Delta, and the night drums with our new friends, their expressive faces illuminated by the bonfire next to our tent, all left a deep impression on us. We decided to return the next summer. But life had other plans: my mom passed away just as we were supposed to head back to the savanna. In hindsight, I was grateful we canceled the trip and spent my free time with her instead. Only years later did I realize that losing my mom early in life meant she would never meet our children. Her hard-working attitude and her endless suffering for our Toni had led to an anemia she couldn't recover from.

At that time, I had just been promoted to a leadership role at DuPont. Work became my best medicine, my antidote to despair. It distributed my grief across time, allowing me to shed only as many tears as my body could bear each day. It took years, but I recovered, and now I embrace her memory as one of the greatest privileges of my life.

Xavi thrived in finance. After graduating in economics, he completed the Securities Industry Essentials to operate in the markets. We spent our summers on the Mediterranean at a village named L'Ametlla de Mar (the Almond of the Sea) in La Costa Dorada of Tarragona province. Winter weekends were abundant with skiing in the Pyrenees, the pure white valleys filling us with peace and joy. We were a hardworking couple who had accomplished the hard part of life, looking forward to professional growth and raising a happy family. I consider myself a hard worker, a fighter, and an achiever. Life had shaped me that way. My brother's addiction had shown me early on that I needed to cherish every moment of peace and joy. Mom's unfair death only confirmed those beliefs, so I savored every bit of our perfect family life.

Sometimes, I think I survived my mom's passing because I had my own new family. I was anchored, having built my little island of safety and happiness.

I was passionate about my job. Promoted to a supervisory role, I led the warehouses and relished being a woman in a traditionally male job. Later, working for DuPont, I was promoted to Supply Chain Manager. I aimed to make the warehousing site operation safer despite having to confront "macho" truck drivers resisting new safety practices. I eliminated unethical practices from some dishonest persons in high positions, ensuring the company's finances and reputation remained intact. Acting according to ethics and values made me feel unstoppable, and DuPont reinforced these in me. During that time, I dressed a bit manly to fit into the still very masculine corporate world. Reflecting on it now, it's clear how hard women have tried to fit in.

I really appreciated the red-line policy that DuPont had in place where any employee could report unethical behavior; it was especially tough on sexual assault. In a former company, I was sexually harassed on a business trip. The aggressor, a higher-ranking director, stopped when I demanded he did so. It was a deeply disturbing experience that kept me awake all night, tears flowing, an overwhelming sense of disgust, rage, shame, and injustice suffocating me. He didn't touch me, so I guess I was one of the less unfortunate victims in the #MeToo movement.

I fell in love for the first time when I was four, in kindergarten. Love found me many times in life, but when I met Xavi, everything fell into place. It wasn't just knowing; it was a deep certainty that he was meant to be my family. His few words are assertive, never doubting. Sometimes, he's right; sometimes, he's wrong, but his confidence is unwavering. When he's bad, he admits it—albeit not as graciously or quickly as I'd like. His British sense of humor, his rare smiles that

63

make me laugh hard, and his posture that some of my girlfriends mistook for arrogance all made him intriguing.

Xavi understands the blacks and whites of life better than the grays. I, on the other hand, see all the grays on this planet and in other galaxies and all their shades. This makes him a mystery from many perspectives, leaving so much in his comments unexplained. I often have to figure it out, make it up, or take a best guess. Sometimes it isn't very pleasant, but usually it's entertaining. There are days when I'm lost in the grays and need rescue. He doesn't notice, but when I ask, he easily extends his hand, helping me land on a more practical world, which I appreciate. He has the character to disagree with me, never swayed by my opinions. I love that about him. We look at things from different angles, enriching both our lives.

Next to him, I felt balanced and safe. Above all, I knew he'd always tell me the truth, whether I wanted to hear it or not. That truth was the solid pillar that anchored me.

I pictured myself in that hospital room, so white and impersonal, a stark contrast to what my mother was in life, full of colorful imprints and exotic textures, her heart a canvas of rainbows. I was twenty-nine, in 1999. Xavi sat on a depressing white chair. I perched on the edge of Mom's hospital bed next to her. She's been hospitalized after years of battling anemia, kept going by cortisone, but increasingly reliant on platelet transfusions. The cortisone weakened her, and now, they tell us, her body can no longer produce or even retain white cells. Surgery is not an option; it's only a matter of time.

Holding her hand, I felt the fragility. *"She looks so pale and fragile, she breaks me down,"* I thought.

She gazed at me with tired eyes, still full of magic candor, and whispers, "Wet my lips…dryness." Silence follows.

Xavi buried his head in his hands; he'd never faced death so closely.

Mom repeated, "Wet my lips…dryness."

Each time, I gently applied a wet gauze to her lips, now as pale as the room. Blood leaves her lips. Her eyes were nearly closed, and her mouth showed discomfort. "Wet my lips…dryness."

I closed my eyes, seeing myself in that stark, hopeless room. I wipe Mom's lips carefully with a cold towel. "Am I doing it right, Mom?" I mutter, my face close to hers.

"Yes, thanks, Silvia," she cracked a smile, that sweet smile transforming her face and illuminating my existence—the smile that made her who she was. Her prominent cheeks are now sunken and not as strong, but she remains beautiful and angelic.

"Mom, how are you?" I asked, desperate to hear her voice, to know she felt me.

"I'm well, Silvia, do not worry, I'm very well," she mumbled. Her words bring peace; she tells me what I need to hear, always giving everything for me, anything.

Moments later, there was silence, the kind that lasts forever. In that eternal silence, I realized Mom had just assured me she was well moments before she passed. *"She had to be kind and caring till her last breath because that's who she was,"* I told myself. Today, I believe she was indeed well because we were together, comforting one another as always; though she comforted me more, she was always more.

She was an independent woman who never wanted to take from anyone, only to create and give to others. This made her so special and made my mom my mom.

Here is when I learned that my job would be my friend, helping me overcome life's difficulties by keeping me focused on stimulating challenges. Compared to the real challenges of life, work was easy and entertaining. My job became the easy part of my life, a place where my effort brought results, a place where I could thrive.

Part II
By the Mediterranean
My life after Marc

"The heart of man is very much like the sea; it has its storms, it has its tides, and in its depths, it has its pearls too."

– Vincent van Gogh

Chapter Five
Watch Out, a Tsunami Is Coming!
Our Lovely Marc is Born!

"You'll Never Walk Alone" by Rodgers and Hammerstein's musical Carousel and in 1963 by local Liverpool group Gerry and the Pacemakers.

Ibiza, one of the precious Balearic Islands, part of the Catalan territories, is renowned for its *"calas."* A *"cala"* is a small bay nestled between cliffs or rocks, rounded like a semicircle, unlike a linear beach. Xavi and I decided to treat ourselves to a summer escape there, choosing the quieter September over the crowded months of July and August.

The Mediterranean sun had given our skin the healthy tone we longed for. We were in love. That morning, the *"Cala"* was ours. The water, pristine blue, caressed my skin as I swam, my movements creating bubbles that danced around me. My senses were fully awakened. I turned onto my back, floating effortlessly under the sun, my body still like a piece of wood. My legs were slightly apart, soaking in the warmth. The sun's rays activated every nerve receptor. My lips parted slightly, and I tasted the salt from the overwhelmingly saline Mediterranean water. I liked the excess salt, rubbing it first on my lower lip and then on my upper lip. Wet and salty made a great combination. Deep breaths increased the oxygen in my blood, stretching and relaxing my muscles, even my pelvic floor. Out of the water, I reunited with Xavi. This *"cala"* was ours today.

The previous night, we had savored a delicious *"caldereta,"* an incredible lobster soup typical of Menorca, another Balearic island. We dined at a beachside restaurant, sharing a bottle of Mateus, a rosé we enjoyed back then. It wasn't the best Portuguese wine, but we found it refreshing. I loved its decadent pink color and the roundness of its bottle.

"Should I stop taking the pill?" I hesitated, touching the base of my neck.

"Yes, why not? We could try to have a child," Xavi asserted, "I'm ready whenever you are." He half smiled.

"I'm not sure if I want to have a child yet," I shuddered. "But I'm thinking that because we might never be able to have one, it probably makes sense to let my body recover the little ability left to conceive by stopping the pill now," I sighed and continued, "so that in a few years when we're sure it's the right time, we might have better chances." I held up my palms and added, "I won't get pregnant anyway." Letting my arms fall by my side, I leaned back in my chair.

I sighed again. It wasn't entirely true that I had no hope left of becoming a mother, but at that time, saying those words felt like a way to protect myself from getting hurt.

It had been a long day at DuPont. We were doing inventory on the two warehouses, a task exhausting enough, but especially so with my eight-month pregnancy. At thirty-two, I was thrilled to be on the brink of having my first child. The hormones gave me extra strength, which was handy for my job. I was very successful. That same day, I had a scheduled check-up at the clinic. The inventory wasn't adding up, and I was close to canceling the gynecology visit. It seemed like just another routine appointment that could easily be rescheduled. Thankfully, everything was resolved, and I could finalize the inventory with finance and leave the site.

I arrived at the clinic a bit late, and five minutes later, I was lying there with wires around my tummy, surrounded by the beeping of the machine monitoring Marc's heartbeat. I wanted to get out of there and go home; I felt so tired. Then, the doctor appeared and introduced himself.

He left me for a while, then started coming and going, making strange faces every time he looked at the monitor. Finally, I got tired of the faces and no words and asked, "What is going on?"

"Silvia, I'm hearing something I don't like. It looks like an arrhythmia," he muttered, his expression unreadable.

"Probably, the baby is playing with the umbilical cord. Some do that!" he said. Now I understand he was annoyed with Marc for playing.

70

"I hate it when they do that," he said, his voice hesitating and annoyed. He moved his hands, looking at my tummy as if lecturing my child.

Finally, the doctor turned to me and ordered, "Go home. It will probably be okay. He must be playing and confusing us."

I think I have to stop here and celebrate Marc's record of a kid with autism, behaviors, and later diagnoses by misbehaving so much as to receive a lecture when he was eight months old and still in his mom's tummy. This is a joke I can only make after surviving all those years of behavior.

At that point, my mind was on fire. My routine schedule, which I almost skipped, was turning into something potentially dangerous for my son. How could he send me home if he heard an arrhythmia? I was determined to get to the bottom of it. I was ready for any sacrifice. I was about to be a mother, and nobody messes with a mother.

I looked straight into the doctor's eyes and hissed, "What do you mean it's p r o b a b l y going to be okay? This is my son you're talking about. Is there anything we can do to reduce any risks?"

His expression changed from la-la-la-I'm-so-relaxed-in-this-routine-test to pure doubt, fear visible in his eyes, now wide open like ping-pong balls.

"So tell me," I insisted, "is there anything we can do to make sure he is okay?" My hormones were jumping, my attitude openly desperate, defiant, demanding a solid decision from my doctor.

"Well, we could do a C-section, but," he said, visibly frustrated, maybe with Marc, with me, or just overwhelmed by the situation.

His voice grew louder, more patronizing. "I'm going to apply oxytocin to you, and you're going to dilate and have your baby. If, for whatever reason, you do not dilate, then you're having a C-section today in hours. Bottom line you're not going home today because you're having a baby."

"Okay, no problem," I replied.

"Worst case scenario, I'll get a C-section. Nothing out of this world," I thought. *"I knew many women who had gone through that. Easy peasy. What does this doctor think, that I'm going to be scared?"* My only thought was, *"Marc will be okay, he will be okay..."*

"Well, if that's what you want?" The doctor paused, seemingly accepting that I was determined to ensure my son's safety before leaving the clinic.

"We are going to admit you, apply oxytocin, and induce labor. If natural birth isn't possible, then a C-section." Now, his frustration seemed directed at me, but I didn't care.

In hindsight, I realize it must not be easy to be a doctor and to make swift decisions with limited information. At that moment, I just wanted my child alive. I was asking him to do his best, and I would do mine, making any necessary sacrifice to help my first child survive.

I called Xavi. During my pregnancy, he had been living in Andorra, a tiny country nestled high in the Pyrenees between France and Spain, a ski paradise. Before pregnancy, I often joined him on weekends, enjoying Andorra's ski resorts like Ordino Arkalis and Pas de la Casa. Andorra is also known for its financial institutions, which is why my husband was there.

"Xavi, you have to come back. I'm at the clinic; we are going to have the baby." I tried to use a calm voice to prevent him from panicking, but the urgency of the message was clear.

"Are you kidding me? No way! What happened? Is the baby okay? Are you okay?" he burst into questions, his voice was trembling.

"Everything is going to be okay. Just take your time and come to the clinic safely."

Meanwhile, I wasn't dilating at all. Hours went by, and the oxytocin had no impact at all on my body. At some point, the doctor returned and announced, "We have to do a cesarean section."

I simply said, "No problem, proceed as needed. Everything is going to be okay."

Just as I was being prepped for surgery, Xavi arrived. He was pale, devastated, his arms in his pockets and his head hanging low, like ripe apples from the trees. We hugged, and I kept reassuring him that Marc would be fine. I felt strong; the doctor and I were going to save the day.

I have a flash of lying in that white room under harsh white light. A huge white sheet blocked my view of the mess the doctor and a colleague were making with my body. I was completely awake. From time to time, they joked with me, trying to ease the tension that filled the artificial space. Everything around me felt deeply uncomfortable, but I didn't care. Throughout the surgery, I imagined Marc. My mind acknowledged the outside world but focused inward, envisioning how the world would shine in colors once this irrelevant thunderstorm passed. I saw myself holding my first child tightly, promising him a life of happiness and opportunity.

Years later, I thought, *"It had to be a cesarean section. Of course, Marc wouldn't make less of a statement coming into this world."*

Marc was born on November 27, 2002, at eight nineteen p.m. by cesarean section. I was only in my thirty-sixth week of pregnancy, the eighth month, so he weighed just 4.96 pounds. Marc was placed on my stomach. I looked at him, and he took my breath away. He was perfect. Despite being small and light, his features made up for it. His lips were full and curled up to his nose as if saying, *"I might be small, but I'm here, and I have personality."* His head was covered in silky brown hair, giving him a surprisingly mature look for an eighth-month-old newborn. In a flash, the doctor took Marc away. I had only briefly felt Marc against my body, and now I missed him terribly.

Later, the doctor returned and told us they had placed Marc in the incubator as a precaution. They didn't even turn it on; they just kept him protected for a few hours because he was a very healthy kid. The fact that Marc was placed in the incubator had a profound impact on Xavi; his face went pale, his eyes anchored to the floor, and he froze in silence. When they finally brought Marc back to us, Xavi did something I've never seen him doing again: he burst into a desperate cry. Men don't cry as easily as women, and Xavi is no different. So I suffered for him, and as we've always done for each other,

I remained strong, pretending I wasn't troubled, trying to dismiss his worries to cheer him up.

"Don't cry, Xavi. Marc was born. They told us he was healthy and we'd be such a happy family. You'll see, we have such a bright future ahead of us," I whispered in his ear, my arm around his shoulder, my hand resting on his chest.

"He looks so fragile and lonely," Xavi muttered. "I can't stand the idea that he started his life alone in that crystal box." Tears rolled down his cheeks. My words couldn't alleviate his suffering; he had a breakdown. Xavi's words seemed like a hunch, but he made a promise to Marc that day: "You will never walk alone."

Breastfeeding lasted only a few months. Marc wasn't gaining enough weight, and I felt terrible, thinking I wasn't producing enough milk for him. I can easily transport myself to that day when another mom multiplied my guilt with just one sentence. "This is common in working mothers. You don't relax enough to feed your children. You're so disconnected from your maternal instinct that you forget the natural postures for nursing. And what's worse is that your poor kids suffer the consequences, having to switch to formula."

I didn't believe the complete criticism, but it made sense that my milk was better than formula. So, I bought one of those pumps meant to draw milk from my breasts. It hurt so much! Soon, I wouldn't say I liked it. It didn't work for me, and after weeks of suffering the artifact that made me feel like a broken cow, one day, I smashed it against the wall. That was the end of my first self-imposed torture of the many to come in my life after Marc. Xavi didn't understand what the big deal was and insisted on being practical and switching to the bottle.

Some weeks before the stupid pump crashed, Xavi had urged me to stop with sentences like, "Just do what everyone is doing, Silvia. This pump doesn't work, and you have the solution right here. Throw the pump away; you're hurting yourself."

And I had responded in a high pitch something like, "Don't you realize I'm a mom on a mission? He has to reach six pounds next month, and I'll make it happen with Mother's milk! It can't be that difficult. Besides, I've always thrived on challenges. Don't worry about me; I'll keep trying."

I'm stubborn and willing to sacrifice for anything my mind deems important. Like all traits, it's sometimes a blessing but often a curse. In the case of the pump, it was definitely the latter. It created unnecessary stress, and my breasts simply weren't producing more milk with that gadget. I was submitting them to torture for no reason. Xavi was totally right, as usual. Many years later, in an interview, I declared, "I love it when people say this is impossible, and I think to myself, this is impossible for you!"

Fortunately, the pediatrician disagreed with my "friend's theory" and urged me to introduce the bottle along with breastfeeding in the second month. That helped Marc and lifted a weight off my shoulders.

I so admired his long eyelashes and his huge, mysterious eyes. He was an adorable child, and I felt whole. I was so in love with his little moves that I often found myself overwhelmed with tears of joy. Then I'd hug him and again hug him or stretch my arms and make him fly like an airplane while I danced around the room. Everything about him was fragile, from his tiny toes to his rounded little tummy, and that made him even cuter. I wasn't worried about Marc's weight because I was fully committed to him—to helping him grow, to protecting him so he would never suffer, and to loving him to the fullest. I'd go above and beyond to help Marc unconditionally.

He was such a cute baby. I see myself changing diapers with a wide smile on my face. Everything about Marc aroused that new feeling of motherhood I had been afraid of for so long, being so attached to my career. Now, I embraced it with all my soul, like a casual ray of sunshine disarming my disciplined, corporate-structured mind. It felt so refreshing.

There was always something about Marc that, at that stage, probably only intrigued me. He spent hours playing with his feet in a real happy baby pose, reaching with his big toe to the funny monkey and the polka-dotted padded mirror hanging from a rainbow above his colorful, squared baby mat. His cute features were relaxed, regardless of my tickling his big toe or making funny faces, doing all the loving demonstrations that moms do to get their toddlers' affection. Then, out of the blue, in the moments when I was just observing him, not interacting, he would crack a smile. Those smiles were my life, filling my lungs with fresh air that smelled like rainbows.

In Spain, one parent gets nine months of maternity leave. I decided to take only two months of full-time leave and then gradually increase my working hours each week. That way, I'd have some fresh air that smelled like rainbows time with Marc until he was one and a half years old. I spent magical hours in the mornings with Marc and drove to work in the afternoons. It was a way to not lose myself completely for too long; I loved being a mother and having a career, too.

My lovely cousin Maite, who was in her early fifties and had taken care of me so wonderfully when she was in her twenties and I was a little girl, babysat Marc during the hours I worked until he was two. This reunited us and made our special admiration for each other blossom again.

Xavi had just returned from the bank. I was already home, feeding Marc a delicious creamy dinner made with fresh, organic veggies that every Saturday morning I'd buy from him at El Mercat de la Independència, a modernist building in Terrassa city center that has been providing fresh products to the city since 1908. Marc loved my purees. His chubby face was decorated with orange cream and full of healthy carrots. It wasn't our first purée, so I bought him an extra-large bib that was a winner. As I moved the spoon from the little Winnie the Pooh plate to his mouth, Xavi sat beside me, and our conversation went something like this:

"He seems only half-aware. He doesn't respond much to me, and when I call his name, he doesn't turn. Maybe I'm not his priority," I said to Xavi. Then I joked, "Imagine if I'm not his priority now; what will happen when he's a teenager? I don't even want to go there." I raised my eyebrows, shrugged my elbows, and made one of my silly faces biting my tongue.

I continued sharing the little magic moments I had spent with Marc. "You should have seen him today when we were watching the Mickey Mouse Clubhouse. When Mickey fell, Marc cracked up laughing. His laugh is so contagious that I ended up having a blast, too."

"What a character!" Xavi said, smiling. Suddenly, Xavi's face transformed; it darkened. "I smell trouble…" he mumbled.

There's one day that stands out from the many memories of Marc's first year of life. I'm in a supermarket in Terrassa, in the city center by the townhouse. I had walked from home, and Marc was in his new maroon stroller. He is eight months old now and can hold his back when seated. I hold him and, for the first time, sit him in the supermarket cart as we set off to do our groceries. He makes me proud. "What a big boy we have here," I exclaim, looking at my handsome Marc.

I started picking up this and that, always fast, always in a rush, to have more time for whatever big thing I have to do next. Despite the rush, my never-still mind bringing me thoughts nonstop and all the interferences my brain gets in public spaces, I can't help but notice another mom with a child in her cart, who seems to be under one year old. What strikes me and gets my attention is their connection. Mom said something; the kid responds, not with words, but with his eyes. They dilate, they look at mom, move around, look at other things, up, down, to the sides… but they always return to mom's eyes.

Looking closer, I captured a moment more relevant than the rest. When mother and son's eyes are completely connected, as if tightened together by an imaginary rope, it is in this moment that all the kid's facial features are in unison, moving together, communicating together. I hear those eyes say, *"Mom, I love you. I want to be seen.*

I want to belong." A second later, mom's features synchronized with those of her son, and she said, "I'm here for you, my baby. I love you back." In this moment, they are connected. The rope is there. Mom throws words into this communication, but they are not really needed; they are just an addition. I know because I'm further away, and her words got lost in the crowd's noise, but I understand their language. It doesn't matter. It is not about words; I know their shared emotion and their connection.

I set myself to replicate the scene with Marc. I breathed in and told myself, *"I will copy that mom's gestures and recreate that powerful rope."* It was Marc's turn to return the ball in that frightening tennis match I had just improvised. The ball never returned. The rope was nonexistent. His eyes didn't look back at me. His features kept doing many gracious expressions; he kept being the cutest kid, looking at the shampoos at the deodorants, but Marc's big brown eyes would not look back into mine. I didn't have a name for what I had just experienced. It felt like a free fall from the seventh floor, and no one was there to save me, to save us from that.

It was Marc's first birthday in November 2003! We invited all our friends and family. It was a big celebration filled with excitement. Our friends brought their children, most of them one-year-olds. Maite got the best present!

"Happy Birthday to you..." I walked into the living room, singing and holding the birthday cake—a cake made with simple organic ingredients that I had specially ordered so that all the little ones could enjoy it. Marc's eyes immediately widened, enchanted by the twilight of the candle. Everything about that moment was adorable.

His shiny eyes succumbed to the magic glow of the solitary candle. In a split second, his chubby fingers, with one flick of his short but swift right arm, were about to touch the flame. Nuri, my mother-in-law, Marc's grandma and lifesaver, prevented it. Immediately, Marc's fingers moved to the cake, scooping some and smashing it into his mouth. His full lips, a copy of his dad's, were covered in crumbs as his jaw moved up and down with intent. Marc's birthdays have always been like that—a refreshing breeze, a time for deep breaths, moments that make life so worth living.

That first year, the unmistakable fascination was unique. It stood out how his attention was laser-focused on the cake and candle, with absolutely no reaction, not even a subtle acknowledgment, to my prominent cheers, the constant movement, mess, and giggling of the other one-year-olds, or the sweet words from Laura and Ester, my gentle nieces, my brother Felip's daughters. His eyes were stuck only on the brightness of the candle and the desire to eat the cake.

Marc loved opening presents. I still hear the sound of crackling paper being tossed and bent in all directions, finally becoming a huge, colorful ball. The sound of the cardboard box dropping to the floor followed, a result of Marc's excited hands freeing it from the never-ending wrapping paper. Then came the part where he opened the box—not at the designated spot, but at a random point. Marc decided to break it open, eager to see what the fuss was about. Inside was a wonderful castle, the height of a one-year-old child. It had some colorful balls that had shifted during the journey from the store to our playroom and now rolled across the living room floor.

The kids immediately grabbed the balls, scooping them up with their miniature but skillful hands, and started placing them into the holes on top of the castle. They watched, captivated, as the balls rolled down through the corridors, past the lion, the monkey, and the chicken, finally exiting through the castle's entrance. Marc sat on the floor, watching the kids take turns, then stood up, approached the castle, and began touching some of the animals. His face lit up with the most wonderful smiles. I rushed to him.

"Look, Marc," I said gently. "Look how Mireia is doing it." Mireia, a sweet one-year-old who would later be in the nursery with Marc, slowly placed the ball on top and, looking at Marc, said, "Here, Marc." Marc never looked at her, the ball, or me. He kept feeling the lion, the monkey, the chicken, and the whole castle with his fingers. Mireia, puzzled, soon chased after another child. I took Marc's precious little hand, placed the ball in it, and guided it to the top of the castle. "Marc, now let go of the ball." Marc stood there, amazed by the castle, with his half-smile, contemplating this new thing, completely unaware of me and my teachings.

Again, I took Marc's hand and, this time, placed the ball next to the lion. "Ro-ro, go ball go!" I said, mimicking the lion's roar. The ball graciously rolled down and exited through the castle's front door. Marc continued to enjoy his castle, his way. I probably experienced frustration for the first time.

Marc moved on to play along with the red balloons that decorated the living room, cracking one of his rainbow smiles from time to time; other times, he had a flat expression all over his face. Maybe Marc was aware of all the toddlers playing around and the loud noise of the adults' vivid conversations, but he preferred his play. One thing was obvious: Marc was clearly having fun during his birthday in an unexpected way, yes, but it was Marc's way. And his happiness was what mattered most.

When everyone left, I told Xavi, "You see how different he is from our friends' kids?"

"Yes, that's going to be a problem," Xavi said with certainty.

"Problem? What problem? You mean a challenge, right? Life is full of challenges, and Marc—well, he has me to help him with whatever he needs." I said overconfidently. But inside, I wanted those balls in the holes, I wanted him to belong with the other kids and show feelings for his family. I started to worry, sensing the troubled waters ahead. However, I knew my resilience and my limitless love for my family, my strongest pillar values, and that gave me strength to keep fear away.

From eighteen months to two years old, Marc was a happy baby. He was also very healthy and absolutely adorable. Xavi and I knew something was off. I hoped he would just grow out of it; Xavi probably did not.

Marc started walking like most kids when he was one year old. I was so happy to celebrate this feat. Little did I know that with early walking came early runaways and the so-called elopements that would haunt us for many years.

Marc has always had great balance and agility. He has been as sneaky, fast, and unpredictably sudden as no other kid I've ever known. Yes, Marc holds many records, I can promise you! He often shows a wide smile on his face, especially when he is being a trou-blemaker and realizes he has the advantage—that's to say, always.

The family loves you and wants the best for you and your child but is not necessarily knowledgeable, and that was our case. We found ourselves alone and isolated, discovering the hard way how to live with Marc.

Marc's first word was not going to be just any word but one that was very meaningful to him. Since Marc was a baby, we took him with us to eat out. He loved napping, and that was gold time for us. When our friends' two-year-olds were no longer sleeping in strollers be-cause they almost didn't fit, Marc was still taking long naps in his foldable baby stroller. He curled himself up, knees to face, to what I guess was a comfortable position for him and slept for an hour or two. That allowed us to have some highly appreciated breaks to re-lax and have adult conversations! It was wonderful to stop the cra-ziness of our lives with Marc for an hour. We often went to a family restaurant; the comfort food they served felt like medicine healing our bodies. Bodies that, although by then we were not yet aware, started feeling the early signs of tiredness of the nonstop life after Marc. The spaciousness of the place was remarkable for a European restaurant, high ceiling and a two story dining room. It was the orig-inal electricity building of Terrassa, the one that generated electric-ity for the city and for some of the privileged families that could afford it when it was created in 1896. As I was living that moment with Xavi, chatting, laughing, and enjoying this small oasis of free-dom because Marc was asleep, I started to grasp the uniqueness of those sacred, privileged times to just be us. Marc would eat first, and his favorite dish was macaroni Bolognese. He loved his macaroni. One day, Xavi, Marc in his stroller, and I were walking to the city center. By then, Marc was two. As we walked, we heard Marc say something. At two, Marc wasn't saying words yet, just some sounds with no identifiable meaning.

"Did you hear that?" I asked Xavi, raising my eyebrows.

"Yeah, he is trying to say something, right?" he responded.

"But what is it? I don't get it," I said, now very intrigued.

Marc looked at us, which was very unusual, and he turned his head in a very assertive way, which he never did. It was obvious that he was trying to communicate with us, but we couldn't understand him.

We continued walking, trying to figure it out. It was only when we got home that I said to Xavi, "I've got it! I know what he was trying to say to us! He said 'macaroni'!" I interpreted the word because now I remembered we had just passed by our restaurant where Marc always ate macaroni.

Xavi started laughing. "So, he was telling us, 'Give me those yummy macaroni from my favorite restaurant!"

"Yes, a long and complicated word, but worth the effort for that deliciousness." I had long tried to get him to say mom, dad, and Marc, but those words were not as interesting for Marc. I get it. I'm a foodie, too!

85

Chapter Six
Drowning at the nursery

"The sea knows no limits, makes no concessions. It has given us everything, and it can take everything away from us."

— John Ajvide Lindqvist

Marc was two years old. Like many working moms in Spain, I enrolled Marc in daycare so I could return to work full-time. It'll be a great chance for Marc to start socializing with other kids, I thought optimistically.

A couple of weeks later, I got a request for a meeting with one of the daycare teachers.

It was a Thursday, and I was having lunch with Titin, my closest friend. Since Marc's birth, she had been my rock—the one I could vent to, reflect with, laugh, and cry over all the ups and downs of motherhood. Most importantly, spending time with her reminded me I wasn't losing it—or losing myself. Laughter and a little fun, even just two hours a week, were my saving grace during those tough times.

"So, Marc's only been at daycare for two weeks, and they already want a meeting? Really?" I said, exasperated. "I bet they're going to kick him out! I've been navigating Marc's quirks, his unique traits, and his unpredictable behavior, and I have no clue what I'm doing! Am I an educator? An experienced mom? No! He's my first child, for God's sake! But what do I do? I just do it. Is it easy? No! But is life always easy? No, it's not!" I proclaimed, throwing my hands up and smiling as I spoke with raw honesty.

Titin squinted in disbelief. "Are you serious? That's ridiculous! Give me easy kids, please, and send the difficult ones home! Shame on them!"

I kept going. "They've had Marc for two weeks, and I can just picture the teacher, hands over her mouth, yelling, 'Oh my God, Marc took the elephant toy from another kid! He's not following directions!' Really?" I said, mimicking the teacher, arms out, palms up. I was on a roll now. Venting was starting to work, and the suffocating feeling I'd had since their phone call that morning was slowly fading.

"People today are so lazy. Anything that requires effort is a problem. I know Marc is a little different, maybe a bit behind other kids his age... but come on, it's daycare! Aren't they the experts on kids? Just do your job while I do mine!" I said, waving my hands in frustration. I've always had a flair for the dramatic.

"Exactly!" Titin chimed in. "You should go to that meeting and tell the teacher, 'The problem isn't Marc—it's YOU! You're just lazy! Do your job, you lazy teacher!" she said, imitating my gestures. We bursted into laughter, tears streaming down our faces.

Deep down, I'd sensed from day one that Marc's quirks might be an issue at daycare. It felt unfair, but I knew life wasn't always fair.

I was wrapping up a warehouse meeting at work when I got the call. I was fully back in my job and loved it. We had just restructured two warehouses, a major project for my team. I'd managed to overcome that "abandoning mom" guilt from my first month back—when I was physically at work but mentally with Marc, constantly wondering what he was doing at daycare. It's something only working moms can truly understand—a tightness in your chest that makes it hard to focus. Your entire being is wrapped up in being a mom, and it resists being anything else. Your mind knows you need to work, but your body aches for your baby, pulling you in different directions. It's like being kidnapped.

Eventually, though, I replaced that overwhelming mom guilt with my "kick-ass professional" mindset. Moms have to fight harder just to feel like themselves. It's a fact.

That day, though, I was almost fully Silvia again—just Silvia—at work. But of course, when Marc needed me, I had to go. Mom's duty never stops. Every working mom knows that. I stood up and said,

"Excuse me, I have to leave a little early for personal reasons," and headed out.

In the car, my mind shifted back to Marc and the upcoming daycare meeting.

"What's their problem? I know Marc's developing a little differently, but they should be able to handle it like I do. It's not always easy, but a meeting after just one month? Sounds like they're already giving up. Seriously? I rehearsed my lines out loud as I drove. *Just adapt and help him. You've got way more experience with kids than I do. It's my first child—don't you have the resources to handle this?"*

In my mind, I could picture the conversation. They'd say, "Marc is different from the other kids, Mrs. Prats." And I'd respond, "Yes, I know. He's a wonderful kid who's different. What's the issue?" I imagined going further (though I didn't plan to say this part out loud): *"I've been raising him at home for two years. You've known him for a few weeks. Do you think you're telling me something new? I know he's different. So what? Let's keep moving forward. Solutions, please. That's what I need from you."*

I pulled into my garage and walked to the daycare, which was just a short distance from my home in Terrassa, a city about thirty minutes from Barcelona. I hurried over, arriving right on time, ready to show them the "strong me."

I entered the meeting room, a small, white space at street level with a tall wooden window offering a view of one of the most beautiful streets in my city: El Passeig del Comte de Egara. It's the noble heart of Terrassa's city center. Just north of El Passeig Street is Garcia

Humet Street, where I lived until I was five, in a house later owned by my brother, Felip. To the west, El Passeig Street connects to Font Vella, a steep commercial strip, and north of that, you can walk up to Cardaire Street, where Xavi and I bought an apartment near my childhood home. The houses along El Passeig Street are part of the city's cultural heritage. Numbers 2 and 4 are Casa Benert Bedrinas, built-in 1916 by Lluís Muncunill, the most celebrated architect in our town. A master of Catalan Modernism, he's renowned for transforming factories and warehouses into architectural gems. His work left a mark on Terrassa, turning industrial buildings into symbols of elegance and innovation. One of his most celebrated achievements was using the arcs to install windows that allowed for both illumination and ventilation of warehousing spaces.

The beauty of the place humbled me. The grandiosity of the architecture made me feel small, uncertain of what this meeting would bring. I knew Marc was different—he didn't respond to his name, preferred being alone, rarely made eye contact, and hadn't yet said "Mom" or "Dad." But I had pushed my worries aside, convincing myself with my usual optimism. I believed my passion and energy would help Marc catch up and that he would grow into the child I knew he could be. *"The nursery will help, too,"* I told myself. *"They're the experts."* These thoughts churned in my mind like a blender set on high.

After what felt like an eternity, Marc's teacher arrived and invited me to sit. We settled into white office chairs, and after a polite introduction, she began, "Marc stands out from the other kids in my class, just like other children have stood out before. It's in the way he relates—or doesn't relate—to others, the lack of words, the way he moves…" Her words hit me hard. *"In the same way, other kids have stood out before."* I kept replaying that sentence in my mind. It was unexpected and deeply unsettling.

I couldn't let her go on. I stood up, staring out beyond the room, her words triggering something inside me. It was like a curtain had been pulled back, exposing a stage I was unprepared to step onto. For a moment, I felt a complete disconnect from reality, as if I were floating in the same haze Marc often seemed lost in. Eye contact was the last thing on my mind. In a daze, I asked, "Are you sure about what you just said?" My confidence and belief in myself shattered in an instant. The ground beneath me felt unsteady, as if I were being tossed about in rough waters. The assured, upbeat version of myself dissolved, leaving nothing but my deepest fears.

The teacher stood too, her voice calm but firm. "Yes, Mrs. Prats. Marc needs something different. He needs more than what we can offer here."

I forced myself to meet her gaze. "But…are you sure?" I asked again, clinging to any shred of hope.

"Absolutely," she replied with quiet certainty. "I've worked with many children over the years. I just know." Her voice was steady, deliberate, and confident.

I sat back down, feeling utterly lost. My face felt numb, like it was melting, and I could barely swallow or breathe. The teacher's words became muffled, and her movements blurred. It was as if I were sinking, drowning in a sea of fear and confusion. All the hidden anxieties I'd been carrying since Marc was born came crashing down on me like I was gulping down water, helpless to stop it. This night-mare, with its unfamiliar and terrifying shapes, was real. And now it was my life—mine and Marc's.

Eventually, I dared to look at her again. She stood there, unwaver-ing, with years of experience behind her, leaving no room for doubt.

At that moment, I realized everything I had believed about Marc, about his future, was crumbling. My optimism, my plans, my expec-tations—they all belonged to another world, another me. This new reality was harsh, unforgiving, and completely out of my control. Marc was different, and his future—our future—was uncertain. I didn't understand this new world yet, but Marc's teacher did. Her honesty was undeniable. Something was wrong, and I had no idea how to fix it. I was completely unmoored, drowning in the nursery.

From somewhere deep within, I found a way to speak. A new ver-sion of myself—fragile, uncertain—emerged and asked, "Yes, I see the differences in Marc. I understand. But what now? Can't you help him?"

By then, another person had entered the room. While I was lost in my thoughts, the teacher had left and returned with someone else. This new person, the principal, calmly addressed me. "We can't give Marc the help he needs here. He can stay with us, but he needs some-thing more—something we can't provide."

Like the teacher's, her face was serious, professional, and without doubt. The words hit me like a tidal wave, leaving no room for hope or maybe. It was a devastating truth, washing over me all at once, leaving me gasping for air.

I looked at the principal, feeling as fragile as a newborn. She added gently, "We're here for you, and we'll support Marc as much as we can. But you need to find help for him. It's the most important thing right now."

I bowed my head, gravity pulling it down as if it carried the weight of the entire meeting. With effort, I slowly raised it and looked at the principal. "Yes, of course," I replied, though I had no idea what I was supposed to do to help Marc. Then, almost like a child seeking direction, I quietly asked, "What do I do?"

She handed me a simple white card with a woman's name and phone number printed on it. "Call her. She'll be able to help," the principal said.

I looked at the card, but the title under the name meant nothing to me. I was still utterly lost.

Looking back, that meeting was the first real warning about Marc's "thing." Neither the teacher nor the principal gave it a name, but they knew. They likely understood exactly what was going on, but they didn't consider it their role to label it. No one said Marc had a condition or needed to see a doctor, but their certainty spoke louder than words. Marc's first diagnosis didn't come from a pediatrician, a family doctor, or a psychologist—it came from a teacher. Teachers hold knowledge beyond what's in books; they know truths about life, often before anyone else. Today, I admire their quiet bravery. They didn't label it, but they shared their concerns with me and prioritized Marc's well-being. These teachers dared to confront me with a difficult truth, and I'll always respect them for that.

As I left the nursery, I felt completely detached from my body. My stomach was knotted, still full of the emotional water I had been drowning in, and my limbs hung uselessly by my sides. I was a wreck. I could barely breathe, and soon, the tears that had been welling up began streaming down my face, salty and unstoppable. I was a shell of the person who had walked into that meeting that morning. The tears distorted everything about me—my confidence, my strength, my very sense of self—all being pulled down by this new, unfamiliar gravity. It was time to go home, to find refuge. My entire body felt like it was breaking apart, like a dying lightbulb flickering before it finally burned out.

When I picture myself walking home that day, I saw a ghost dragging through the empty streets of Terrassa. In my memory, the streets are dark, and it's raining, though I know that's not what really happened. The meeting was in the morning, so it must have been around two p.m., the time when everyone heads home for lunch. It was probably sunny, as it often is in Spain.

In reality, as I walked home, I ran into my sister-in-law, Carme. She took one look at me with her warm, deep brown eyes and immediately hugged me. I broke down, crying in despair, my body trembling.

"Silvia, what's going on?" she asked, looking directly into my eyes. Carme, with her sharp and no-nonsense demeanor, was the principal of a school. She knew kids, and she knew how to handle difficult situations with families.

After I explained everything through my sobs, she gave me some advice that I would cling to in my "new me" life: *"ocupació, no pre-ocupació"*—in Catalan, it means "do something about it instead of worrying." That sentence became a guiding principle for me.

When I finally got home, I washed away the tears and made a promise to myself: I would be the go-getter mom that Marc deserved.

The unknown has a way of paralyzing you, making you feel completely vulnerable. I've never handled the unknown well, and my immediate instinct is to try to replace it with something I could hold on to as quickly as possible. My resolution was clear: *"I need to make sense of this new world we're stepping into; this 'thing' that others have pointed out is affecting Marc, setting him apart."* The situation felt abstract and overwhelming, but I could at least begin to define it. That was something. The second thing I did was accept that I was not equipped, at that moment, to understand what was happening to Marc, let alone figure out how to fix it. But one thing was undeniable, and I repeated it to myself over and over that afternoon: *"Silvia, this f***ing 'thing' is here to stay. You knew it before the teacher told you. We knew it. And it's serious. It's affecting Marc in everything he does unless I do something."*

With Carme's advice in mind, I detached myself from the overwhelming emotions and called the number on the card as soon as I got home. I scheduled a visit.

The office of the woman whose name was on the card was in one of the noble houses on El Passeig Street. I walked there. A dark, weathered wooden door greeted me, its knob worn down from years of use. The place had the eerie feel of entering a haunted house. Inside,

95

the dim light made the white walls appear gray, casting a cold, unsettling atmosphere. The corridor seemed endless, with its high ceilings adding to the sense of isolation and unease. When I reached the office, it was as unremarkable as I had imagined. A single chair next to a bare table. I sat down, bracing myself.

"This is where the torture begins," I thought.

The woman was dressed professionally and spoke with a calm, measured tone. As I sat there, I couldn't help but wonder what exactly her job was. She was empathetic, and I appreciated her kindness, especially at a time when Marc and I felt like we were drowning, desperate for any help we could get.

I figured she was involved simply because the nursery had flagged our situation. Even now, I'm not entirely sure what her role was, but I do know this: she did help. She set me on the right path, one that would eventually lead me to Amaia Hervás, a person who would become a game-changer for our family.

Back in that noble house with the kind woman whose job title remained a mystery, I sat across from her as she continued to speak. She wore a black skirt and a blouse, her demeanor professional but with a softness in her voice that was, at the very least, reassuring. It was clear she had experience, but she wasn't an expert. Her answers were distant and vague—like an artist painting an abstract picture, leaving it up to the observer to interpret the brushstrokes. She avoided responding directly to any of my questions.

I understand her approach now, but at the time, it was maddening. Every sentence was wrapped in layers of caution, as though she were afraid of liability. It was clear she knew more than she was saying, but she held back, and each evasive answer felt like a theft. Every time I thought I'd pinned down a solid plan to help Marc, she would add another layer of uncertainty—her words turning once-clear actions into mere possibilities. I felt like Alice in Wonderland, stumbling through a maze when all I wanted was solid ground.

Now, I realize she wasn't there to diagnose Marc or give me definitive answers. She was simply a guide, someone who knew a little and wanted to point me in the direction of real experts.

"Yes, some kids develop differently," she said at one point. "He might have autism. Many improve with support over the years, while others don't. I understand what you're going through…" Her voice droned on, lost in a sea of vague, non-committal phrases. I barely registered the word *autism* when she dropped it in the middle of a long-winded sentence. It was like an atomic bomb, but it was buried so deep in her rambling that it didn't immediately explode.

I knew what autism was, or at least I had heard of it, so I didn't ask for clarification. I simply let her continue, hoping she would eventually offer something concrete.

But she didn't. She kept talking, and I kept listening, though, with each passing moment, I grew more frustrated. I felt like I was sitting there with a giant radar dish for ears, trying to pick up a clear signal from a distant planet. But no matter how hard I tried to listen, nothing she said was concrete enough to hold on to. It was as if I had developed a massive parabolic antenna, scanning every faint sound and searching for anything that would help me understand this new reality.

That day, I wasn't emotional. I had my explorer's hat on. I was on a mission to figure out what this "thing" was that made Marc different and, more importantly, to find the first step I could take to help him. It was the first day of my fight for Marc's future, and I was determined to make sense of it. I knew I had everything to learn, and I was ready. I wasn't afraid—challenges fuel me, and I felt confident that I could build a plan to help Marc. But despite all my efforts, nothing she said made sense.

Realizing that passive listening wasn't getting me anywhere, I switched tactics. I moved into questionnaire mode, asking questions in the hopes of extracting something useful—anything that would give me a clearer path forward, a first actionable step to take when I left her dark, uninspiring office.

But even then, her answers remained vague, offering little clarity.

"How are the kids who overcome it different from those who don't? What works and what doesn't with kids with autism?" I asked, desperately trying to find a way forward.

"It all depends…blah, blah, blah. Many are diagnosed with autism now and need lots of resources at home and school. What's certain is that they develop differently," she said, throwing out the word "autism" again as if I were already familiar with what it truly meant. It felt like an ominous banner suddenly stuck over Marc's head, defining who he was and possibly determining his future.

I wasn't completely unfamiliar with the term. Years ago, I watched a documentary about autism, and what stayed with me was the image of children unable to speak, kids who seemed to have no connection with others and were emotionless. The image that haunted me most was of an adult man sitting cross-legged in a tight shirt and shorts near a wall. He had no expression on his face—he reminded me of the Mona Lisa, so blank, so unreadable. Suddenly, without warning, he started banging his head against the wall. I can still see that scene clearly in my mind. The narrator's voice in the documentary is cold, clinical, and almost devoid of compassion. He explained that the man had autism, a condition with no cure, and that he lived in an institution because he couldn't integrate into society.

That documentary terrified me. Beyond that, I'd never really heard anyone else mention autism, nor had I met anyone with it. My mind switched to practical mode as I sat in that office, and I reassured myself: Marc wasn't like the man from the documentary. He had some words. He wasn't hurting himself. None of it seemed to add up. Maybe autism was broader than what I had learned from that frightening and misleading film.

Then she mentioned another word: "resources."

"Resources? What resources?" I wondered, feeling more lost than ever. With my business background, I was used to thinking of resources as money, people, or materials. I'd never heard the term used in the context of autism or education. Did she mean money? Did kids with autism need expensive treatments? And why would schools need resources for this? My brain was swirling with confusion.

I couldn't take it anymore. "So, do you think Marc might have autism?" I asked directly, hoping for something concrete.

"Well, I don't know him, and I'm not a doctor, but yes, it could be, probably..." Her response was evasive, like a politician dodging a

99

straightforward question. She answered with ambiguity, leaving me more frustrated than before.

I pressed on, this time with a double question: "How can I help Marc? And what does it mean to 'develop differently'?"

Each question was met with a flood of vague information, none of which gave me the clear direction I needed. It felt like she was speaking a language I didn't understand, leaving me grasping for meaning. The terms she used felt distant, abstract—noise in the middle of a storm, none of it useful for charting a path forward.

We talked and talked. She wasn't in a rush, but I was struggling to make sense of it all. I couldn't untangle the vague content, and I was no closer to figuring out what to do next for Marc. Nothing solid, nothing actionable.

Finally, I gave up. I was overloaded with information that led nowhere. Sometimes, things make sense later when they have time to settle, but in that moment, I felt like I was sinking under the weight of it all. I stood up and thanked her, ready to leave, feeling as lost as I was when I first walked in.

Just as I was about to go, she said, "Wait a minute..." She murmured it quietly, like a secret, something she wasn't supposed to do. She disappeared into a smaller office next door and returned with two pieces of paper. She had written on them hastily and ripped them out of a notebook. Handing them to me, she whispered, "Don't tell anyone I gave you these names. Especially call Amaia—she has a great reputation for working with autism."

Her words were low and conspiratorial as if she was doing me a favor that wasn't entirely within the rules. And just like that, she handed me the first real clues for my journey into the unknown.

Chapter Seven
Navigating the Ocean Depths -Clues to the Unknown

"You can't cross the ocean of life just by dreaming about it; you have to jump in and swim."

— Debasish Mridha

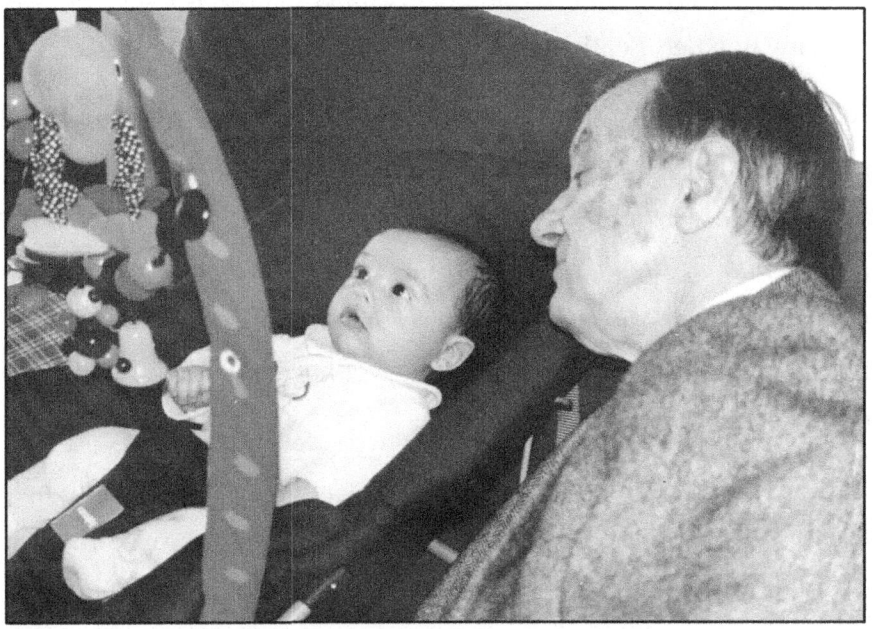

I held the papers in front of me, frozen, my eyes locked on the two torn scraps of paper the woman had handed me at the last moment. To me, they were golden tickets to Marc's future, clues to the unknown. One read "Amaya Hervás," the other "Carina Robles." The sweat that had built up during the long, stressful conversation seemed to evaporate. I wasn't losing the game of life anymore—I had just been dealt a joker card, the one that says, "You're not saved, but you're not out either. Keep playing." I left that haunted house with one scrap of paper carefully folded in each pocket. As I walked out, I looked up at the sky and realized for the first time that *"This wouldn't be a simple journey from point A to point B. But I was ready for the ride—or so,"* I thought.

I called Amaya that very day and every day for the next two years, but she never answered. Her assistants always picked up, telling me they'd pass the message along, but Dr. Hervás was fully booked. I felt like I was chasing a ghost. On the other hand, Carina responded right away when I called.

At that time, I felt invincible, convinced there was no problem I couldn't solve. I was unstoppable, and I knew it. I kept telling myself, *"I'll be on top of Marc to make sure he progresses. I'll bring experts into his life, like Carina now, and many others I'll find along the way. We will overcome whatever he has."* I was certain I could fix the problem, even though I didn't yet have a name for it. Everything was in my hands.

Carina was a therapist employed by the Catalan government to help families like mine. A couple of weeks later, I found myself sitting with her at a public center funded by La Generalitat de Catalunya, the Catalan government. She introduced herself as a psychologist who would work with Marc. She didn't label him with autism or anything else—she just wanted to help him. That sounded perfect to me, the newcomer on this strange new planet.

"So, Silvia, tell me about Marc. Have you been home with him, nourishing him these past two years?" she asked, dropping what felt like a bombshell question to any working mom in 21st-century Spain.

"Well, I love my child, and of course, I've been nourishing him," I replied, thinking it was such an obvious answer that it didn't even need saying. But my gut told me she was asking something deeper, so I felt the need to defend myself.

"I guess, but have you always been there for him?" she asked, closing her eyes and stressing the word *always* as if driving a nail into the conversation.

"Well, I need to work. I have to take care of the house and do a million other things like any mom, I guess," I mumbled, suddenly unsure of my answer.

"I see. So where was Marc when you were doing all these things?" she asked, sounding like Sherlock Holmes grilling a suspect.

"When I was working, Marc was with my cousin Maite. She's incredibly kind and loves him. She's thrilled to spend time with him!" I stretched my neck and looked her straight in the eyes, confident in my response. I couldn't imagine a better person to help care for Marc than Maite, who had practically been my second mother. Still, Carina's scrutinizing gaze told me she didn't think this was the right answer.

"My mother passed away before Marc was born. Maite took care of me when I was a baby, and my mom needed a break," I added, hoping to win Carina's approval. But her expression didn't soften. She looked right through my clarification as if I were standing in front of a judge about to deliver a verdict.

Carina pressed on with her strange line of questioning. "Okay, but what did Maite do when *she* needed a break? When she had to do something around the house or take a phone call?" Her voice turned detective-like again. I felt horrified, confused, and caught off guard.

I hesitated, feeling cornered, then snapped, "Obviously, she put Marc in a safe place with a toy."

"I see, I see. And how many hours a day was he in this… safe place?" she asked, again elongating the word *safe* as though it held some hidden meaning. Her eyes narrowed, round and probing, like something out of a cartoon, and I suddenly felt like a cartoon villain was grilling me. I couldn't escape her gaze until I gave her a number.

"Maybe two hours a day," I muttered, doing quick mental math. I guessed Maite might spend twenty minutes here and there—eating lunch, using the bathroom, making phone calls, talking to her husband, chatting with neighbors. I assumed this all added up to about two hours.

"Two hours a day alone? That is a **lot**!" Carina said, her voice loud as she pressed her palms together against her chest like she was praying. Then, silence. A long, painful pause followed as she pursed her lips tightly and shook her head from side to side repeatedly. I watched her, paralyzed, her reaction so exaggerated that my imagination spiraled. I started to picture her as the possessed kid from *The Exorcist,* her head spinning around like Regan MacNeil in the 1973 movie.

Her voice—now low and funeral-like—brought me back to reality. Her head hung down, still shaking slowly from side to side, in rhythm with her grave tone and hopeless eyes. "That definitely must have had an impact on Marc," she finally sentenced, as if struggling to breathe. Just like that, I was condemned as a bad mother. My

105

sweet Marc was going to have this terrible "thing" for life, and it was all my fault for being a horrible mom. I had ruined my son's future, and Maite—my beloved cousin who had helped me so much—had contributed to it too by leaving him alone, unattended, for two hours a day.

My neck, which had been stretched in defense, was now bent in defeat. I didn't say a word. My mind was spinning, desperately trying to make sense of it all but failing. There was silence for a moment before Carina spoke again, this time in a condescending tone, the kind you'd use with a child after scolding them for being "very, very naughty." It was like she had just roasted me, and now she was offering me a shred of advice—but only after making it clear that the consequences of my actions were severe and irreversible, something only I was responsible for, something only I would have to deal with.

In that tone, she continued, "Let's see what we can do. If Marc were older, I'd start by talking to him to understand the trauma that was caused. By resolving that trauma, we might be able to 'remove' his condition, which is nothing more than a strategy he developed to cope with an inadequate environment." She paused for effect. "But since he's only two, the only option is to do therapy through play and hope it helps."

"What??" I exploded, my voice cracking. My mind was torn in two directions. On the one hand, my judgment told me that what she was saying simply didn't hold up—it didn't make sense that Marc's "thing" could be caused by being left to himself sometimes. But on the other hand, I couldn't ignore the fact that I was sitting in front of a licensed psychologist appointed by the Catalan government to help families with children like Marc.

I tend to consider perspectives that don't align with my own, even if that means that I might have made a mistake. I like to explore new ideas and entertain possibilities, and I pride myself on being humble enough to change my mind when necessary. Life's truths aren't black and white, after all. I've always believed in the gray areas, the nuanced truths that evolve. But in this case, I was almost certain my initial perspective was right. Still, the mere suggestion that I had harmed my son, even remotely, was devastating.

I felt like I was drowning again in the ocean of guilt, and confusion was pulling me under. The thought that I could have caused harm to my child, to Marc, tore me apart inside. It shook my entire sense of reality like I was on a sinking ship. Desperate to understand, I asked, my voice trembling, "Is it really possible that Marc has autism because he was left on his own for a couple of hours a day?"

"Most probably," she said firmly.

I sighed, drained, and looked into her eyes. At that moment, this was the only person who seemed educated enough to help Marc. With what felt like a prayer, I asked, "Can you still help him?"

She looked back at me with full confidence. "The past is the past. My job is to try to help him."

That was all that mattered to me—Marc. Everything else was secondary. The waters inside me calmed, and I regained some of my confidence. Whether I was guilty or not, whether I had made mistakes or not, I was doing everything I could now to help Marc. The blame faded, and my focus shifted entirely to helping Marc through the therapy Carina offered. Was she the best? Was she the worst? It didn't matter at that point.

For three years, I visited Carina twice a week. I never missed a session. She became my go-to person, the one who listened to me for ten minutes and then spent fifty minutes working with Marc. Sometimes, I sat in the room with them; other times, she asked me to wait outside. I didn't challenge it. I was simply grateful to have someone who was there to help Marc, no questions asked.

As I look back, I see myself walking alone across Sant Pere's Bridge in Terrassa. The bridge, built in the 16th century over the Vallparadís stream, feels monumental. Today, the stream has been transformed into a green lung that stretches from one end of the city to the other. The bridge itself is a humble construction, made by and for the people, linking the town of Terrassa to the village of Sant Pere, which is now just another neighborhood in the city. It has a magical quality to me—so narrow that it only allows one lane of cars, with the thinnest sidewalks squeezed in on either side. Every time I crossed it, I felt like a tightrope walker in a circus. The bridge didn't belong to this period, and that's exactly why I loved it.

In the background, I had just left the monumental Churches of Saint Pere, part of La Seu d'Egara complex, a site that holds some of the most significant archaeological and artistic heritage in Catalonia. It spans an uninterrupted timeline from the Iberian era to the present day, and it is considered one of the jewels of Catalan Romanesque art. The largest of those churches, Sant Pere, was where Xavi and I were married a few years earlier. The beauty, history, and pride I felt for my city made it the perfect place to begin my life with the man I loved. To me, it was a sacred place—not just in a religious sense, but as a symbol of centuries of resilience and endurance, dating back to the founding of Egara by the Roman Empire in the 1st century A.D.

The structure feels like a testament to the passage of time, and as I crossed the bridge, I let the energy of that ancient place wash over me.

Yet, despite the beauty surrounding me, my thoughts were focused on what Carina had just said. Marc had already returned to nursery school, and I had taken a stroll to collect myself before heading back to the German company where I worked. As hurtful as Carina's words were, they didn't sit right with me. They seemed unreasonable. Deep down, I knew that neither Maite nor I were the cause of Marc's autism. It just didn't add up. His condition couldn't be explained by how we had cared for Marc as an infant. Maite and I adored Marc, showering him with affection, hugs, kisses, and lullabies. We loved him in every possible way because that's how our family is. Marc had received all the tenderness a baby could ever need, multiplied a thousand times over.

Carina was wrong. Absolutely wrong.

Years later, I would learn that her ideas were rooted in psychoanalysis, a school of thought that was common in Spain at the time for treating autism. But at that moment, I told myself that if I caused his autism, I still needed to help him. And if I didn't, well, he still needs help, and Carina is the only one here to offer it.

Carina's play therapy did help in certain ways. She gave me useful tips for capturing Marc's attention, and I appreciated the time we spent together. Despite my disagreement with the psychoanalytic approach, I don't regret those sessions with Carina. She wasn't the best, but she wasn't the worst either, and she truly cared. Her play-based techniques did engage Marc, and for that, I was grateful.

That evening at home, I couldn't stop crying. Even though I didn't believe Carina's theory, the idea that I could have caused Marc's autism gnawed at me. It was so evil, so disturbing. That night, I had the worst nightmares, and the emotional wound stayed with me for weeks.

Many psychoanalysts believe autism isn't a neurodevelopmental disorder with a strong genetic component, as is now widely accepted. Instead, they see it as a condition caused by psychological trauma, specifically a disturbed family environment, often pointing to the child's relationship with their mother as the root cause. At the time, Carina's perspective wasn't unique—it was the dominant view held by many professionals in Spain, including the psychologists employed by the government to help families like mine.

On our next visit, Carina didn't bring up the mother-blaming theories again. She just focused on playing with Marc. I saw her doing much of what I was already doing at home—playing with trains, role-playing with dolls, drawing, and building with blocks. She was more skilled at it than I was, and I appreciated her approach. In the beginning, she asked me to leave the room during the sessions, but over time, she realized Marc wasn't paying much attention to me, so she let me stay.

Being there with them was a gift. I learned so much just by observing Marc's reactions to different stimuli in the games, and it helped me play with him more effectively at home.

Those three years I spent visiting Carina may not have helped Marc as much as they could have, but it was better than having no support at all. Carina was kind, steady, and reliable, both as a professional and as a person. One day, she ventured to suggest that Marc might have Asperger's. At that point, I didn't know what Asperger's was, but the very next day, I was reading books and learning about it as fast as I could.

It was encouraging—and even fun—to read about the unique abilities that individuals with Asperger's often have. People with Asperger's tend to focus intensely on their preferred topics, usually becoming brilliant in those areas. Of course, as with anyone on the spectrum, social interactions can be their weak point, posing considerable challenges, no matter how smart or knowledgeable they are in other areas. Communicating differently is always difficult, especially in a world where most people don't understand those on the autism spectrum. This often creates challenges for individuals with autism, who usually struggle to see things from someone else's perspective. In a society as social as ours, being on the spectrum can bring bumps in the road.

As a mom beginning to understand autism, reading about children with Asperger's was like a breath of fresh air. For nearly a year, I dreamed about what Marc's strong interests might be. I was so curious, so eager to find out. *"I can't wait,"* I told myself while turning the pages of yet another book on Asperger's. I imagined Marc belonging to a select group of people who, despite facing social challenges, had unique abilities that made them stand out. *"How cool is that?"* I kept thinking. *"Marc is probably hyperactive now because he's so young, but eventually, he'll grow into a young man with Asperger's. He'll need support in some areas, but he'll thrive in his favorite activities. What a dream."*

But over time, that dream began to fade. As the months went by, Marc's hyperactivity increased, his attention span shortened, and his language skills didn't improve. I can still feel the sting of those tears when I finally accepted that Marc wasn't a genius or even close to that. Marc was just Marc, and while I loved him unconditionally, I didn't consider his autism as a gift. I didn't embrace his autism and didn't buy the idea that it made him special or better in some way. His autism was limiting him. It wasn't a superpower—it was something that made life harder for him and our entire family.

On March 10, 2005, it was my father's turn to leave me. I can still picture it clearly. Xavi and I were lying in bed when the phone rang. It was my brother, Felip. The moment I heard his voice, I knew something was terribly wrong—this wasn't the time for a family call.

"Dad is dead," Felip said bluntly. "He had a stroke in the middle of the night. They found him in a hospital corridor, just ten feet from his room. They think he got up to ask for help, but no one heard or saw him, and he collapsed and died."

Felip's voice sounded distant, detached. Maybe he hadn't fully processed it yet, or perhaps that's just how I perceived him—calm on the outside but deeply vulnerable on the inside. With each word, my breath grew shallower. My gaze drifted to the gardens of "La Casa

112

Alegre," the beautiful Renaissance estate visible from our living room windows.

When Felip finished speaking, I took a deep breath, trying to absorb the news without collapsing the way Dad had. Time seemed to slow down. Minutes felt like hours. Even after the call ended, Felip's words lingered in my mind, refusing to make sense. Dad had walked into the hospital on his own two feet to have an infected pimple removed. *"Who dies from a pimple in the 21st century?"* I kept asking myself. I couldn't comprehend it.

Then Xavi came into the room. I told him the news, and he hugged me, gently guiding me to the couch. As I sat there, memories of the conversation I'd had with Dad just the day before came flooding back. I had spent hours with him right after his surgery.

"Hi, Dad! How did it go?" I had asked, smiling in my professional suit, trying to keep things light.

"I don't know," he replied sharply, barely making eye contact before glancing down, his left eyebrow raised and his lips set in a frustrated frown.

"Does it hurt? Let me see!" I had pressed, eager to help in any way I could.

"No, it's not that. It's annoying, but it's nothing," he muttered, covering his forehead with his hand. "Last night, I had a nightmare. I dreamed I was dying." He paused and looked directly into my eyes. "It was all dark," he continued, shrugging one shoulder slightly. "Maybe it would be better if I did die. Since your mom is gone, nothing makes sense anymore."

I had rushed to reassure him. "What are you talking about? You just had a bad dream because you hate hospitals, and you're feeling depressed."

Now, as I sat there in shock, I comprehended that his nightmare had come true.

I truly believed this, but deep down, I knew how much he missed her every single day. She had been his whole world. After fifty-four years together, it was easy to understand why living without her felt impossible. She was his everything, every day of his life.

We talked for hours in that hospital. Dad rested on the couch, refusing to lie in the bed. He had always disliked hospital beds, and I did, too, especially after everything we had been through. We had spent too much time in hospitals, staring at monitors in silence, as if time itself had stopped. I remembered when Toni, just thirty-six, was rushed to the ER, never to recover. I recalled the distant, cold announcements over the intercom, the endless IV lines fighting a losing battle to keep Mom and Toni alive. Those sterile, mechanical sounds were constant reminders that we were not at home, not in the comfort of our kitchen with Mom's hearty beef stew simmering on the stove, artichokes and "llanegues" mushrooms filling the air with their savory aroma. Mom always threw in a handful of meatballs to make my then-little nephews, Laura and Ester, happy.

We weren't around my parent's dinner table, with Felip, Carme, Laura, Ester, Xavi, and me eagerly awaiting our Saturday family lunch. No, we were in a hospital. Dad on the couch, me on a hard, cold metal chair—just inches apart, but it felt like miles. Since Mom passed, Dad and I had made it a habit to spend one afternoon a week together at my parents' apartment, just talking. We found comfort

114

in each other, talking about everything from world news to memories of the past, my work, and, of course, Marc. That day, he even asked me for advice on how to reconnect with his friends in this new chapter of life without Mom. I tried to guide him, helping him to soften his sharp edges, be a little kinder, a little more of a people-pleaser, something that didn't come naturally to him.

It was amusing to see his reactions. "Do I really scare people with my sarcasm?" he asked, wide-eyed with curiosity, his forehead creased. "I made a joke the other day, and to my surprise, everyone laughed!" he continued, raising his eyebrows in disbelief. "Maybe I should learn more jokes and work on my delivery."

Dad was authentic to the core, with values that ran deep. Even when he thought he was being harsh, he was genuinely kind underneath it all. But that day, I made a terrible mistake—perhaps the biggest mistake of my life. I didn't stay with him that night. My rational mind told me, "It's just a pimple," and I left, not thinking twice. I should have stayed. I should have had the patience to consider the unpredictable nature of hospitals. I will never leave a loved one alone in a hospital at night again.

When Dad passed away, I didn't have time to mourn. Marc needed me. He had autism with high support needs—what some call severe autism—and extreme ADHD, along with more diagnoses that would come later. Back then, none of those labels hadn't yet been placed on him, not even the autism, and certainly not the high support needs, but I knew something was significantly very different in Marc. By then, I had met other children with autism, and their families were struggling too, but not with the same intensity our family was struggling. I had no energy left to grieve for Dad.

115

Now, in my fifties, I dream about my family. I dream about Mom, Dad, and Toni. I cry for them and think about them nearly every day. When you have a child like Marc, with autism, with high support needs, there's no time for sadness, no time for healing.

Thankfully, Dad never worried about Marc. To him, Marc was perfect. All my anxieties—"*Don't you see? He's not doing this, he's not doing that,*"—were irrelevant to him. Back then, I thought Dad was just too old-fashioned to understand. But now, I see that I was the one who didn't understand. Marc *was* perfect. He *is* perfect.

The thought of Dad calling out for help, only to be unheard, of him dying alone on that cold hospital floor, haunts me. But I told myself he was ready to leave a world without Mom, and I kept my focus on Marc. When you're drowning, your only job is to survive. There's no time for anything else—not even to mourn your dad.

117

Chapter Eight
Unveiling the Secrets of the Enigmatic Ocean – The Stickman World

"We are like islands in the sea, separate on the surface but connected in the deep."

— William James

Marc, at two years old

That morning, Marc had therapy, so I dressed him up, and we left home. We walked to Carina's—not close, but not too far either. Marc loved the exercise, and he had started moving too much in the car, even unbuckling his seatbelt and jumping toward me. Even short drives felt risky, so I decided we'd walk unless Xavi could drive while I sat in the back, keeping Marc safe.

For some reason, Marc wasn't in a good mood that day. Lately, he had started collapsing onto the pavement during walks, refusing to stand. We'd walk a block, and then he'd melt down. Each time, I had to pull him up by his arms. "Marc, please, it's not time to play. We have to see Carina," I urged.

He didn't respond, just kicked at the ground, making it harder to lift him. Finally, I managed to pull him to his feet.

As we crossed El Passeig Street, he did it again. "Marc, no! The ground is dirty. You'll get sand all over you. Please stand up."

He laughed and began rolling on the ground. His hair, jacket, socks, shoes—his whole body—were now covered in sand.

It was winter, and winters in Catalunya can be cold. I wore three layers of clothes and a thick black suede coat with a blue wool scarf wrapped around my neck. Each time I bent down to lift Marc, the ends of the scarf dragged through the dirt. Annoyed, I kept pulling it back with my left hand while holding onto Marc with my right. The scarf kept falling, but I couldn't tie it up without using both hands, and I had to hold onto Marc. He had run off a few times recently, so I never let go of his hand.

Marc looked up at me from the ground, laughing. I finally gave up on the scarf and focused on lifting him. Bending low with both hands, I managed to get him back on his feet. Now my scarf and coat were filthy. We walked two more blocks, hand in hand, with Marc humming a song. Then, in a split second, he yanked his hand free and ran. By the time I reacted, he had already darted into a Chinese restaurant.

"Marc!" I yelled, but it was too late—he was inside.

Panic surged through me. The other times he'd run off, Xavi had been there. Xavi, who once was the fastest kid in Barcelona in the 200 meters, is a race that demands speed and endurance. I was sure Marc had inherited those genes from his dad, which, combined with his autism, made him explosive.

I ran to the restaurant. The door was open. Inside, it was a huge space—tables, chairs, a fish tank full of golden Chinese barb fish, and red lanterns hanging from the ceiling. The place seemed empty.

"Marc! Marc!" I shouted, my voice echoing through the room. No answer. My heart stopped. My throat was dry, and I swallowed hard, panic rising. I had lost Marc. Frozen in place, my eyes darted around the room's red hues, searching. Then, I spotted a red screen with golden rivets that matched the wallpaper. I moved toward it, and behind the screen, I saw a door—probably leading to the kitchen.

Suddenly, a Chinese cook burst through the door, nearly hitting me with the double swinging doors. Behind him, I saw Marc running with something in his hand. I chased after him. He ran to a table, and there we were—the cook on one side, me on the other, and Marc in the middle. He was holding what I thought was a kitchen utensil. Marc ducked under the table and bolted toward another. We chased him again. Finally, I caught him, his little hands gripping a beautiful porcelain centerpiece. He looked into my eyes with a wide grin ear to ear and, as if it were a game, flung the piece into the air.

The sound of shattering porcelain filled the room.

"Marc, NOOOOO!" I cried a desperate, useless plea to reverse time. The Chinese cook, now furious, started shouting in what I assumed was Mandarin. Holding tight to Marc's arm, I bent forward in a gesture of apology and respect.

"I'm so sorry," I murmured in English, hoping he'd understand. "My son has autism." Marc hadn't been formally diagnosed yet, but at that moment, I decided he had autism. It explained everything.

The cook didn't seem to understand much of what I said, but he made some gestures and spoke rapidly. I didn't want to understand, thinking it was better that way. But then I caught a phrase: *Que tinguis molta sort amb el teu fill. Ja veig que té autism. Tot anira be!* It took me a moment to realize he was speaking Catalan, heavily accented, saying, "Good luck with your son. I see he has autism. Everything will turn out okay!"

From a distance, I yelled back, *"Moltes gràcies. Sí, tot anirà bé!"* which means, "Thanks a lot. Everything will turn out okay." Few people in my country recognized Marc's autism or that he had a condition, but that Asian chef did. I always thanked him for those kind words after the whirlwind Marc had created, like a force of nature.

Five minutes later, we arrived at the therapy center. Carina came out to greet us.

"How are you today?" she asked cheerfully. As always, she looked flawless. I wouldn't say I liked her style, which was too dark and boring for my taste, but you could tell she had time to choose what to wear. Her whole demeanor was relaxed. *"How fortunate she is,"* I thought.

Meanwhile, I was a mess. My body was both hot and cold, an unsettling mix of sweat and shivers. I was overheated from the physical effort of pulling Marc and chasing him, but the dampness of my clothes had cooled me down, giving me that shivery, post-fever feeling. My face was pale, my hair disheveled, and my mouth was half-open as I tried to catch my breath. My eyes brimmed with tears from the stress of that short walk and the realization that raising Marc was far more intense than I'd ever acknowledged. Even the Chinese cook's parting words—"You'll need luck with Marc"—echoed in my mind, a reminder that with just average luck, Marc's future, and mine, seemed precarious. I wasn't keeping up. I wasn't providing Marc with the safety he needed.

Lost in these thoughts, I suddenly remembered Carina's greeting and mumbled, "I'm a bit tired. We had an interesting walk with Marc." I glanced down at him. He was grinning ear to ear, clearly thrilled about another day of playing with Carina.

After leaving Marc at the center, I rushed home. No time for a shower, despite being sweaty and dirty from all of Marc's escapades. Self-care wasn't a priority. I had an operations meeting at ten, and after that, I needed to prepare for a presentation at our Mechelen site later that week. In a rush, I applied some deodorant. "That'll do," I muttered to myself. I threw on a gray suit and a blouse, grabbed my metallic red Volvo—my company car—and headed to the DuPont site, thirty minutes away.

In an instant, my mind switched to work. "I need to discuss the Operations meeting text I just received. Some of the paint is showing craters at the VW site. Damn, this is a real crisis! We'll need to expedite some batches in production. We can't afford to stop the line—that would be catastrophic. The penalties would kill us for the quarter. We're supposed to have the Just-In-Time system back up by the end of the day. But to move batches up, I'll have to reschedule some Jaguar and Toyota orders. Customer service will need to contact the account managers to prioritize their orders. The mills are at capacity, and the production planner is going to clash with the manufacturing supervisor, who's not exactly productivity-driven. The demand planner will have to step in, and the QC lab needs to test the VW samples first thing..."

When I was working, Marc didn't cross my mind. Work was my therapy, a mental and emotional escape. On top of that, I earned a good salary and was surrounded by smart leaders and team members. How lucky I was to do what I loved—leading, strategizing, managing teams, handling crises, and crafting ambitious action plans. It energized me.

Some years later, DuPont organized a seminar on managing stress at work. I stayed for five minutes, then left, shaking my head and laughing. *"Stress? What stress?"* I thought. Managing a site's supply chain wasn't stressful. My stress came on weekends, being a full-time autistic mom to Marc.

My job was my anchor, grounding me through all the chaos of Marc's behaviors. It reminded me that I could handle anything. I was growing in my career with relative ease, and it felt so rewarding to know that I could be both a successful professional and Marc's kick-ass mom. There was a certain pride in being able to juggle both—they complemented each other.

But the moment I got back into the car, I transformed into Marc's mom again. *"Hopefully, Marc hasn't picked on any kid today... What if they kick him out of school? Oh no!"* The thought paralyzed me. My crisis-manager self kicked in: *"I need to explain to the teacher how she can prevent these incidents."*

At five p.m., I picked Marc up from the nursery. The teacher wasted no time filling me in on the day's "highlights."

"During recess, Marc took all the snacks from the other kids. He ate Maria's raisins, Pedro's cookies, and Jose's banana. Jose cried for hours; he loves his banana," she said, shaking her head slightly.

I nodded, half empathetic, half exhausted from hearing these stories on repeat.

"Then Rosa fell to the ground. Marc wanted her Lego piece, and she wouldn't let go. He backed her into a corner until she fell. Then Marc laughed, which made her cry even harder."

With each word, my head drooped lower, my neck straining under the weight. I could only manage a soft "I'm so sorry."

I had seen Marc's behaviors play out so many times—at the park, on the street, with guests at home. I knew he wasn't trying to be mean. Something must have been misinterpreted in his mind. Was it just the way he was wired? A reaction to something? His way of expressing a need? At the time, I had no idea.

Just as I was thinking, *"At least no one was hurt today."*

The teacher added, "He also bit Joan." Her eyebrows shot up so high that they seemed to stretch toward the ceiling.

I pressed my eyebrows together, trying to think of a suggestion. "Maybe you could keep Marc a bit apart from the group…" I trailed off, knowing it was a flimsy, unrealistic idea. My neck ached from the tension, and I squeezed my eyes shut to stop the tears from escaping. *"Poor Joan's family…"* I thought, imagining Joan's mom coming home from work to find out her perfect two-year-old had been hurt at school.

I couldn't hold back anymore. Oceans of tears flooded my face and soul.

The teacher returned with Marc. I looked into his eyes, but as usual, he didn't meet my gaze. "Marc, Marc," I said, more for the teacher's sake than anything else, knowing it wouldn't change a thing—it never did. "Don't bite, okay? Be a good boy at school tomorrow."

Once we left the premises, I pulled Marc close and kissed him. "I missed you! Let's go eat in the park and then head home." He did not react, but I had learned to understand his emotions without needing facial cues anymore. I just knew he was happy.

On the way to the park, we stopped by the local bakery. In Spain, buying freshly baked artisan bread is a daily ritual. The crunchy crust and moist, flavorful inside make it irresistible. I picked up a baguette wrapped in a brown paper bag.

Marc, who had been silent since we left the nursery, started making sounds. "Thrma," he said.

"What do you mean, Marc? Thrma?" I asked, knowing I wouldn't get an answer.

"Thrma, thrma," he repeated. He'd been saying it for weeks, but the word had no meaning to me, though he spoke it with unusual intention.

I gave Marc a piece of bread, and his eyes, which rarely met mine, darted around like a bee flitting from flower to flower, absorbing everything around him. As he savored the bread, though, I saw a light in his eyes, his tongue flicking out to catch the crumbs from his upper lip.

We crossed the large wrought iron gate that led into the Casa Alegre garden, a luxurious, decadent space right in front of my apartment on Sant Fructuós Street. The garden had once been vegetable plots, but now it was a tranquil haven, rich with the scents of spring. We sat down on one of the walkways, surrounded by flower beds, soaking in the peaceful atmosphere. I felt so blessed to spend these moments with Marc in such a historic setting. From where I sat, I could see another grand iron gate decorated with garlands and roses, the one separating the garden from the house.

The house itself, dating back to the 18th century, had belonged to a successful textile entrepreneur—the Sagrera family. Terrassa, my city, had been shaped by the Industrial Revolution, its very identity woven into the spinning machines and looms that powered the textile industry. I admired those early entrepreneurs, the creators of opportunity for so many families, just like my own family would later be. The past of my city felt as real as the air I breathed, as if those historic machines still influenced my life, constantly pushing me

126

forward. Those machines, like me, never stopped working, never surrendered. Their goal was to produce perfect yarn, and mine was to help Marc, to somehow level him with the other kids—to make him "perfect," like the yarns that had spun Terrassa's success.

But wasn't it from the Industrial Revolution that we inherited this obsession with perfection? The idea that everything must be uniform, fast, and cheap? The imperfect threads, the flawed yarns, were discarded, much like how Marc and I were being pushed aside, day by day, in our city by people who believed in the myth of normalcy. And I was one of them, raised in this culture of perfection, I didn't know any better.

Now, I've come to see that not all perfect yarns are special. In fact, I've developed a passion for thick-and-thin yarns, the ones with slubs and imperfections, the bobbly bits that stand out. To knit them, you need a larger needle to accommodate their differences. The thick bits bunch up, and the thin parts look lacy, but over time, when they come together as a finished piece—like a sweater—they create something unique. It's those diverse threads that bring life and movement to what would otherwise be a dull, plain knitting pattern. And haven't we all seen enough dull, plain patterns around us? It's the diversity that makes something truly beautiful.

I snapped back to the present, sitting in the park with Marc. The smell of roses and lilies filled the air as I gave him his dinner: homemade grilled sole with pureed veggies. He made a mess, but I didn't care. He was having such a pleasant time under the warm Catalonian sun. I reassured myself, *"Soon, I'll get him into the bathtub and his clothes into the washing machine. No worries,"* trying to shake off the stress of the day.

I turned my eyes to the romantic central pond, its statue of a baby holding a goose reflecting in the water. Disconnected musings all over my mind. Seconds later, I heard myself screaming, "Marc! Stop! Stop!" In a flash, he let go of my hand and darted toward the pond.

Marc adored that pond, captivated by the busy tadpoles we visited regularly to watch their transformation into frogs. That day, he decided to get an even closer look. Before I could react, his shoes were still on the ground, but his waist was bent forward, and his head and body were fully submerged in the water as if he had plunged into a science experiment. I ran, heart racing, and pulled him out with one arm.

"Marc! Marc!" I repeated, hugging him tightly, feeling his soaking wet sweater pressed against me. "Let's get you into a hot bath—you need it now!" Marc was laughing, having the time of his life, his eyes sparkling like stars. His head, covered in water plants, couldn't hide his big, curved smile of satisfaction.

I noticed one of the people sitting on a bench, reading peacefully, suddenly raising his head in shock. The tranquility of the park had been broken, and so was mine. You never really get used to living in "red code" mode, always on alert.

That evening, Marc entered the bath as happy as a clam, his lips curved into a smile, showing his front teeth—similar to mine, just smaller and without the gap. His little body twisted and turned in the water like the tadpoles he had just been watching in the Casa Alegre garden pond. Knowing how much he loved bath time, I poured in extra soap, turning it into a bubble bath. Water and bubbles splashed everywhere, but I didn't care. He was so happy creating waves with his hands that I didn't want to spoil the moment. I had bigger challenges than cleaning up a wet bathroom. Yes, it was exhausting, especially at the end of the day, but I still chose to do it every night.

Suddenly, Marc paused. "Thrma, Thrma, Thrma," he said. I looked at him, surprised. He was still only two years old and had very few words. His eyes were locked onto the shampoo bottle, fixated. I wondered why. I looked at the bottle, trying to figure out what was so special about it.

Marc didn't point to show me, and I knew better than to expect him to. Pointing, or following someone else's point, is such a natural skill for most people, but not for Marc. It wasn't instinctual for him to use pointing as a way to share information. It's part of communication, a skill that might be taught through therapy, but it wasn't something Marc did naturally. When you pointed at something, Marc would look at your finger, not in the direction you were pointing. He didn't understand that my finger was trying to guide his eyes toward something specific.

Since Marc couldn't show me what he saw, I scanned the shampoo bottle myself. Then I noticed it—a tiny stickman at the bottom right corner. Suddenly, it clicked.

"Thrma, Thrma, Thrma," Marc repeated excitedly.

"I got it! You're saying, 'the running man!" I said, smiling.

Marc's eyes locked onto mine for a brief second, his face lighting up with a wide smile.

In Spain and other countries, there's a sign used to show the exit in public spaces—a green rectangle with a stickman running toward the exit. Marc had noticed this stickman and identified him as part of his world. While Marc showed little interest in real people and rarely said "mom" or "dad," these stickmen were different. They were simple and easy to understand. They didn't have complicated facial expressions or overwhelming body language. They weren't too much for Marc to process—therefore, they were his friends.

The good news was that Marc's stickman friends were everywhere. When we parked the car, I saw the exit sign, but Marc saw a friend saying, "Now you can sit in the car, listen to music, and watch the world from the window, Marc!" When we bought bread, the recycling symbol on the paper bag was just a reminder to me to care about the environment, but to Marc, it was a friend saying, "This bread is so good, Marc!" Even in the bath, the symbol that reminded me to recycle plastic probably told Marc, "Bubble time! Yay!"

It was fun for me, too, and I love fun, so I embraced Marc's stickman world like a ray of sunshine after a storm. Suddenly, I had something to connect with Marc over, a way into his world. He couldn't submerge himself into mine, but I could swim in his. It became easy for me to live in "Stickman City," and with all the signs everywhere, we were never lost again.

Of course, there was a learning curve. I tend to talk too much, and my overloading language was probably overwhelming for Marc. Sorry, Marc. You were trying to show me how to be the mom you needed, the mom you deserved. But back then, I was still just starting to learn, like a newborn myself, ever since the day I had drowned in confusion at the nursery.

Marc had different interests than typical kids, and he experienced human interaction in his own way. Looking back, I now realize that I was oppressing him with too much communication—he couldn't process it. At the time, I was just starting to understand Marc, but my actions were still too focused on "fixing" him. I thought that with enough effort, he would learn anything. I was just beginning to notice some of the unique abilities Marc had. I started to grasp that even though he was not a genius, he did indeed have exceptional abilities. Those abilities didn't seem to help him much with his daily life, but they were there. I was learning that fun, concrete, and specific visual signs were far more effective for communicating with Marc than my long directions, explanations, or repetitions. But I was an achiever, so I always pushed the limits—pushed Marc.

Marc liked signs, so I thought, *"Let's work on signs for half an hour."* But that was too long, and I didn't know. I put all my energy into helping him, sometimes forgetting about Marc's boundaries, so we often ended up with Marc yelling, even though he loved the book of the sign. I need to explain myself to explain to Marc why I was doing it. But the truth is that I can't find a better answer than "You don't know what you don't know." It took me years to understand that sometimes trying hard is not enough; how you construct your demand for your child determines success, too. We have to challenge our children with realistic requests. If Marc's attention span was five minutes, I had to squeeze my demand into only five minutes; that way, Marc had been successful, and we both had a rewarding experience. Today, I think that sometimes when we do not know better, it helps us to practice some "stopping, observing, and reflecting" to improve our experiences. These practices require us to slow down and allow ourselves to learn from our child's reactions so that next time we can incorporate new approaches to our propositions that lead to better experiences and results for our child and us. I could have seen your frustration building up, but I was too busy focusing on unrealistic results.

Still, despite all that excessive effort, which put so much strain and frustration on both of us, we had some remarkable successes, Marc.

Marc tore up all the pages of his books. The fox, Little Red Riding Hood—they all met the same fate. Every book turned into scattered pieces of paper on the floor. A bit of the red hood here, a brown leg of what used to be a scary fox under the chair, too far for me to reach, so it stayed there for months. It was a constant reminder that I couldn't even read a simple children's book to Marc. How heartbreaking is that? Isn't reading an illustrated book with your child one of those perfect, heartwarming moments you assume every kid would love or at least appreciate?

It broke me inside every time. With each torn book, each renewed attempt to create that magical experience I had shared with my mom, it felt like a knife being driven deeper into my chest. The pain grew stronger with each ripped page—pure torture, pure suffering from not knowing *why*. "Why are you doing this, Marc?" I would whisper, tears rolling down my cheeks, soaking the pages of books full of unheard stories. I couldn't understand what was going wrong, and I started asking Marc in sheer desperation. But Marc could never answer my questions. Obviously, he didn't know why he was acting that way; Marc didn't understand abstract questions and never answered a "why" question. Now, I grasp that many of his conducts were triggered by sensations he noticed on his body, a world of sensations that invaded Marc in a way that most typical persons have never experienced.

Still, I kept asking. I kept suffering. I kept gluing those torn books back together, hour after hour. *"I can fix this,"* I'd tell myself. *"I'll read the book to Marc again tomorrow; I'll simplify the story, and I'll hold the book tight this time."* And day after day, I did. *"He'll love these books and respect them because they're perfect and precious,"* I reassured myself. But I was exhausted. I was losing weight, losing my appetite, struggling to survive—but I didn't stop.

Then, one day, I woke up with a new notion: *"Maybe most kids love these books, but what if Marc isn't interested in them at all? What if he doesn't understand any of the stories, I assume he does?"* Instead of rushing to work that day, I stopped by a driving school and grabbed a driver's manual. When I came back home, I handed him the manual. I didn't say a word. I wanted to, but I held back, not wanting to overstimulate him.

Marc's face relaxed, his eyes lit up, and he smiled wide—his teeth and even the tip of his pink tongue visible. I pointed to the stop sign in the manual and said, "Stop."

Marc repeated, "Stop," pronouncing the word as if talking had suddenly become easy for him. Two minutes later, he was reading out all the sign words from the manual: "Stop," "Do not cross, the train

133

is coming," "Bicycles only lane." Every word was clear and intentional.

Tears rolled down my cheeks, but this time, they were tears of pride and joy. I was in awe of Marc, my heart swelling with admiration. My mouth hung open in amazement, and I felt like I was witnessing a miracle.

With the concrete language of signs and the ever-stable, always-smiling stickmen, Marc was thriving. We both were immersed in that subworld of ours. Those experiences in our little world didn't stop me from believing that he would eventually succeed in "normal" life, too, the mass of typical people I had always known. Following all the books and advice I read, I tried to use those successes to push Marc to do what he was "supposed" to do—what "all" kids did in my mind. For years, I kept repeating, insisting, fighting, and never giving up on changing Marc, which, to me at that time, meant helping Marc.

Now, almost twenty years later, I comprehend I may have spoiled many of your moments as a child, Marc. But I tried. I got better each time, and you gave me more of those butterfly smiles that I love to the moon and back. Sometimes, though, I wish I had focused more on the stickmen and their colorful world in the here and now instead of being frustrated because you didn't follow my directions. Directions that likely meant nothing to you, Marc, because you didn't understand them. Those directions were probably too full of words and unnecessary detail; sorry for stressing you out, Marc.

I wish I could erase all the times you saw desperate Silvia—sometimes angry Silvia—because I didn't stop, observe, and learn who you really were. I didn't take the time to understand your needs. The stickman was a good hint, Marc. Thank you for teaching me. I know it was hard, and I regret it. It wasn't tough because you didn't communicate—you did it in your way. It was hard because I thought I knew it all.

At the time, I was fascinated by the stickman world you opened up to me, and I'm so grateful that I at least discovered that, thanks to you. But I was unable to take the lesson further. I wish I had been able to let go of my beliefs about what I was "supposed" to do to help you and just embraced that fun new world. I wish I had left my Agenda aside, my rationale, my plans, and we had just flown away together with the stickman. I wish someone had helped me see that, but there was no one there, and I wasn't intuitive enough to figure it out on my own. For years, I suffered endlessly trying to change you. Now, I wonder, *"Why did I even try?"* For years, I didn't get it.

The girl who thought she had a plan and an imagination big enough to solve anything didn't register enough of your gifts.

I was constantly looking for answers from the so-called professionals. Some did help, but now I see clearly that all those years of seeking answers, all those restless days of asking others to help me "fix" you, were full of wasted time. I thought it was worth it because I believed I'd eventually make you more "typical." How wrong I was.

People can't change people, and they shouldn't even try. I'm so sorry, Marc. I didn't understand until now, twenty years later, that what I thought was my struggle was really *your* struggle—the struggle to be understood, loved, and accepted as you are. I've always believed I was an empathic person, that I could connect with anyone,

135

no matter what. But I failed to understand that real empathy is about stopping, observing, and delighting with what my child had to offer, not rushing to shape him into what I thought he should be or what society had shaped me to believe Marc was supposed to be.

Chapter Nine
A crumbling shipwreck – A family decaying, a mother not giving up

"There's nothing more beautiful than the way the
ocean refuses to stop kissing the shoreline no matter
how many times it's sent away."
— Sarah Kay

Xavi's side of the family around the Christmas tree. There are only a few ornaments left on the top of the tree. Only the top ones survived Marc's attempts to bring the ornaments down.

I was so wrong. Why didn't anyone tell me? You couldn't, Marc. You could only endure my constant efforts, my tears, and my relentless push to "fix" you. I was frustrated and tired because I couldn't overcome your autism. It never crossed my mind that *you* must have been frustrated and exhausted, too. Tired of having a mom who, instead of comforting you in a world that was probably already overcomplicated and overwhelming, was often sad. Instead of making the world easier for you to live in and thrive as you were, I was too frequently wrapped up in my sadness.

I wish I could turn all that sadness into acceptance and just have gone with the flow.

For years, I was psychologically exhausted, searching for answers that no one could give me. *"Will he be independent when he grows up?" "Accept? Accept what? I'm willing to accept, but please help me understand! How does the definition of autism, assuming Marc has autism, relate to him?" "Will Marc overcome this autism?" "How can I help him overcome it?" "Why is he misbehaving so much? Why can't he stop moving? Why does he always do the exact thing he's not supposed to do?"*

Now, I know those were the wrong questions to ask in the first place. But nobody ever told me that. In my defense, Marc, I wasn't the only one in the dark about autism. Almost everyone around me was too. At that point, no one had even formally labeled you with autism—no one. Even if the professionals had understood autism better, they couldn't have answered my questions. Why? Because Marc, before any diagnosis, is a person—a unique individual like we all are. Nobody can predict someone's life, whether they have autism or not.

But no one ever told me those questions were wrong, and some professionals even tried to answer them, sealing your future with statements like, "He will never learn a second language." Carina once told me, "Don't expose him to English—it will just confuse him."

Today, I can only say, "Ha!"

That evening, we found a letter from Carina's office in the mail. It was from the local government in Catalunya, La Generalitat de Catalunya. For the first time, I saw the words "developmental disability" as your diagnosis. It was the first formal diagnosis—nothing about autism. I shared the letter with Xavi. He didn't understand what it meant, so I explained, "I guess it means Marc isn't developing typically. It'll just take him longer to learn and grow, but I have the passion and energy to help him catch up and be the kid he's meant to be."

"I had never been so mistaken."

Now, it's hard to imagine not immediately searching for a term online, but back then, we just went with what we thought, waiting until we could ask another "expert of weird names"—doctors, psychologists, neurologists, therapists. None of them, except Amaia Hervás (whom I hadn't yet met), had the knowledge I so desperately needed about autism.

Marc, at three years old

At three years old, I moved Marc from nursery school to a transitional kindergarten. It was there that we had the fortune to meet Olga Carretero. Olga understood Marc, which triggered moments of unparalleled connection.

No new activity was ever easy for Marc, and TK was no different. "Today we went to the pool," Olga wrote in our communication notebook. "He didn't like it at all! Marc was asking for mom all day, especially when we went to the pool." "Today, he saw the water and just said, 'no, no, no, no.' Every day, Olga shared kind notes with details about Marc.

One day, he came back from school, and I knew it had been a pool day. I remembered that same pool from my childhood, where they attached colorful plastic seahorses to the right side of our bathing suits to separate kids into swim skill levels.

I asked Marc, "Marc, where did they put the seahorse on your bathing suit?"

He said, "The butt."

I cracked up laughing and told him, "No, Marc, it can't be on the butt. They normally put them on the sides."

"The butt, the butt," he insisted. My exaggerated expressions made him laugh, creating one of those fun shared moments I'll never forget. When he was three, he loved all the silliness around butts, farts, and poo. These topics were perfect for bringing him closer and having a good time. In fact, they remain some of his favorite jokes to share with the family today.

One day I asked Olga about Marc's insistence that his seahorse was placed on his butt when I had clearly seen it attached to the right side of his Speedo. "Do you think he told me that just to make fun?" I asked. *"Normally, Marc doesn't make things up."*

"Kusu, kusu," Olga chuckled as she explained. "The swimming coach gave Marc one of those floating foam tubes to help him with buoyancy, and he was sitting on it in the pool, one leg on each side. That was definitely his 'horse,' and yes, the 'horse' was on Marc's butt. He was absolutely right," she said, waving her bent arm and moving her hand toward her stomach in a solemn gesture to emphasize the "absolutely right."

We both cracked up, laughing until our stomachs hurt. "Marc never lies," I added.

It took Marc months to accept the pool. Now, I know that Marc thrives on routine, and introducing him to new activities is always challenging. His initial reaction is as solid as a rock—he never wants to try it. After those troublesome months, though, he eventually came to terms with the water. The only reason he ever wanted to get out was because it was a bit too cold for my tiny, skinny Marc at that age.

That afternoon, Marc was very communicative. I asked him, "Marc, what was the best thing you did at school today?"

He responded, "Time out."

Marc rarely answered questions, so whenever he did, it filled me with joy and gave me enough energy to keep going for the rest of the month. However, what he said often didn't match what had actually happened. He frequently repeated things from the past or movies.

I decided to check Olga's magic notebook, my window into Marc's school day. "Olga, Marc just told me he was in time out. Is that true?"

"Yes, he is correct! He was misbehaving with a girl, so I asked him to sit in time out for the first time. It worked! He didn't like it at all. He enjoys being included and getting my attention, and you could tell by his eyes that he understood the consequences."

I was delighted and surprised that he had communicated this to me. It meant he really understood the situation. Olga had established such a good relationship with Marc that he behaved well just to keep her approval. She was always straightforward with him, and there was real chemistry between the two. She was the best.

When Marc turned four, it was probably the first time in my life that I felt like I wasn't succeeding the way I had expected to. I had been trying to change Marc for two years with no substantial results. At the time, failure wasn't even a word in my vocabulary. I had no plans to give up or do anything different. I was like a bulldozer—determined, relentless. I believed in learning, but with no one to show me alternative ways, I kept trying the same strategies over and over. I'd tweak them, adapt, improve them, and hold on to any small improvement as a sign that I was helping Marc, that I was moving forward, even if I couldn't say I was truly succeeding. There was always some small battle won, some hint of progress that gave me hope.

As Amaia once told me later, *"We all evolve; even the most compromised people evolve with support, even if it's not exactly the support they need most."* But evolving means becoming more of who you are—not transforming into someone else. Back then, I couldn't see that. My ambition was to change Marc, but that was an unrealistic goal. I know that now, but at the time, I celebrated every tiny success as if it were proof that he would "recover" and that he would one day overcome autism.

I'd share every sign of progress with Xavi, trying to convince him that these small wins were leading toward a bigger victory—a new Marc. But Xavi never saw the success. He didn't even appreciate the small improvements; they were too insignificant for him to see them as accomplishments. No matter how tiny the changes or how frustrated I became seeing my husband give up on Marc from the day he was born, I kept going. I kept adjusting, adapting, educating those around him, teaching Marc, and tracking everything—updating files, graphs, notes to Olga, and visits to Carina.

I spent countless sleepless nights holding Marc down with my arms and legs, physically restraining him so he wouldn't stand up. I was not just psychologically exhausted—I was skin and bones.

"Silvia, you look tired. Have you lost weight?" That was the daily comment I'd hear from people in the community when I walked through the streets of Terrassa with Marc. He was always ahead of me, pulling my arm, eager to go faster. My arms hurt like tree branches weighed down by heavy snow in winter, bent and strained under the load. Marc's feet were always bouncing, sometimes tiptoeing, his eyes scanning everything but mine. He'd speak in broken sentences, random words he'd picked up elsewhere, or lines from movies that made no sense to me.

Sometimes, the words he repeated were from conversations he had overheard from family, school, or TV. Sometimes, they were bits of songs mixed with sounds or words he made up for his pleasure, pronounced so inwardly that I couldn't even make out what they meant. Later, I would learn that this was echolalia—repetition of words or phrases. Often, just to be part of his world, I'd sing along with him or say something like, "You look so happy today, Marc. I love seeing Marc happy—it makes me happy too." I tried not to use pronouns with him. I had learned intuitively that they were too abstract for Marc.

There I was, being dragged by this force of nature, my body aching, my mind fully depressed. When people stopped to ask about my health or comment on how I looked, I'd brush them off. "I'm okay, I'm okay. I have to go—Marc doesn't like to stop."

In the past, I had tried stopping to chat with acquaintances in the city center, but Marc quickly found a way to escape those moments. Marc's nature to keep his little body always in action made it really hard for him to wait. His different relationship with words made him explore other ways to escape the situation. He'd pull down his jeans zipper and pee right there, holding himself with one hand while I held him with the other. His strategy was disturbingly efficient. My friends or whoever I was talking to would immediately be horrified by the scene, and passersby would turn their heads in shock. Everyone stared at my terribly "rude" child, and then, a second later, they turned to judge me, the "weak" mom who couldn't control him.

I'd saw the disgust in their faces—eyebrows raised, wrinkles on their foreheads, their eyes squinting as if to avoid witnessing the scene, and their noses wrinkled in disdain. I bowed my head, mumbling, "I'm so sorry. Marc doesn't do 'wait.' But in my mind, I could

144

still hear them thinking, *"What does she mean, 'he doesn't do wait'? She needs to teach him that this is unacceptable!"*

Day by day, I changed my routines to adapt to Marc, often in desperation. As much as I tried to teach Marc patience—using the stop sign I had taped to every door in the house—the results seemed so bleak to me. The stop signs helped a little inside, teaching him that he couldn't dash from one room to the other without asking me first. From today's perspective, I recognized these achievements were actually huge. I just didn't fully understand the degree of challenges Marc was being asked to overcome—challenges that were simply unattainable without his many special needs being properly addressed.

Marc's mind did indeed understand the stop sign and the requirement to ask me first because I had given him the right communication tool. But even then, it wasn't enough to prevent him from running off here and there. Why? I was assuming that all our actions depend solely on the mind. I didn't realize that our bodies play a role, too, and that being in control of one's body varies from person to person. Just because it was easy for me and seemed to be easy for everyone I knew didn't mean it was easy for Marc. Marc's body couldn't stop, even when he wanted to. His impulse often was the one in control of his body. He wasn't even aware of where his body ended, and space, air, or water began, whether he was in the ocean or just taking a bath.

This was unimaginable to me back then. I had heard about ADHD—Attention Deficit Hyperactivity Disorder—but that didn't mean I understood it. I had only encountered it in passing, often overhearing other moms say things like, "There's such an overdiagnosis of ADHD these days, right?" And another would chime in, "Totally. Teachers just want all the kids to behave like soldiers. They use ADHD meds as a tool for control." The conversation would be ended with one of them raising her eyebrows in disgust.

Nobody had diagnosed Marc with ADHD—or catatonia, specifically a type associated with autism, which can affect people whose muscles are in such constant movement that their bodies end up like those of marathon runners or earthquake survivors trapped under rubble. This kind of catatonia is severely underdiagnosed, and, as I know now, it can be treated. ADHD and catatonia, when they present with autism, are named comorbidities—they come as a bundle deal with autism, if you will.

Marc also yelled—long, piercing yells that filled more and more of his day as time went on. It was like being caught in a tornado at its peak, and I was spinning around with no direction and no control. I had no clue then that Marc was probably trying to communicate his frustration when other forms of communication failed or when Marc was sensory overloaded.

In my persistence to get Marc into books, I bought him *The Hundred and One Dalmatians* children's book with illustrations. When I first picked it up to read to him, he rejected it as usual. And, as usual, I persisted. This time, I'm so glad I did. Don't get me wrong—I still believe that persistence and endurance are valuable traits. But like everything in life, persistence has its downside, and this was no exception. After many days of pushing through, I did the same as I had done so many days before with so many other books: I sat next to

Marc with *The Hundred and One Dalmatians* book open on our little green round IKEA table and started reading.

I was there then. But Marc was having his usual reaction. He was not grabbing my hands to close the book right away. I took a deep breath and looked up. Marc was sitting still. I was astonished—he was actually pausing, giving me a momentary break, like a fantasy. My mind, which is always scattered by nature but has been forced into constant focus over the last two years, starts to wander. Like a prisoner whose warden forgot to lock the cell, my mind wanders freely, unaware that it's doing so.

In that sudden freedom, I visualized Marc closing the book with his usual impatience. *Bang!* I heard the imagined sound of the book slamming shut, my breath caught, and for a split second, I heard it thud to the floor. My heart races—*thump thump*—followed by the imagined sound of Marc's footsteps, like a bolt of lightning across the corridor. I pictured the loud crash from the kitchen, probably a heavy object slamming against the wall. My heart pounded harder, and panic flooded me. But then, I blinked and returned to reality. Marc was still there, glued to his stool.

It's my frayed nerves that made me relive one of my daily nightmares, but that day, Marc was not running off like a free spirit with no destination, like a cheetah stalking its prey. He was not grabbing the book from my hands, ripping it apart, throwing it through an open window, or hurling it at me like he'd done so many times before. He was not racing down the long corridor, which had become more like a home racetrack for him.

I was never gifted as a runner, but need and desperation turned me into an Olympic athlete of sorts, sprinting after Marc through that corridor every day. Marc was always the champion, and I was always left behind, never making it to the final race, constantly hearing crashes from the kitchen—glass shattering, pans clanging. I tried so hard to prevent the inevitable, but no matter how fast I ran, I could never stop the disaster: eggs and cheese smashed to the floor, pans collided midair before leaving a dent in the kitchen table, and water spilled everywhere. Every time Marc bolted, the result was the same. A constant loop that played out multiple times a day. I'd catch my breath after the chase, only to find Marc already on his way to pee on the carpet. It was a cycle I couldn't break, no matter how many strategies I tried, and it was killing me—mentally, physically, emotionally.

But now, in this rare moment, Marc was still. He was looking at me, and for the first time in what felt like forever, his eyes were locked onto mine. I'm tired, and he hasn't misbehaved. He was giving me time, but I was so overwhelmed by everything going on in my life that I felt like a bird whose cage door had been opened but who's lost the ability to fly—trapped on the bars, unable to move or chirp. Dead inside.

Marc was still, and it seemed that *The Hundred and One Dalmatians* book had the power to keep him glued to his green IKEA stool for ten minutes. I started reading. Marc listens. Marc looked at the pictures. Then, Cruella de Vil made her first appearance. I impersonate Cruella, and Marc's face softens—his jaw dropped. He was captivated by my portrayal of her.

It was as if, with my Cruella performance, I'd shot a web from my hands, just like Spider-Man. The web connects Marc's eyes to mine, and like Spider-Man's web, it's sticky and strong, holding him in place as long as I'm Cruella. I was witnessing a miracle! I've found water in the desert! For about a year, Marc became fascinated by my Cruella impression. He started repeating the lines in the same tone I used all day long.

Cruella, that villainous character for most children, became our special connection. Until it faded, it was our secret code. Like the stickman world or the signs universe, it was the fine thread that tied his world to mine. To an outsider, it might have looked like a weak thread, but to me, it was the most precious, unbreakable silk string.

The images of that day have stayed with me to this day. It was in the evening when my energy was almost depleted. It had been a long day, one of those days that keep you dragging in this world for no reason. A tough night with Marc, followed by a grey day at work, and I had just had to do the groceries in a rush, holding hands with Marc. With his free hand, he had decided to remove one cookie box from the base of one of those beautiful and, for my liking, too unstable supermarket pyramids, so yes, all the cookie boxes on that gorgeous display were now scattered on the floor.

We had just arrived home, and still holding Marc's hand, I plunged onto the couch and let it all go. I cried and sobbed like a little girl, tears of exhaustion. Marc watched me. He didn't run away. That was unexpected. Marc observed me and all of a sudden, I noticed the warmth of his face against mine, and then he kissed me. The singleness of this intimate moment is with me forever. Words fail me to describe my emotions. Marc didn't kiss, and today Marc had not only kissed me but had done it when I really needed it the most. I was so grateful to you, Marc! You cheered me up and were there for me when I needed to see a light at the end of the tunnel.

I'm an incontinent kisser. Kissing is essential to me, maybe to everyone or to many of us at least. It was so painful that Marc was not kissing me. I could rationalize that it was not in him to do it, but still, I suffered from the missing kisses. For months I had taught Marc how to kiss but he didn't seem to get it. It sounds weird, right? But kissing was not in him, as so many aspects of communication that some of us often assume we all know how to do and that we never needed anyone teaching us.

Well, typical people imitate easily, so maybe that's why it seems it's natural to humankind, only that we are not all typical. I've had the privilege to talk to someone with Aspergers who shared with me that for him to feel an emotion, something impactful needs to happen. That insight makes me think that maybe Marc was not kissing me when I was teaching him how to kiss me because, at that particular moment, nothing that he considered impactful had happened to display his emotion with a kiss. However, seeing mom desperately crying lying to the coach, who might have spoken to Marc.

Marc, at four years old

When Marc turned four, his body grew stronger, his behaviors intensified, and his energy seemed endless, with no apparent need to recharge at night.

I visualize those nights...

None of this power ever slept. Since the day he was born, Marc had never slept through a single night. Not once. Xavi and I had to learn to take turns at night for years. As a baby, he would cry and cry. When he turned three, he started yelling—yelling so piercingly that once the sound entered my head, it possessed me. I couldn't shake it off, and it felt like being dragged into a torture chamber from which I couldn't escape until Marc, unpredictably, decided to stop. Sometimes, it went on for hours, and there I was—consumed, sleepless, exhausted in body and mind, with no escape. None at all.

One night, I took my pillow and Xavi's and tried to cover my head. I could still hear Marc. I felt utterly miserable, defeated. Xavi, always the reliable teammate, took over. I felt a brief relief, a moment to catch my breath and let go of restraining Marc in his room. It wasn't just the yelling; Xavi or I had to physically hold Marc in his bed so he wouldn't get up and continue destroying things around the house. So many objects that seemed harmless to others were powerful weapons in Marc's hands. Our house was already adapted for his needs, but it was never secure enough. He would find something new to misuse.

He threw forks at the TV—Marc probably holds the record of TVs broken by a kid: four. He tossed chairs into the air; lamps were smashed to the floor, leaving deep gouges in the wood. Bulbs shattered. All of this happened on nights when our bodies couldn't keep up with the boundless energy contained in our sweet, playful, adorable Marc. Because even in the midst of this chaos, Marc was still cute. His butterfly smiles would appear after the most intense bouts of noise he caused. I see him now, running gracefully in his black-and-white Mickey Mouse pajamas, his long lashes and sweet, naïve

151

expression never fading—not even when he was breaking a TV, an activity that seemed to give him particular joy. Allow me the irony; I know he didn't mean it but put for a moment in the parents' shoes. I've used irony so many times in my life; to me, it's a great way to escape the heavy emotions that really hurt inside.

That night, like so many nights before, at four a.m., Xavi and I knew exactly what would happen if we weren't on top of Marc, physically restraining him from getting up. These were our nights for fifteen years. Well, not quite—every year was worse. As Marc grew stronger, Xavi and I grew weaker and more drained. Sometimes, I think we were just ghosts dragging what little energy we had left around the house, waiting patiently for our turn to collapse into bed. Even though the yelling didn't stop, our bodies were so exhausted that we could sleep through alarms blaring at full power.

Xavi was stronger than me, and he knew it, so he took longer shifts. I appreciated it, but at the same time, I felt guilty. I felt useless, like a failure. I couldn't "fix" Marc. I couldn't even slightly change his behavior. I had no idea what to do. I was lost and exhausted, and depression began to take hold of me.

Mornings were unbearable after sleepless nights. Xavi left for work at the bank very early, and I stayed home to take Marc to school. Every morning, he dumped his milk and cereal on the floor. By the time he was four, he had almost broken all our glassware and dishes. I switched everything to plastic—not just for Marc, but for all of us. The sound of glass breaking had damaged my nervous system so deeply that even now, decades later, I still get anxious holding anything made of glass. My stomach tightens as if my brain is still warning me that glass is unreliable and dangerous.

When Marc was finally ready for school, I faced the same terrible decision every day: should I take the stairs or the elevator? If we took the stairs, he'd try to break free from my hand and dash down three flights, smash open the building door like The Hulk, and run out into the street until he'd found a random person to latch onto. Then, I'd have to chase after him, all sweat and exhausted, and apologize to a stranger before my workday even began. The other option was the elevator, which carried its own risks. Once inside, Marc would jump, and I'd make one of those frantic faces, my voice rising in that high-pitched tone that made him laugh so hard. The more he misbehaved, the more I lost my temper. And the more I lost my temper, the more Marc laughed.

It was a vicious cycle. By the time I realized it, it was too late—Marc already knew all my buttons. He knew exactly what would trigger those exaggerated reactions: the funny faces and flapping hands. It was pure entertainment for him. He couldn't read my emotions or understand that I was angry. To him, it was just a game—a mouth opening wide, hands moving up and down, a voice getting louder and faster. He was delighted with my "shows."

He never understood the impact of his jumping or why sometimes the elevator actually stopped working, and we were stuck in that small space, waiting for a kind neighbor to rescue us. So, he yelled and yelled, trapped in something that he did to himself, but one he didn't comprehend. Now, I understand it all more—but back then, I didn't. Every morning, I felt miserable, with only two horrible options: the chaos of the stairs or the risk of getting stuck in the elevator. Neither felt like a way out.

When Marc was four, I started working remotely from my home office while also traveling around Europe for work. That meant I was the one taking care of Marc during the weekdays when he was not at school, in addition to providing him with all the resources he needed. I fought for his resources—or rather, the lack of them.

At DuPont, I led projects across Europe. I resolved operations crises in different countries and deployed SAP systems throughout the old continent. My job was once again my lifesaver. I loved being up there, above the clouds. It was a literal escape from the sleepless nights, from the constant worry about Marc's future and the immediate crises. The unbearable behaviors, the red codes for the next day or night—all of those thoughts disappeared as I prepared action plans to deal with leadership problems in Belgium, lack of collaboration with someone in Germany, or warehouse configuration issues in Portugal.

Challenges that might have been stressful to others were pure medicine to me. I let them consume me completely. I shut my eyes, picturing myself seated on the plane, feeling my muscles relax. The tension would drain from my toes to the top of my head, turning fire into refreshing cold water and pain into a wellness spa. I'd look out at the clouds, knowing there was nothing I could do for Marc from up there. So, I surrendered and embraced my best friend with love: my job.

These trips lasted about a week. I remember one particular trip to Köln. After my last meeting, everyone at the site thanked me for my support. *"Mission accomplished,"* I told myself, with that comforting feeling of a job well done and being appreciated by others. I returned to my hotel and started packing my trolley. Suddenly, a wave of pure mom essence hit me—a hole in my stomach. *"I want to be home. I need Marc."*

My brain, my muscles, my skin needed Marc. Everything changed in a second. Imagine a perfect summer day, the sun caressing your skin, and then, out of nowhere, a thunderstorm rolls in. That's how it felt. In a rush, I packed my trolley and took a taxi to the airport. My body ached for my family. I needed to hug Marc, read Olga's notebook, kiss my son, and hold him in bed at night—no matter what.

Suddenly, all sorts of bright ideas filled my brain. I could see my thoughts racing through every curve of my brain, filled with cortisol. I had to organize them and wrote them down. I needed every detail in place to put into action when I got home. At the airport, sipping coffee, I created an Excel sheet on my laptop. I knew exactly what to do when he jumped in the elevator or to stop him from peeing on the street when we met someone. I even had a solution for the yelling—I was ready not to react and avoid reinforcing the behaviors that he did to seek my attention, even my negative attention.

I checked the monitor. My flight was boarding. I rushed to the gate. Then I heard the announcement: "This flight is overbooked. We have randomly selected a list of passengers to board. If you don't hear your name, you'll be compensated and flown to Barcelona to-morrow morning."

I had flown countless times in my career—cancellations, overbook-ings, even missed flights. It wasn't very pleasant, but it was never the end of the world. But now, with Marc, everything was different. My stomach knotted with pure stress. *"I need to board. I have to be with Marc. Let me be with my son,"* I pleaded in my head.

The agent started calling out names. My heart pounded as if my life depended on it. My name wasn't called. Uncontrollable tears poured from my eyes, instantly soaking my cheeks—like Niagara Falls, the kind of tears a three-year-old cries when their balloon pops. My mind couldn't process it, but I couldn't stop. Completely broken, I sat down in one of those impersonal airport chairs, curled up, my neck and business shirt collar wet. I felt lost. Again, like a child. I didn't belong there. My skin needed Marc's skin. My soul needed his smile and the bubbles we made together during bath time. I missed his giggles when I squeezed the rubber duck, and I even missed the water that splashed all over the floor, the towel he would pull into the tub, swirling it around him like a playful baby seal.

Immersed in my thoughts, I didn't notice a man approach me. "Why are you crying? Do you need help?" he asked.

I burst out, "I miss my son! I need to be on that flight. He needs me, my husband needs me, I need my family. My son has autism. He needs me."

The tears fell harder. I didn't recognize myself.

"I hear you," the man said softly. "Take my ticket. I'm on the boarding list, but I can wait—you can't."

I jumped up and hugged this stranger. "Thank you!" It was the most precious act of kindness I had ever experienced.

Wherever you are, you have shown me the power of human connection, one of the most important reasons for our existence. Someone once told me that the most common regret of the elderly as they approach death is having missed opportunities for human connection. That will never be my regret. I embrace connection as the powerful force it is.

I went home and extended my arms to Marc, who was running down the corridor. "Marc, Marc," I called out with all my heart. He kept running, crossing right past me without looking—no glance, no gesture, nothing. It hurt, just for a moment. *"Marc doesn't connect... and moms need this connection. We need it, I need it."* I chased after him and hugged him, but he broke free.

There was a sharp pain in my chest, a pain I couldn't undo feeling or erase. I acknowledged it, then turned to Xavi. He gave me the connection the affection, and welcomed me home. It was brief—too brief for me—but I know why. He was busy making sure Marc was safe, while the housekeeper we hired months ago to make our lives a bit more bearable prepared dinner for Marc and Xavi.

I retreated to my room to unpack. I adjusted my expectations—I still have enough energy to do that. *"Tomorrow, I'll put my action plan in place to help Marc. Tonight, I'll let Xavi sleep. He must be exhausted."*

In the following days, my pain or emotional state was the least of my concerns. My sole focus was Marc—his progress, his learning, everything to give him a better future. One by one, I feverishly implemented all the strategies I had carefully planned. I tracked Marc's development with scientific rigor, updating his files daily while he was at school after my long work days. All of them filed under *Overcoming Marc Crisis*.

Xavi and I had a saying: "Only if he could stop sometimes." His extreme difficulty in communicating, which was at the core of the issue for most children with autism, wasn't even our biggest challenge. We would comment: "What's really hard is that he never stops moving and has no sense of danger or control over his actions. How can Marc strategize three different misbehaviors in a row?"

I vividly remember the day he opened a window and threw a toy out, then ran and squeezed a juice box with both hands until it exploded like a fountain, spraying juice all over the corridor walls. While I was frantically cleaning that up, he ran to the bathroom and flushed a Lego firetruck down the toilet. This was our life—every single day, multiple times a day, for years.

But some days, Marc surprised me with the unexpected and made my day. That day, his gift was improved communication. It was a winter day when he brought home "Pam the Elf," a puppet that Olga Carretero had lent him for a week. Pam the Elf was the class mascot. We were wearing our winter ropes while sitting on Marc's cozy room carpet. I took the elf in my hand, just like I did with Chow Chow, Marc's favorite doll, and asked Marc, "Hi Marc! How are you today?"

158

I knew for sure Marc wouldn't respond—greetings didn't register for him. But I was wrong. He replied, "I'm good!" I jumped up from the floor like I had witnessed another miracle, overcome with emotion.

I continued the conversation, "What color is my shirt, Marc?"

"Green," he replied.

"Do you want to play with me?" I asked.

"Yes," he said, smiling. I couldn't believe it. Moments later, I noticed Marc coughing and looking tired. I took his temperature, and sure enough, he was sick.

From that day on, I noticed that every time Marc was sick, his communication skills improved tremendously. My theory was that Marc's hyperactivity and attention deficit were so extreme that his attention span was usually just seconds. But when he was ill, his body was too weak for the ADHD to dominate, and his attention span lengthens enough to allow for his communication to appear timidly. I'm no scientist, but I know there's a correlation. In fact, I could often predict Marc's illnesses before any symptoms appeared just by how adorable and communicative he became.

Xavi and I used to take Marc to the zoo. Kids love animals, right? We'd point at the animals, but Marc would just watch our fingers. No matter the animal, he wouldn't look—he didn't care. What he did care about were doors, mechanical parts, and random objects left behind by the maintenance staff. Motors, metal pieces, plastic scraps, wheels—things most people would never notice. He tested every door, trying to enter ones the staff had forgotten to lock.

"Marc, nooooo!" I shouted one day as he slipped into the polar bear zookeeper's door. As always, Xavi, quick as ever, ran after Marc and saved the day. I just stood there, mouth open, in disbelief at what we had just witnessed.

We left the zoo feeling frustrated. A simple walk in the park seemed like a better idea. But then something happened that lifted my spirits. Marc eloped, as he often did, and Xavi was about to chase after him when suddenly Marc stopped in his tracks in front of a huge pile of fallen leaves.

Watching Marc delight over this carpet in shades of yellows, oranges, and browns was an utter bliss, a rainbow amid the storm. His entire body moved with intention, stomping on the ground to hear the satisfying crunch of the dry leaves. He'd throw himself into the pile and comfortably submerged himself as a fish in the water, waving his arms and legs, completely unbothered by the dust rising around him. He was throwing himself into the hands of Mother Nature—experiencing the world on his terms.

One day, we visited a rural house. Marc had never been exposed to an old, rustic place like that. As soon as we stepped out of the car, his eyes locked on the house, and he said, "It's dirty. I'm scared."

I couldn't believe it. He had qualified an object—something he had never done before—and expressed an emotion. That gave me so much hope. It didn't go much further, but it was enough for me to know that if something impacted Marc deeply enough, he was capable of identifying and verbalizing his emotions. That was huge.

A similar thing happened when we started taking him to Tibidabo, an amusement park in Barcelona. Marc loved some of the rides so

160

much that just a couple of days later, back home in Terrassa, he looked me in the eye and handed me one of his communication cards. He never used those cards, but this time, he gave me the one showing a simple black-and-white roller coaster. "Here, here, I want to go here!" he said.

Marc blossoms with music. He dances and dances, especially to percussion. He won't say a word, but his smile and the way his body groves said it all.

Christmas, a time for families to come together, was always special to me. Despite the challenges, I held onto those traditions for my family's sake and for myself. As a child, I relished all the magic around Christmas. In Spain, the Three Kings traditionally bring gifts on January 6th, but many families, like mine, also decorate Christmas trees. However, when Marc started walking, things got complicated.

I close my eyes and remember playing with stuffed animals alongside Marc. "What's your name?" I'd ask with my most masculine voice, speaking through his favorite plushie, Messi—yes, the Barça player replica. Marc would look at Messi but remain silent. "Tell me, tell me, what's your name?" I'd insist, still using that voice. Marc wouldn't meet Messi's eyes or mine; instead, he'd looked up at the ceiling and quietly, almost as if talking to himself, said, "Marc."

"Hello, Marc! Do you want to play with me?" I'd continue. Silence again, his eyes were lost somewhere. Then, suddenly, Marc would jump up and start running. I'd leap to my feet, ready to chase him down, thinking, *"What is he planning now?"*

161

Like Speedy Gonzales, he'd race down the corridor, through the hall, and into the living room. There, right in the middle, stood our shiny Christmas tree, its lights blinking and adorned with red and green ornaments—very traditional. Xavi and I had put it together with joy for ourselves and Marc, hoping he'd revel in the colors and shapes.

But now, Marc was charging straight at it. I sprinted after him, but it was too late. Balls shattered, ribbons tangled, lights flickered out. Marc layed on the floor, laughing, delighted by the chaos. He loved the noise, the visuals, and, of course, my frantic attempts to stop him. The look of frustration was on my face must have been the icing on the cake for him.

I tried to pull up the tree and rebuild it with Marc, but it wasn't realistic. Or maybe I should say it wasn't physically possible. Once Marc started walking, I always needed at least one free hand to hold him, ready to grab him if he made a break for it. If I had the tree with one hand and tried to pick up ornaments with the other, I wasn't stable enough to chase him down. This was my daily life with Marc.

So, my strategy became one step at a time. Ball after ball, ornament after ornament, I'd guide his little hands in picking each one up and placing it in a container. Then, I'd wait for Xavi to come home to help reconstruct the tree while he held Marc. This routine repeated itself at least twenty times during the Christmas season. The tree was up with its ups and downs from the week before Christmas until January 7th, the day after the big celebration of the Three Kings in Spain.

The sparkles going out of Marc's eyes when he opened a present had an out-of-this-world beauty. I told myself this was so meaningful to me that I would keep having that tree, no matter what. Otherwise, it would feel like there was no Christmas in my life, and that would have been wrong. My family celebrated Christmas every year, and I poured my heart into cooking my most cherished recipes. For many years, we celebrated our Christmas lunch—traditionally held in Catalunya—just the three of us. More people meant more unpredictable behaviors, so that's how we managed it.

Even though I never had time to savor the meals because Marc would throw his plate and mine to the floor, it didn't matter. I was happy because it was Christmas, and I had a wonderful family that loved me and that I loved unconditionally.

We have a couple of Christmas traditions that are very Catalan, and they seem to have been created for Marc. He absolutely loved them. My theory is that it's because they're pure fun—our ancestors knew how to live in the here and now, enjoying the things that were part of being human without judgment. They had a deep connection with nature, and their lives didn't require all my plans. They lived one day after the other, just like Marc.

One he particularly loved was El Tió.

El Tió is a log—yes, a simple log that kids find in the woods and bring home, along with some sticks. The sticks will come into play soon. During the holiday season, the kids "feed" the log. I know it sounds strange if you're not Catalan, but that's how it works. The log gets raw carrots, potatoes, or whatever else the family decides.

The children take care of it for weeks before Christmas, even tucking it under a cozy buffalo-check wool blanket.

Then, on Christmas Day, the kids—well, I'll admit it—torture the log. They beat it up hard with the sticks. I know it sounds a bit un-Christmas-like, but bear with me. They hit the log because they want it to "poop." Yes, you read that right. The goal is for the log to poop turrón, a traditional sweet, while also hoping it doesn't poop sardines because they're too salty. It's an odd image for Christmas, but remember, we're Catalans. We do things differently.

The kids sing while beating the log, full of excitement, asking it to poop treats. When they're done, they run to another room to sing Christmas carols. Meanwhile, the adults pretend to suffer. The log, of course, starts "farting" before the grand finale of "pooping." The adults complain about the smell: "Oh, this is unbearable!" "What a sound—this means a lot of poop!" The kids get hyped up, knowing that after the farts come the presents. They rush back, rip off the cozy blanket, and uncover all the gifts that the log has pooped out for them.

This was Christmas in its purest form for Marc. He was as typical as all the other kids in Catalunya during this tradition. He loved everything about it—cracking up at the farting, getting excited for the pooping, and thriving on the log beating. At home, we'd do three rounds of *"Fer cagar el Tió,"* the Catalan way of describing this pagan tradition passed down through generations. The phrase translates to "Make the log poop." It's a tradition so old that it's stripped down to pure essence—no sugar coating or pretending, just fun. It was perfect for Marc.

164

I remember being in the woods with Marc, showing him mushrooms for the first time. From that moment on, they became his friends. The forest was full of sticks, and Marc, shocked by how many logs there were, expressed himself in a way that surprised me. He said, *"El bosc es brut, i el bolet es verinós,"* which means, "The forest is dirty, and that mushroom is poisonous." It was a brand-new, perfect sentence from a child who hadn't spoken a word for days.

Marc didn't care much about saying common words like "carrots" or "potatoes," but he'd use them when it came to feeding El Tió. He didn't care about dressing dolls, but he treated El Tió with care, fixing its blanket whenever it fell out of place. He learned the Tió song with ease, singing it every year. His eyes lit up when he saw the presents, and I treasured those eyes as the most special moments of my Christmas days with Marc. They were my antidote to cure all the suffering, my whole me filled with straight-up love and fascination for Marc.

Year after year, Christmas after Christmas, I'd tell myself, *"This year, Marc is doing better. He won't feel the need to charge at the Christmas tree."* But he never stopped. I adapted sturdier ornaments, higher-quality lights, and an artificial tree to avoid sweeping up needles after each reconstruction. But the tree was always there. It was my statement that Marc's autism wouldn't define him—or us.

Now, when I think about it if El Tió was so successful for Marc and the Christmas tree so useless, why did I cling to it? I guess I needed it to avoid losing myself. Or maybe I was too stubborn, using the tree to convince myself I had control. But the truth was, I was completely out of control and overwhelmed from every perspective, but I was still celebrating Christmas.

Chapter Ten
The eerie silence of some dreadful ocean depths
- Autism? Accept? Accept what? Accept HELL?

"If they give you ruled paper, write the other way."

— William James

Two years had passed, and I still hadn't been able to reach Amaia Hervás—the name on the second piece of paper handed to me by a mysterious professional. I later learned that person was a social worker, a resource schools often turned to when faced with students in need. Frustrated by the lack of assistance, I told the receptionist I had an urgent, private matter to discuss with Dr. Hervás and asked her to leave a message in Amaia's voicemailbox. The next day, I finally had an appointment. Looking back, I now realize that this was probably the first time I thought outside the box in my efforts to help Marc. It took facing a new level of difficulty to jolt me into finding alternative strategies—ones that would change our lives forever. Doors that once seemed locked were never really locked at all; we just hadn't been trying the right keys. Learning to find those keys became a constant in my life, much like solving the puzzles in an escape room.

Two months before Marc turned five, we had our first visit with Dr. Hervás. Marc was still attending El Pi Elementary School with the ever-sweet Olga Carretero and visiting Carina Robles regularly.

Amaia was an exceptionally knowledge able expert, uniquely qualified to support individuals with autism in Spain. At the time, she was one of the few psychiatrists in the country with specialized training in autism and a strong belief in the effectiveness of behavioral therapies. Behavioral intervention was virtually unknown in Spain then, with maybe just one company offering the service—at a price only a few wealthy families could afford. Worse still, that company seemed more concerned with protecting what it claimed as proprietary practices than truly serving the needs of those with autism.

Amaia, however, was different. As a highly sought-after psychiatrist with a long waiting list, she was doing everything she could to support as many children and families as possible. If there's one thing I did right, it was being persistent. Once I met Amaia, I began to learn which strategies would work for Marc and which wouldn't. We became very close. She cut through the stigma and helped me understand the sheer scope of services required to support someone with autism. It was through her that I first began to grasp what "resources" really meant in this context. From diagnosis to early intervention, therapies, and finding the right schools, Amaia and I started piecing everything together. It became clear that I would have to work smarter if I was going to help Marc. Dr. Hervás became a pivotal figure in our lives, explaining the root causes of many of Marc's behaviors—behaviors that had long caused me frustration and heartache.

"Silvia," she said, "you have to understand that because Marc doesn't imitate others, it's very hard for him to acquire new skills. His imaginary play is also extremely limited." I immediately thought of myself sitting on the floor with Marc's favorite doll—Chou Chou, it was a baby doll. I held Chou Chou in both hands and, using a playful voice, said, "Hi Marc, do you want to play with me?" But Marc, as always, just walked around the room in circles, tiptoeing. I tried again, this time with an even sillier voice: "Marc, I want to play with you." I finally got a smile from him, and that smile made my day. He didn't imitate me, nor did he respond to Chou Chou's question, which wasn't surprising since I'd tried this many times before without success.

Occasionally, Marc would echo the question, saying, "Do you want to play?" But that was it.

Amaia continued, "From what you've described, Marc doesn't seem to have any appropriate responses to other children and hasn't picked up on typical preschool habits." While she was in part putting in words what I'd already told her, reading her summary helped me deeply understand how Marc must have been struggling, for instance, in class—how lost he must have been, unable to grasp the social interactions happening all around him. At that moment, I appreciated even more the kindness and understanding of his teacher, Olga Carretero. She never judged Marc. She smiled at him and gave him only simple instructions—things she knew he could manage—without expecting more than he could provide.

In her visit notes, Amaia wrote: "Normal development of first words but delayed in forming sentences; poor qualitative speech. Repetitive behaviors, including body stereotyping and tiptoeing. Interests at age five: electrical boxes, elevators, *The Hundred and One Dalmatians,* and fluids. Displays oral stimulation."

"Of course, it was oral stimulation, now I understand why Marc puts dirt, sand, and anything really in his mouth so many times, thinking he did it because of a low IQ."

This world I had been living in with Marc—so confusing and overwhelming—was suddenly summarized and made much more understandable by Amaia. It all made sense to her, and with that, plus a series of tests, the diagnosis was undeniable: Marc has autism and Attention Deficit Hyperactivity Disorder (ADHD).

There was one diagnosis, however, that Amaia was reluctant to make. She didn't diagnose Marc with an intellectual disability despite all the tests indicating that he fell within that category. She believed the tests weren't adequately adapted to accommodate Marc's autism.

To this day, I still believe that Amaia's insights in this area are invaluable.

I hope that one day, science will evolve enough to create tests that can measure what we could call the "raw intelligence" of individuals with autism.

Once Marc was diagnosed, my self-education began in earnest. I used to read book after book on autism—written by doctors, people with autism, therapists, and experts, books written from all perspectives. While these readings didn't erased my uncertainties or resolve all my issues, they were a game changer. I now had the theoretical knowledge, but the real challenge was applying it to help Marc. I had some tools, but I knew I didn't have them all, and I understood there was a long road ahead.

One thing became clear to me from several books and articles: psychoanalysis therapy was not only ineffective for treating autism from a modern psychiatric perspective, but it could also be harmful to the mothers involved. At that point, I felt deeply betrayed by my country. I wished I had spent those past three years engaged in useful therapies rather than wasting Marc's precious developmental time on psychoanalysis. It was then that I began to realize how ill-equipped my government was to handle autism. They were wasting taxpayer money on therapies that didn't help individuals with autism while simultaneously stigmatizing and burdening the already overwhelmed mothers.

Marc, at Five Years Old

When Marc turned five, we decided, under the guidance of his psychiatrist, to explore medication. This was the only way forward. Psychiatrists are the only professionals qualified to discuss medication options with families. Up until then, though, I hadn't fully grasped how critical my input would be—not just my decision to medicate Marc or not, but also my interpretation of how he was responding to those medications. Parents play a key role in this process, more than I initially realized.

For Marc, medications did help. They made him more manageable. Marc was still Marc, but some of his more challenging traits became a little more mellow. There was no radical change, but a combination of medications gave him a bit more self-control, reduced his hyperactivity slightly, and helped him sustain his focus a little longer.

The medication didn't transform Marc, but it made a difference—it made him more receptive to the behavioral therapies that, combined with the meds, had a more positive impact on him. At the same time, I've heard that some individuals with hyperactivity experience dramatic improvements from medication; it's a complex, individualized process. The psychiatrist can only suggest options, and the parents must assess the results for their child. For us, the fact that Marc became more manageable was a significant win. But this was my judgment based on our specific situation.

This experience taught me that medication is a challenging journey for many parents. When Marc wasn't on medication, his attention span to any request was mere seconds. After medication, it stretched to about a minute. I often found myself wondering, *"What if we increase the dosage and get two minutes? Two minutes provides more opportunities for learning than one, so let's try it."* Then, there were times when I thought this particular medication hadn't worked for Marc, but the psychiatrist mentioned an alternative that has worked for other children. *"I'll try that one. Imagine if it really helps slow down his hyperactivity and boosts his focus—it's worth a shot."*

The entire process was one of trial and error, trying to find the optimal balance that would offer Marc the most improvement. But how do you know when it's time to stop? When do you decide that the results you're seeing are enough? I don't recall how many times we adjusted Marc's medications, but it was many. Each time, I convinced myself, *"We can achieve better results."* So, we'd change the medication, hoping to see improvements. But each change disrupted Marc's stability. Sometimes, these adjustments triggered even more challenging behaviors, leaving us all dealing with a situation worse than before.

What I didn't fully consider back then was the toll all these changes were taking on Marc. He had to endure the effects of those chemicals—sometimes they helped, but sometimes they had the opposite effect. Medications meant to increase his attention span and reduce hyperactivity occasionally made his hyperactivity and irritability worse. I can't imagine how confusing and difficult it must have been for Marc to go through all those changes, side effects, and stimulants.

I'm sorry, Marc.

Even now, I still believe it was worth trying. It's an incredibly arduous process, and finding the right balance—knowing when to keep going and when to stop for the sake of the child and the family's well-being—is a fine line.

We all experience mood changes—days when we feel energized and days when we're completely drained. Marc was no different. The difference was that whenever Marc had one of those days or even weeks, he couldn't tell me. The only way I knew something was off was through his behavior changes. When we were trying a new medication, it was nearly impossible for me to determine whether his behavior was due to him feeling unwell or if the new medication was the cause.

Marc, it was so hard for me to separate what you needed help with from what you were simply reacting to because of a bad day. You couldn't tell me, and I couldn't always read you. At that time, the channels of communication just weren't there. Psychiatrists, of course, work closely with families and base their decisions on the specific needs of each patient, but parents are the ones who talk to the psychiatrist. If you're not satisfied with the progress, they'll try to help using the tools they have, but ultimately, it's up to the parent to decide whether to settle with the results or push for more. In that sense, parents are the ones who implicitly decide when a medication is working or not.

Life, however, is constantly in flux, so ideally, you would want all the other variables to remain stable during this trial-and-error process with medications. But life doesn't pause for you. Beyond the changes in Marc's body, there were environmental changes that impacted everything. Now, looking back, I wonder: *"When my son was having tantrums, was it because he needed a different medication? Or was it because he needed a change of school or a new therapist? Or was it me—was I demanding more from him than he could reasonably handle? Or was it some combination of all of these factors?"* So many variables were shifting while I was trying to assess if a medication was truly working.

174

Later, I learned that medication needs can also change over time because children grow and people evolve. I gained a lot of knowledge throughout this process, but even now, I consider navigating medications one of the most challenging experiences I've ever been through.

Despite all the difficulty—and I recognize that even with a world-class psychiatrist, making decisions about psychiatric medications is incredibly stiff—I have to say that for us, medication was essential in helping Marc. This is my truth, and I would do it again. It often intensified our crises and caused additional suffering, but it was a risk I was willing to take for Marc at the time, and that's okay. In our case, it took many different medications to achieve a meaningful result. This made the process even more complicated because we had to test each medication individually and then evaluate how they worked together. At one point, we were juggling up to five different medications at once. It was extremely hard for Marc and our entire family, but for us, it was worth it.

At the same time, Marc was undergoing every kind of test imaginable. We were constantly visiting doctors, checking his brain, his ears, and his blood... despite being a healthy kid, Marc became very used to doctors. In fact, it became such a routine part of our lives that I decided to start playing doctors and nurses with him at home. It was a huge success—he loved it! In Spain, doctors and nurses visit schools once a year to do physical exams so that families don't have to schedule them on their own. Olga, Marc's teacher, told me that he was very cooperative during the exam. *"He's so used to it,"* I thought.

At the end of that day, after all the white-coated medical staff had left the school, Marc turned to Olga and said, "I'm cured now." That made us laugh so hard. Marc's unique way of interpreting the world always surprised us. It was also amazing that he could string together those sentences so perfectly, only to go back to being almost nonverbal for weeks afterward.

One day, Olga took Marc's class on a field trip to Tibidabo, the iconic theme park in Barcelona that Marc adored. She brought them to the Marionetarium, a puppet show that I had always thought would be impossible for Marc to sit through, as it required sitting still for thirty minutes. But in our little notebook, Olga wrote that after the show ended, Marc turned to her and said, "I love them all; I love them all a lot!" I was astonished. Not only had he expressed how much he connected with the puppets, but he also felt the need to repeat it, ensuring that his beloved Olga understood him. That moment showed me that Marc had hidden abilities to communicate—he would express himself deeply, but only when something made a profound impact on him, not in everyday situations. At that time, I thought I could harness that string of connections and make it universal across all aspects of his world. When he didn't communicate in the same way during ordinary moments, I felt frustrated. I felt like I hadn't succeeded in changing Marc and that I wasn't a good mom—I thought I was failing. Instead of celebrating those special moments, I became fixated on wanting more of them. I didn't know any better, and no one guided me just to let those moments be.

Michael Jackson, the King of Pop and my teenage idol, became another way for me to connect with Marc. Marc thrived on music and loved to watch me dance. He wouldn't dance in the conventional sense; instead, he'd spin in circles, following the rhythm with his feet and head. When we danced together, we were in sync—he did not need to misbehave; it took us both to a happy place. I can still see Marc in his cotton pajamas with little blue dogs scattered across a white background, his butterfly-like smile lighting up his face. His entire body radiated relaxation as he spun around and around in the living room. His eyes stared into the air, his head moving slightly forward in time with the music while his right arm bent, making circular movements like a fan on a hot day—never stopping, never pausing. I joined him, dancing alongside him. He glanced at me briefly before I grew tired and sat down. I watched him, mesmerized by how handsome and perfect my son was.

Marc started behavioral therapy at five, and through it, he discovered candy—particularly M&Ms. Behavioral therapy uses what the child enjoys most as a reinforcer, rewarding desired behavior with something they love. For Marc, that was M&Ms. On his birthday, I gave him a bag of M&Ms to share with his class. Since he usually only got them for doing good work, it was a very special treat. Olga had a plan: she gave a bag to each child and saved Marc's for last, hoping the delay would help keep him calm while she handed out the treats. Marc's eyes were glued to the bag of M&Ms. At five, Marc didn't often ask for things. Typically, he would either try to take the bag himself or grab Olga's hand to show her he wanted it. But that day, feeling happy and special as the center of attention, he decided to use words. With his eyes half-closed and his shoulders shrugging, he looked at Olga and asked, "And for Marc?" Olga was so delighted by this that she changed her plan and immediately gave Marc his candy before finishing with the rest of the kids.

On another day, Olga wanted Marc to complete some classwork that he hadn't managed to do earlier. While the other children were at recess, she gave him some one-on-one time. Marc, however, was watching the other kids play through the classroom window. He turned to Olga and said, "I play, I."

She responded gently, "Yes, Marc, you play later, but first, you finish your work."

And he did it! Olga had intuitively applied a strategy that I had learned from behavioral experts—she reinforced his good communication and calm behavior while guiding him to complete a non-preferred activity by promising a reinforcer (playtime). How I wished I could have had more of that patience and ability. How I wished I hadn't lost my temper so often. But I was so stressed, so frustrated, so utterly exhausted. I was disappointed in myself, feeling lost and unsure of how to keep going.

My job at DuPont kept me sane. At work, I had a list of issues to fix; I love fixing, so that was fun. There, I was just Silvia—the Silvia with plans and backup plans, the one who met challenges head-on and achieved results. I thrived in that environment. When the corporate leaders of the company I worked for decided to shut down our plant, I was part of the team leading the closure. It was a tough job, but I understood my role. My responsibility was to support those corporate leaders in executing their business strategies, which ultimately benefited the shareholders—the people taking risks with their dollars to make everything possible. However, beyond being a professional, I am also an empathic person and value other's efforts, and while I embrace capitalism, I believe in putting people first, especially those who have demonstrated merit and dedication. For me, the path was clear. I supported the decision because it wasn't my job to question it but to implement it. At the same time, I did everything I could to help my team—the people I worked with and genuinely cared about—transition to other roles within the company. I also worked closely with the sites receiving our production to minimize the impact of the shutdown on customers and the overall business. I approached it with humanity and honesty while staying focused on doing my job with excellence, as I was paid to do. This dual approach—caring for people and executing my duties—came naturally to me.

No one told me what would happen to my own job after the shutdown, but I wasn't worried. I knew my duty, and I was confident in my skills. I thought, *"If I'm let go after this, I'll just find another job."* Everything about that process was so predictable compared to raising Marc. Managing the shutdown was, in many ways, far easier than managing Marc's needs.

I don't want to downplay what happened—it was a difficult process for many, and there were some intense moments. I saw my name scrawled on walls, and at times, I was physically intimidated by employees and stirred up by union leaders. I vividly remember one day when all the unionized employees barged into the office where the operations team was meeting. They kept coming and coming, packing the room until we were trapped like sardines. They chanted populist slogans, including, *"¡Nos quitáis el pan! ¡Nos quitáis el pan!"* which translates to, "You're taking our bread away!" While I firmly believe in private property and the right of corporations to decide where to place their operations, the physical proximity of that situation was unnerving and claustrophobic.

DuPont, very thoughtfully, offered psychological support to leadership, and I took advantage of it. It was my first time seeing a psychologist. But by the second minute of the session, I was already talking about Marc. Life had thrown far worse at me than anything my professional life ever could. Compared to the overwhelming responsibility of raising Marc and ensuring his well-being and future, business challenges felt like a breeze. In fact, they became my therapy. I knew I could accomplish anything at work, and I did. I thrived in that environment, contributing with my tenacity and hard work to a science-based company that allowed me to grow and compensated me fairly for my efforts.

The psychologist, however, quickly turned the conversation toward handling my concerns about Marc. I broke down, crying for what felt like an eternity, overwhelmed by the ocean of uncertainty I was carrying inside. She had no answers. She didn't understand autism or how deeply I was struggling. I poured all my questions out to her, hoping for clarity, some way to replace the unknown with facts, or, at the very least, strategies for managing the weight of it all. The day I quit therapy, I scoffed and told myself, *"She is as lost as I am. The difference between us, though, is that I admit it while she keeps collecting a paycheck in exchange for my tears. Not cool! And incredibly painful to get nowhere."*

Reflecting on that now, I recognize that I did learn something. She was the first person to help me be in touch with my physical body. It was there that I discovered I was living my life only listening to my thoughts and emotions, never considering my body. She taught me how to notice my body. This was probably a very useful experience for my growth, but physically, it was very painful. Once I started listening to my body, every part of it was talking to me by hurting. I noticed such unbearable discomfort everywhere—my joints, my stomach, my neck, my back, my brain! It was all aching. In the months following therapy, I visited many doctors who could not come up with any diagnosis. One day, I decided this whole new body discovery was not practical and was taking me nowhere, deviating me from my plans. Because my mind ruled, I was numb to my body again. Long years passed until I could reconnect with my forgotten body, which I had been dragging along with me wherever my mind led.

It was a beautiful sunny day when we took Marc to the Aquarium. I thought *"My passion for the ocean would be contagious, and Marc would fall in love with all the colorful fish swimming around, just as I did."* Xavi and I tried to get Marc to look at the fish. I vividly remember a small octopus in one of the tanks. *"What a great start! What could be more captivating than this mysterious creature?"* I wanted so badly to dive into the tank, hold the octopus's soft, slithering tentacles, and dance with it. But I pulled myself back to the present, to Marc. I placed my hands on either side of his face, my body right behind him.

"Marc, look at the octopus. It's one of the most beautiful creatures in the ocean."

But Marc didn't react. I turned to look at him, and his gaze was fixed elsewhere, his eyes darting to the right, focused on some fences in the distance. *"Is he trying to avoid the octopus?"* I let my hands drop—they were useless. As incredible as it sounds, I'm almost certain that Marc didn't saw any marine creature that day.

Instead, we discovered that the darkened pavilions, meant to highlight the illuminated tanks of exotic fish, were full of hidden doors—painted black and draped with dark curtains, blending into the background. For most people, these doors were invisible, but not for Marc. Like a commando from an action movie with night vision, but without the need for any technology, Marc spotted things we couldn't see. He managed to find and open every single door. The result? Xavi ended up exploring all the behind-the-scenes areas of the aquarium, places no one but the staff ever ventures. Their exploration was so fast-paced it felt like one of those sped-up videos you make on a smartphone.

Meanwhile, I was captivated by the lionfish, utterly mesmerized. It swam toward me, its body covered in a perfect pattern of brown and white stripes, surrounded by spines that gave it an otherworldly elegance. The spines reminded me of those retro lamps from the 70s—white when turned off but glowing in vibrant neon when lit. The long, symmetrical spines on either side of its body were so surreal they felt like they came straight from my imagination. Then, a door slammed, jolting me out of my trance. I turned to see Xavi and Marc darting in and out of doors like characters in a Benny Hill sketch. I sighed. *"I'm so fortunate Xavi is here,"* I thought. I turned back to the tank, only to see Marc holding a fire extinguisher. Foam covered the room, and Xavi was talking to security, looking defeated. No one cared about the ocean life anymore—Marc was now the main attraction.

Back at home, I tried to process everything that had just happened. I held Marc by the shoulders to keep him still and asked, "Marc, what fish did you like best at the Aquarium?" I was persistent—you know that by now.

He looked straight into my eyes and, with confidence, said, "The fences."

At that moment, I realized something important: whether Marc liked or disliked the octopus didn't matter. What was clear was that he was totally into fences and doors—and today, I say that's okay.

There are two memories from Marc's school that still hurt me deeply when they surface.

One day, while I was working from home, my phone rang. It was Marc's school director. "Ms. Prats," she began, "I need to inform you about something you might not be aware of. Marc is misbehaving during lunch, and it's become so difficult that we'll have to ask you to start picking him up for lunch. We simply don't have the resources to manage him."

I was in shock. No one had ever mentioned any problems with lunchtime before. I had always assumed that no news was good news, but that wasn't the case. The very next day, I had Marc home for lunch.

That marked the beginning of the worst crisis we had ever faced with Marc. It was a crisis so profound that even today, as I write about it, I feel a tight pressure in my chest, my lungs constrict, and my breath trembles.

Many children have eating challenges that cause their mothers to worry and lead them to seek support—some are picky eaters, others refuse to eat altogether, and some struggle with textures or making a mess with their food. And then there was Marc. Like many aspects of daily life, his eating disorder was extreme. He had all the usual challenges, but those were the least of my concerns. When Marc was five, the behaviors surrounding his eating during dinner were among my biggest worries. Adding lunch at home after being asked to pick him up from school took those worries to a new, unbearable level. My anxiety peaked, feeding into and reinforcing Marc's behaviors, turning mealtime into an impossible nightmare that consumed me twice a day, every day.

I could see Marc at lunch. He sat at the end of our kitchen table, which was pushed against the wall on the left side. I sat next to him in the right corner. Our white table held two plates of spaghetti Bolognese—one of our favorite comfort foods, made with love from scratch, as all the dishes I prepared every day for lunch and dinner. The smell of tomato sauce and melted cheese filled the air, but I felt uneasy. Eating was troublesome for Marc, and I braced myself for what was to come.

Marc looked at me, and with a sudden sweep of his right arm, his plate flew, crashing to the floor. Spaghetti and sauce were everywhere. I sighed and cleared my throat, my frustration rising but contained.

"Marc, no! It's not okay to throw your plate."

If Marc is not angry, Marc says, "I'm not hangry." He looked at me again and started yelling—a sustained, high-pitched scream, then a

184

pause. He left out the piercing yell again. And again. "AHHHHH!" It was ear-splitting, and my blood boiled inside, but I remembered the therapy advice to ignore the behavior. I struggled to stay calm, my voice tight but controlled.

"Marc, now you have to pick up the pasta."

With my hands modeling the movement, he reluctantly picked up the pasta and put it back on the plate. I handed him a paper towel, and together, we cleaned the table. I'm not a patient person by nature, but I tried. I really tried. I took him to the trash, and he threw away the pasta and the dirty paper towel. We returned to the table.

"Marc, do you want to eat the pasta?" I asked.

"Yes," he replied.

"Are you sure? Are you hungry, Marc? It's okay to say no," I gently added.

"Yes, yes," he insisted.

"Okay, Marc," I said, trying to stay calm. "This time, Marc would not throw the pasta. If Marc throws the pasta again, there will be no more lunch. No more food. Do you understand?" I tried to pronounce each word carefully and calmly despite my mounting frustration.

"Yes," he responded, a slight curve forming at the edges of his lips.

I served him more spaghetti. Marc picked up his fork and, smiling, began singing. As if to match the rhythm of his song, he started rattling the fork on the table.

"Marc, the fork is for eating, not for playing. It's not safe to play with a fork," I said, trying to be the perfect mom. But have you ever heard of impostor syndrome? It's when you're doing something but feel completely unqualified—lacking the skills, training, or confidence to succeed. That's how I felt.

Marc intensified the clanging, now banging the fork against the wall while singing louder. The fork was clicking loudly against my wedding porcelain plate now. He looked at me, defiant, seeking negative attention. I saw it coming. In one sweeping motion, the fork bounced off the wall and came dangerously close to my eye. I was scared. I lost control.

"Marc, STOP!" I shouted, much louder than I intended.

Marc threw the fork across the room, narrowly missing the TV, and then hurled his plate onto the floor with such force that, despite being plastic, it shattered. Spaghetti sauce splattered all over me. I was hyperventilating. My frustration boiled over, and I grabbed Marc by the shoulders, holding him tightly.

"Marc! W-H-A-T A-R- E Y-O-U D-O-I-N G?" I yelled, spacing the words to control my anger. "I CAN'T STAND IT ANYMORE!" I screamed, letting all my anxiety, frustration, and exhaustion pour out. "STOP IT!"

I let go and collapsed to the floor, sobbing. I felt utterly defeated, like a failure as a mother. My tears flowed, not just from exhaustion but from the overwhelming sense that I had lost control and couldn't raise Marc properly. I was hurting a helpless, wounded animal. But the moment of self-pity lasted only a few seconds—I couldn't afford it. I didn't have time for it.

"What is Marc doing right now?"

That terrifying thought pulled me from the floor. I inhaled sharply, pulled myself together, and left my misery behind as I rushed to Marc's room, where I heard a commotion.

When I got there, Marc had just knocked a row of books from his shelf to the floor. He smiled, his body moving frenetically. He was in full "tornado mode," as I called it. I hadn't yet learned to interpret the signs, but I knew he was overwhelmed with anxiety, overstimulated by everything happening. He charged toward the second shelf, full of heavier books. I tried to block him, but I wasn't fast enough. The heaviest book fell directly onto my bare foot, the pain mixing with all the emotions swirling inside me. It was a dangerous cocktail.

I grabbed Marc and pinned him to the floor, holding his little hands down by his sides. His back was pressed against the floor, and I was crying. "Why do you do this to me, Marc? Why? Why? Why?" I mumbled. "Autism? Accept it? Accept what? ACCEPT HELL?!" I screamed so loudly that the one book still left on the shelf toppled off.

I sniffled, sighed, and crumbled. I let Marc go, and he sat up, crossing his legs and leaning back against the wall like an angel, smiling at me. He looked relaxed now. I was exhausted. As long as he stayed still, I was okay. I let my tears flow freely, wetting everything around me. He didn't move. I breathed deeply, in and out, finally feeling some relief as I rested for a moment.

Marc and I repeated similar scenes every lunch and dinner—always dramatic, always intense. The apocalyptic nature of these moments

187

wasn't entirely Marc's doing; my own passionate personality fueled it. I tried countless strategies, but nothing seemed to work. His intermittent deafening yelling at full blast was the constant reminder that chaos was reigning, and I felt like I was melting, disappearing a little more with each passing day.

One evening, Xavi came home earlier than usual and witnessed the full scene unfold. He immediately stepped in, taking my place in the kitchen, and gently asked me to finish my dinner in the living room on my own. From that day on, Xavi made it a point to come home earlier, taking over Marc's dinner routine. I vividly remember sitting in the dining room—the "never-to-be-used-except-for-Christmas-or-birthdays" dining room. Both dining room doors were closed, along with the corridor and kitchen doors, in an attempt to insulate me from the chaotic sounds coming from the kitchen: Marc's persistent intermittent yelling, the clattering of cutlery, Xavi's calm voice trying to soothe him. But it didn't matter how many doors were shut—the sounds and the tension still reached me.

Xavi always seemed more composed than me, but it wasn't that Marc wasn't engaging in the same behaviors. It was that Xavi, with his more grounded personality, didn't let those behaviors get under his skin the way I did. I sat there eating, though my stomach was churning with anxiety. I knew I was lucky to be at the dining room table, away from the battle in the kitchen. But I was also acutely aware that this reprieve was only possible because of Xavi. He was the one fighting the war for now, and eventually, when he could no longer take it, I would have to go back to the trenches, like any soldier.

So, I ate. I needed the food—the protein, the vitamins, the carbs—all of it. I sighed and ate and sighed again. My mind was still focused on what was happening in that kitchen. It screamed at me, *"Silvia, get up and help!"* But the practical side of me fought back, saying, *"Silvia, you don't know how to handle the kitchen war anyway. Stay here, recover, recharge, and be ready when you're called."* I turned up the volume on the TV, hoping the Catalan news would drown out the chaos from the kitchen, but even at max volume, it couldn't completely silence the sounds of our twice-a-day kitchen battle.

The kitchen battles raged on for several long, painful months. Our family was saved—literally—by a behavioral therapist named Ana Miralles. Ana was one of the sweetest, most humble people I had ever met and, without a doubt, one of the most skilled. She had been trained in Barcelona through a program initiated by a collaborator of Amaia Hervás. Ana was much younger than me, small in stature, with delicate features that made her seem fragile—but that was just on the surface. Truly kind people often appear fragile, but Ana was anything but.

She came to our house daily at lunchtime, stepping into the kitchen during our battles. Marc would perform all his usual behaviors—throwing his plate, yelling, refusing to eat—but gradually, Ana took control of the situation. In a couple of months, the situation improved dramatically. To me, she was a magician or a genie from a bottle, working wonders in our home. What was even more extraordinary was that she mentored me along the way. I learned how to manage Marc's behaviors on my own. While his behaviors at lunch haven't completely disappeared, and there are still random days when he'll throw his plate with force, he always looked at the person

189

next to him as if to say, "Yes, I'm still Marc." His therapist today, Rubit, said that it's as if Marc is reminding us all, "I'm still here."

What we eventually learned was that the main driver behind Marc's behavior was control. He had figured out that by pushing certain buttons, he could control the situation, and for Marc, that was huge. Autism and ADHD left him with little control over so much of his life, so once he discovered a way to exert some control, he clung to it fiercely. It wasn't something he was willing to give up easily, and I now understand that more than ever.

If the "kitchen crisis" caused by Marc being expelled from the school cafeteria wasn't enough, the school director called again with more bad news. "Silvia, I see that you've enrolled Marc in the summer camp. Unfortunately, we don't have the resources to care for Marc during the camp, so we will have to tell you that he is banned."

It was the first time I truly felt the sting of discrimination hitting me in full force. I hung up the phone and, in a fit of rage, kicked my dresser over and over, sending the drawer pulls clattering to the floor. Pure anger coursed through my veins. At that moment, I realized how important Olga had been in our lives—she had shielded us from what would have been Marc's harsh reality at school. She had cared for and nurtured him, protecting him from the rejection that now came crashing down.

The next day, I picked up the shattered pieces of wood from the floor. They were no longer drawer pulls, just splintered remains. I threw them away. Then, I picked up the scattered pieces of myself and pulled them together. I refocused on the battle ahead: finding a place where Marc would be accepted and embraced. I knew I would find it, and I did—in the most unexpected place. It wasn't perfect on the surface, but it was perfect in the ways that mattered. We found the human connection and pure kindness at an organization called Esplai El Timbal.

Esplai El Timbal was a youth organization that offered recreational activities for children on weekends and during holidays. They had a small budget and some space provided by the city to run their programs, offering a safe and fun environment for children when school was out. I met them in Parc de Sant Jordi next to the spectacular Masia Freixa, a modernist building by Lluis Muncunill inspired by the Catalan genius Antoni Gaudí. I got straight to the point. "Hi, I'd like to enroll Marc, but Marc is… well, he's special. Marc has autism and ADHD. He has significant needs—he can put himself and others in danger. He elopes, takes his clothes off in public, pees for attention, breaks things because he likes the sound, and he's fast, uncontrollable, and dangerous. His communication skills are limited to his immediate needs… would you still have him?"

The young woman listened patiently, her eyebrows lifting as I spoke. I knew my list was long, but I felt it was necessary to be completely transparent about Marc's challenges. I wanted to give them the chance to make an informed decision. She looked me in the eyes and said, "We love supporting all kids, and we've worked with children with disabilities before. We'd love to have Marc. What strikes me most is that you're the first parent to be so open and honest about your son's needs. That will help us so much to meet his needs from day one. Thank you!"

I was stunned. That was the last response I had expected after dropping that bomb of information. My heart leaped out of my chest, and a huge smile spread across my face, showing every tooth. I wanted to hug her, maybe even kiss her, but I held back. Instead, I said, "Of course! How could any caregiver not share their child's needs?"

She replied, "Many parents don't accept their children's disabilities or differences. Others are ashamed, or they tell themselves, 'Maybe no one will notice...' Not everyone has your courage." She paused, then added, "The challenge is that when we don't know about special needs, we can't prepare, and that can lead to avoidable incidents. But once we know, we can handle it."

At that moment, I exhaled deeply, feeling the release of tension. I mentally drifted away, imagining myself in paradise, swimming in crystal-clear waters, surrounded by colorful coral reefs and bubbles caressing my face. It was a sound from Marc that brought me back to reality. I looked up and saw Marc playing with one of the coaches—also named Marc—who later introduced himself to me. My Marc was dressed in a Halloween costume of Scarface, with both hands raised above his shoulders, pretending to scare the coach. The other Marc, a tall, kind-looking young man with a humble expression, played along. His empathetic, tiny eyes squeezed shut, lips pressed tight as if truly terrified by my son's costume. Then, my Marc did it again—the same sound that had pulled me from my imaginary island. He let out his second-ever attempt at a spooky "Boooo!" It was feeble, almost inaudible, but it instantly became my "most precious sound of the day."

As I relaxed, my mind wandered again back to that serene island. But this time, Marc was with me, happily playing among the fish, just like any other kid in the ocean—free, joyful, and completely at ease.

The team at Esplai El Timbal was like another version of Olga Carretero—a shining example that with kindness, positive energy, and a willing heart, you can make a meaningful difference in the lives of people with autism, even without formal training or resources. For years, we entrusted those remarkable young adults with Marc. I'll never forget the time they took him on an overnight trip to a cabin in the woods. It was an adventure that could have been overwhelming, but instead, it turned out to be an amazing experience for Marc. I remember receiving texts from them late at night, letting me know he was doing great and even sending photos of him fast asleep. I was in awe of their courage and dedication.

Then came the third and final call from Marc's school director. This time, it was to tell me that Marc could no longer continue at the school. He had completed first grade but hadn't met any of the academic milestones expected of a typical child. More importantly, he wasn't showing any signs of adapting to a mainstream educational environment. From today's perspective, it seems unreasonable to have expected that in the first place, but back then, there were many voices—including the school psychologist—telling me that some children with autism had developed those skills in the early years of school. We had hoped Marc might be one of them, but it was clear that wasn't the case.

El Pi School was the perfect place for me when I attended it as a student. It was a small, private school that not only prepared me well academically but also focused on character-building. The talented teachers provided an additional layer of safety and support that complemented my family's care. I had hoped that the same environment would be right for Marc, but it wasn't.

Chapter Eleven
The Breaking Point of False Promises

*"Waves tossed themselves against the shore, drag-
ging grit and sand between their nails as they were
slowly pulled back out to sea."*

– Holly Black

My brother Felip and Marc

As we looked to the future, we were left with two types of schools
for children with autism like Marc: regular schools or special education schools, both available in private, public, or charter options.
Around that time, a new project was being piloted in some public
and charter schools. The initiative involved creating specialized autism units within mainstream schools. These units allowed children

with autism to spend part of their time in regular classes and part of their time in a special needs classroom, guided by a dedicated special education teacher.

I was immediately drawn to this idea and was excited when I found out that a nearby charter school, El Romaní K-12 school, was part of the pilot project. It seemed like the perfect opportunity for Marc—a balance of integration and specialized support. At this point in my life, I had begun to understand Marc a little better. I had managed to accept many things that were once difficult to grasp, especially before meeting Amaia.

I found my notes from back when Marc was still five and about to attend El Romaní K-12 school in September 2007:

How do I feel?

I would describe it as a bittersweet experience. What does a mother love more than her child, her only child? That simple fact explains why Marc's condition impacts me so profoundly, why it shatters my most secret and intimate emotions—the ones that live deep in my subconscious, built on my most basic beliefs and values, the same ones that have guided me for so many years. On one hand, as painful as it is, I have no choice but to dismantle some of those beliefs. They are an intrinsic part of me, but today, they're creating barriers to helping Marc. That's the bitter part. I know these old beliefs won't help Marc, so I've had to replace them one by one with new beliefs that do. I'm proud of my transformation into a better mother for Marc—and that's the sweet part.

I had to redefine what celebrating achievements meant. In my mind, celebrations were reserved for big life milestones—graduations, weddings, promotions, or receiving a prestigious award. But the joy I felt when Marc kissed me for the first time, after teaching him for months, was a happiness I had never known existed. The celebration we had afterward was unlike anything I'd experienced. I deeply believe most people will go through life without ever feeling that level of joy after such an accomplishment. Many of us don't express gratitude for the little things in life because they seem to come so easily, so effortlessly. After Marc, I understand that effort and hard work—especially when the results aren't obvious—always pays off. When hard work and suffering lead to any kind of result, they bring a unique type of joy that cannot be achieved without hardship. So now I embrace having Marc and fighting for him because, in the long run, I know it will be worth it. I celebrate every little thing he accomplishes.

I had to come to terms with the fact that Marc will learn at a different pace than other kids, that he will struggle to connect with his peers, and that his behavioral challenges, all due to his autism, might persist into adulthood. This realization is tough. I've been told that some parents of children with developmental disabilities like Marc never go through this process—it's too hard for them to accept, and they live in denial. But accepting is a must to help Marc. I began the process when I first received hints from his nursery, but it was a slow, drawn-out process for me. To accept, you have to understand, and I didn't find anyone capable of truly educating me until Marc was nearly five. Accepting doesn't mean giving up; it means being realistic about the impact and severity of the situation today so I can find the best support for Marc and develop a realistic plan of action to help him reach his potential.

It saddened me to realize how many resources are required to support Marc. I never fully understood how much my country's policies ignore people with autism. It's as though their existence isn't even acknowledged. Pediatricians don't screen for autism, and the lack of support continues as these children grow up. There's no assistance from the government to provide the professionals that are so desperately needed at every level—mental health, therapy, education, leisure, research… This is happening in a country with world-class healthcare available for everyone—everyone, that is, except for people with autism. It's a disgrace.

I've learned that the ability to communicate in the way most typical people do is something that comes naturally to most individuals—but not to people with autism. It was incredibly hard to grasp that not only spoken language but also gestures, facial expressions, and all the non-verbal cues I've always used to communicate weren't understood by Marc. I had always assumed these forms of communication were inherent to all humans, but they're not. Mainstream communication—the kind most of us take for granted—is not part of Marc's world. He has to learn it from scratch in order to fit, somehow, into a world dominated by typical people.

Amaia explained to me that it was as if someone expected me to live in China and have a typical life without first teaching me Chinese. Based on that, I wonder, *"How would I survive? How would I get along at work? How would I learn at school? I'd probably use signs or try to communicate with someone who spoke another language. But what if no one around me spoke another language, and I didn't have the option to use signs? How would I survive then?"* Well, that's Marc's everyday life. It's no wonder that, from time to time, he displays challenging behaviors. When I look at things from his perspective, it seems far less surprising. Marc will never be a native speaker of communication, in the same way that I'd never be a native Chinese speaker, no matter how hard I tried. That's just a fact.

I've also learned to be grateful that Marc is happy—he's always been a happy kid. It's been a process for me to accept that I'm the one who struggles with happiness sometimes. Maybe part of Marc's happiness comes from the fact that he's unaware of the many challenges I see for him. But that doesn't make him any less happy. So, I need to remember to be happy because he is happy. Of course, I worry about the future, especially about his ability to be independent to some degree. But even if he never becomes fully independent, he could still be happy. I keep telling myself to keep working hard for him but not to let the worry consume me.

It's been demanding, and I know it's going to continue to be tough. I've accepted that this isn't a phase of life that will eventually pass—it's here to stay. There are moments when I feel really low, but I've learned from experience that if I stay down for too long, my overall performance slips. So, I try to pull myself out of those lows as quickly as possible and keep fighting. The fight is necessary to ensure I stick to the action plan I've made to help Marc and to keep pushing for improvements.

The word "normal" has a completely different meaning for me now. Normal, for me, is what I'm used to. With Marc, I've gotten used to things that I once thought were anything but normal, but now they are. This shift has been helpful because no one else gets to define my reality. I decided what was normal in my home. I no longer worry about what others think is normal or abnormal. Their opinions don't affect me anymore. I know that my normal has changed, and I no longer judge anyone for not realizing that their own version of normal is just as fluid and dynamic as mine.

I'm also aware of how much I don't know and how much I'm willing to learn to help Marc.

It was the meet-and-greet at the new school, and I was filled with excitement and hope. The school director, Mr. Smart, came to meet Xavi and me. I had high hopes for this new school model, and Xavi was there to support me as always. After our experience with full integration at El Pi School, where it became clear they didn't have the resources to help Marc, this new approach seemed to be arriving at just the right time for his future.

I couldn't wait to share everything I had learned about Marc—the areas where he needed help, the strategies I knew could support him—with a staff that was presumably more prepared, more educated, and trained for this role. In this school model, a special education teacher would focus on Marc's specific needs, while the mainstream teacher would understand his differences and make accommodations for him in the regular classroom. They would also help other students understand that there was more that united them than separated them. I believed that this school would champion diversity and inclusion, creating an environment where students and families could grow together, an example for the rest of society to follow.

El Romaní K-12 School was a school I knew well. After finishing elementary school at El Pi, I continued my education through middle and high school there. It had been a good school for me—although I always felt El Pi prepared me better academically and personally, El Romaní K-12 School had done a decent job, too. It was a much larger school, so it lacked the personal touch of El Pi, but I always felt welcome and somewhat supported.

I had been watching Mr. Smart as he moved around the meet-and-greet. We knew each other and had interacted multiple times over the years when we crossed paths in the streets of Terrassa. He looked particularly happy that day, darting from one family to another, greeting everyone with a big smile. It was nice to see him so joyful and eager to engage. I felt proud of him—admiring his tenacity in making it all the way to becoming the school's principal. I thought, *"Because we knew each other, it would be even easier for him to show empathy toward Marc and our family."*

When it was our turn, Mr. Smart approached us with open arms, a huge smile on his face. He greeted me warmly, and right after he pronounced the words, I would later realize they were the biggest lie anyone had ever told me.

"Silvia," he said, "this school is for everyone. Marc will thrive here because it's a school for *everyone*—and when I say everyone, I mean E-V-E-R-Y-O-N-E."

Looking back now, my response would be a simple, "Ha!"

As soon as Mr. Smart finished his sentence—*"Marc will thrive here because it's a school for everyone, and when I say everyone, I mean E-V-E-R-Y-O-N-E."*

I felt a wave of uneasiness start to replace the excitement I had felt just moments before. His optimism was so over-the-top, so sugar-coated, that I began to doubt everything. I've never been naïve, and I knew Marc had significant needs, no diagnostic was needed anymore. Overconfidence wasn't the right approach; it was a red flag. Instead of going along with the butterflies, the hippie flower-power vibes, and the hallelujahs he was chanting, I switched into my usual "hands-on, practical" mode. I tried to steer the conversation toward something more realistic, something useful.

In my most professional tone, I said, "This sounds very promising. However, you don't know Marc yet, so I'd like to propose a meeting with the involved parties to discuss the approach, the goals, and the plans for Marc's education. As Marc's mom, I can offer support to help you understand what works with him and what doesn't..."

"Oh no! That won't be necessary," he interrupted me abruptly, "Our team is specialized in autism. That's why we're so thrilled to have been selected for this pilot project. He's going to be in the best hands—guaranteed."

I couldn't believe my ears. Right at that moment, I knew this was trouble. A person has to be full of themselves to reject help before even starting one of the most challenging jobs of their career. But there I was, caught up in the excitement of this supposedly great opportunity. I was hopeful my action plan was ready, and part of me wanted to believe that maybe her team really would surprise me with a thoughtful, effective education plan for Marc, even if they didn't involve me from the start. It was hard to swallow, but I swallowed it. After all, I didn't have a lot of options in my city, and I tried to convince myself that maybe Mr. Smart was naive, but his team wasn't.

Marc had just been dismissed from his first elementary school, and this was his first opportunity to attend a school that was supposedly specialized in autism, with a special education teacher who would be an expert. That alone sounded like music to my ears. I told myself, *"Whatever, if he doesn't want the meeting, so be it. The important thing is that Marc is finally in a place designed for kids like him. This has to make a difference! Finally, Marc is in the place where he belongs."*

It was a terrible mistake. Every time I ignore my gut instincts, I regret it, and this time was no different.

Marc started at the new school. His special education teacher was kind and humble, but that was about it. Every day, I'd pick Marc up and ask the same question: "How was Marc's day at school today?" The response was always the same—an uneasy look on her face, a mix of gentle disapproval and forced kindness, trying to soften the blow.

"Well," she'd begin, "he's struggling with the plant on the stairs. Once again, he threw the pot with the plant. It wasn't very easy. He has to learn. He's sweet, though—he has a beautiful smile..."

Every report was the same: behavior after behavior, pitfalls with no learning or progress in sight. She never mentioned anything she had done to help Marc, never talked about any strategies she was using, just a bland recounting of the difficulties they faced with him. As I walked through the streets, I often asked myself if it was even worth it to ask the same question, knowing I'd get the same answer. "We're struggling. We don't know what to do with Marc, but I'll keep being nice to you."

Did it make sense to keep asking and hurting myself with every reply? Probably not. But I kept asking because I didn't know what was really going on with Marc, and that teacher was my only source of information. And so, I suffered through it every time. Marc was suffering, too. His behaviors at home had only gotten worse since starting at the new school, but back then, I didn't see the connection. Now, in retrospect, it's obvious.

A month passed, and the principal, who had previously rejected the idea of a meeting, now requested one. Xavi and I went. I was over-prepared, as always, but what I didn't expect was the complete lack of interest in hearing me out. Mr. Smart had invited his counterpart from the OAP (a department of the Catalan education system that guides schools on placements for children with special needs). As is often the case with arrogant ignorance, they both dismissed any input from us as Marc's parents. They weren't interested in hearing our observations or our understanding of Marc's strengths and challenges. To them, our insights were just annoying distractions from their predetermined agenda.

The two "experts" clearly believed they knew everything they needed to know about Marc. They were there to judge, to be heard, and to deliver the first warning.

"We've called this meeting to inform you that Marc is not benefiting from this environment. He doesn't fit here," they said, their voices were firm. They backed up this harsh statement with a precise list of all the things Marc couldn't do and all the behaviors he had exhibited over the past month—an array of "proof" to justify their decision.

That meeting was the second worst of my life—there was no room for my voice, no empathy, no respect. It was the perfect example of how a combination of ignorance, unpreparedness, and arrogance can deeply harm a child with autism and his family.

I went home filled with rage, unable to believe what I had just experienced. It was the time when the "Yes We Can" campaign had paved the way for President Barack Obama in the U.S. I resonated with that slogan on a deep level. It reflected one of my core values: *effort pays off*. If you want to achieve something, you roll up your sleeves and make it happen. That was my attitude toward Marc's situation, and I couldn't accept anyone in his life not sharing that mindset.

I kept asking myself, *"Do these people—the main teacher, the special ed teacher—have milk in their veins instead of blood?"* The injustice, the betrayal, the abuse of power, and the sheer ignorance in the face of a family crying out for help, support, kindness, and understanding were unbearable. For the first time in my life, I felt real hate. Writing about it now, I realize it's an emotion that I carried on for a long time.

At that point, I had read so many books on autism and had been in close contact with professionals who were helping me understand Marc's condition. I had worked hard to come to terms with his autism, to accept him as he was. That meeting should never have happened. It was like a tornado suddenly ripping through the house I had been carefully building, shaking my family to its core and leaving our dignity shattered on the ground. We were left wounded, crawling in the dust, marginalized, and abandoned. It stirred a fire in me, an indignant rage. *"Nobody disrespects my family. Nobody gets to be unkind to Marc—not while I'm still breathing."*

But the harsh reality was that I couldn't stop it. I was vulnerable, made powerless by autism. *"Autism sucks!"* I thought. All those books about the road to acceptance felt like lies. *"Accept? Accept what? Autism? Accept Hell?"*

As summer approached, I needed a place for Marc. I reached out to Esplai El Timbal, the youth-run organization that had been so helpful in previous summers. Their young leader, full of energy and kindness, asked me a favor. "Silvia, could you ask Marc's school to fill out this form? We've realized Marc needs one-on-one support, and we want to ask the city council for funding to have one of us dedicated just to him."

"Of course!" I said, loving the idea. "They'll totally support it because Marc already has an aide in class."

The next day, I handed the request to Marc's teacher. The day after that, the principal came to me, his tone dripping with condescension, his eyebrows practically jumping off her face.

"We are not signing this form. How dare you ask for a teacher's signature and a recommendation?" he snapped, his voice smug and condescending.

I was speechless. My blood was boiling again—anger rising through my body like steam under pressure. "WHAT?" I interrupted him, unable to control my disbelief. "You just need to state what you already do for Marc. All you have to do is confirm that he has an aide in class. It's not official; it's just a simple statement that would help Marc during the summer, and you refuse to sign it?"

"No," he said, with unwavering arrogance. "This is none of my business."

There was no sympathy in his words, no sense of responsibility. Signing the form posed no risk to the school, no liability, no impact at all. Yet he refused, as if Marc's well-being—and mine—didn't matter. It wasn't his problem.

I folded the paper, shoved it into my pocket, turned, and slammed the door with all the strength I could muster. I had never been so furious. My frustration was overwhelming, the injustice unbearable. It felt like I was burning in hell, the boiling rage coursing through every vein and artery in my body.

My friend Titin once again became my lifeline, pulling me out of the burning rage that consumed me. Our Thursday lunches were sacred, a much-needed oasis of understanding and common sense. Titin's love and wisdom were like cold, refreshing water that helped me slowly rebuild my self-esteem and dignity, which had been so brutally attacked. My most sacred values had been shaken, and I needed heavy doses of her support to stand on my feet again.

Then came the day when Mr. Smart fired Marc—and our entire family—from the school. Like a coward, he kicked Marc out without a moment of reflection on how the school was failing him. Their mission was to help children like Marc, but no one ever told them they were doing a bad job. The director and her partner from the Catalan government, who was clearly calling the shots, repeated their favorite line: "Marc is not profiting from this environment. He doesn't fit here." Their faces were plastered with hypocritical smiles as they uttered the words. Hand in hand with the government official, they not only expelled Marc but destroyed our family, especially me. And they dared to call us into a final meeting to formalize the decision.

So there we were, in another meeting—this time with the two "bosses," the special education teacher, the regular teacher, government representatives, and Xavi and me. The meeting began, and we were nothing more than "mom and dad" to a room full of people I had never met before, alongside the two leading persons who had orchestrated this disaster. They even had the nerve to hand out an agenda. *"At least there's some organization,"* I thought and asked for my copy.

But their response? "No, parents don't get a copy. This is confidential information."

"What??" I couldn't believe it. Xavi and I exchanged a look that said it all—we were being bullied. The entire meeting had been pre-decided and pre-discussed, and we were the least important people in the room. We were just there to listen, to comply with hidden agendas prepared by people who were supposed to serve our children. But instead, they were using my own taxes to attack my family and my son. That meeting was the worst of my life. My anger and frustration were infinite. I felt completely alone in a country that had turned its back on children with autism. All my dreams and hopes for Marc had been dismissed.

After that horrible meeting, I tried one last effort. I thought if I could meet with Mr. Smart in a more casual setting, I might change his perspective. I could appeal to him as a person. Maybe he would listen.

That Wednesday, I approached him in the schoolyard before picking up Marc. After some polite chit-chat, I said, "Do you know that Marc loves M&Ms? You'd be surprised at what he can do for an M&M. I've used them at home with spectacular results."

He nodded, his expression vacant, and then leaned in, lowering his voice as though he was about to share a piece of juicy gossip. "Silvia, you can't imagine what Marc is doing at school… He can't even go to the bathroom on his own," he said, his face twisted with disgust. "I found him throwing the toilet paper roll into the WC," he added, his eyes wide with horror as if this were the most grotesque thing he'd ever encountered.

His words hit me like a slap in the face. He thought he was shaming me as if I didn't already know Marc's struggles. For six years, I had gone to the bathroom with Marc every time he needed to go—and every time I needed to go. His attempt to horrify me with Marc's "gross" behavior only showcased his ignorance and lack of compassion.

"Give Marc a chance," I said, trying desperately to maintain my composure. "I've seen improvements at home. I could sit with the specialized teacher; I could connect her with Marc's therapist…"

But the answer was always no. His features remained unchanged, that same arrogant smile stuck on his face. His blonde hair perfectly parted in the middle, his perfectly rounded blue eyes, his static sug-arcoated smile and he rarely blinked —it all reminded me of a wax figure: lifelike on the outside but dead inside.

In my desperation, I humiliated myself. "What school will I find for Marc? There are no other openings for children with autism right now. Everything I've done, every improvement Marc has made, every bit of support Xavi has given us—all of it led us to this school, the one that's supposed to support families like ours. And now you're saying Marc doesn't fit here? It doesn't make sense. Please, give him a chance, give us a chance!" My hands were clasped to-gether in a silent prayer, my lips trembling as I fought to hold back the flood of tears. But they came anyway, pouring down my face in a thick, unstoppable stream.

I was able to taste the salt of my tears as they fell, my mouth dry and aching. There were no more tears left in me, just a constant flow of grief spilling out. My sobbing stopped, but as I looked at Mr. Smart again, he was looking like a statue—completely dehumanized. His ears, his heart, were closed. His mind had been made up long before we even sat down in that first meeting. He was just following his protocol, carrying out the final execution, no matter the setting, no matter the tears, no matter the desperation.

He wasn't human.

After that experience, I began to realize for the first time that Marc's condition—his struggles with tasks or his inability to do certain things—wasn't necessarily the main barrier to his happiness and growth. The true obstacles were people like those I had encountered:

dishonest individuals who refused to give him the chance we all deserve. The cruel irony was that these people had been paid for years to do the exact opposite. It would take me more time to understand that not everyone who serves in roles meant to help others is motivated by a sense of duty or a desire to provide quality care. Some are simply there, performing their jobs with a lack of care or skill, guided by motivations that have nothing to do with the people they are supposed to serve.

Looking back, I've learned to recognize that not all individuals in humanistic services are truly passionate about their work or interested in making a positive impact. Sometimes, they are too arrogant to admit they don't know enough, and other times, they just aren't invested. They go through the motions with a confidence that far exceeds their abilities. I learned to spot these people, and now, when I encounter them, I make it a priority to distance myself from them as quickly as possible.

Back then, I believed I could change those individuals, that I could appeal to their humanity and find the kindness I assumed was hidden within. But it was damaging for both Marc and me. I was vulnerable, uncertain about how to help Marc, and unsure of how to navigate his challenges. It was easier for people to blame Marc, rather than admit their limitations or wrongdoings.

With time, I now see that I should have trusted my instincts more. I knew Marc could be helped, but I doubted myself. Today, I would tell my younger self to believe in her own strength. Sometimes, instead of trying to convince people who don't want to be, you have to let them go. When someone hands me a ruled piece of paper, I

now write in the other way. If something doesn't add up and someone tells me, "That's just the way it is," I find a way out. I no longer
waste my energy on people who aren't interested in helping Marc or
me.

Marc, at Six Years Old

That school experience took a toll on my health. When Marc wasn't
around, I would cry and cry, feeling as small as an ant. Not that ants
should be underestimated—they're one of the creatures I truly admire in the animal kingdom. Humble, small, but capable of incredible feats. Scientists say ants can carry more than a thousand times
their weight. I always wished I could be that strong. But at that time,
I felt weak, depleted, and so small.

That time, it was my sister-in-law, Gina, who helped me. During a
phone call, I confided in her about how low I was feeling. She gently
suggested, "Maybe you're suffering from depression?"

"I don't think so," I answered quickly. "My tears come from real
problems." But as often happens, her words planted a seed of doubt.
Eventually, when I hit rock bottom, I told myself I had nothing to
lose and made an appointment with a psychiatrist.

The medication was exactly what I needed. The conversation with
the psychiatrist helped, too. She explained, "You have to understand
that reality is one thing, but how we see it and live it is something
else. The way you're experiencing your reality with Marc is overwhelming because your brain chemistry is working against you. It's
not a weakness; it's chemistry."

She then drew a diagram of an eye with low serotonin and another with a "happy" eye and a full tank of serotonin. "Once your serotonin levels are back to normal," she said, "that's when you have to do your homework. People often feel better and stop there but don't. Once you feel stable and in control again, work on your issues. Figure out what triggers your sadness, how to cope with it, what works and what doesn't. Don't let the good feelings distract you from working on yourself."

It was an eye-opener and a game-changer. I had never heard anything like that before, and I was amazed at how the lesson started with chemistry but didn't stop there. In two weeks, I began to feel better. Silvia was coming back, all because of one tiny pill in the morning. What a discovery!

I stayed on the medication for several months. After making some changes in my life, I consulted my doctor about reducing my dosage. He gave me very specific instructions on how to taper off slowly, and I eventually reduced it to half a pill. After more progress, I was able to stop the medication completely. I had recovered from my depression.

However, the psychiatrist warned me, "Depression may come back. If reality ever becomes too much again, don't hesitate to level your serotonin. Depression can return, but you'll know what to do."

Depression was gone, at least for now. My attitude had shifted, and although Marc's behaviors were still a constant battle—a permanent "red code" in my life—I approached it with passion, love, and acceptance. It was tough, but it was my priority, and it no longer made me sad. I told myself that I'd had my share of pleasant experiences growing up, and now it was Marc's turn. My role was to support him, no matter what. Everything else became secondary.

That didn't change the fact, though, that physically, I felt fragile—not sick, just delicate. Every day, at some point, I'd feel sick to my stomach from nerves, hoping that Xavi would come home earlier than usual so I could finally take a steady breath, even if it were just for a little while. My ultimate dream became simply spending a moment alone with my breath, just to relax.

On the professional front, however, I was thriving. I had been promoted to a global role in the business platform I was part of and was appointed as the Business Intelligence Leader for Performance Coatings. It was by far the most interesting and challenging position I had ever held. The role was entirely new, and leadership in Wilmington, DE, expected me to create it from the ground up, which was right up my alley. I designed the entire organization and strategy, and it turned out to be a winning structure.

This part of my life brought balance, especially when I felt the weight of my struggles with Marc. Despite all my strategies, I never saw them as major successes. However, looking back now, I realize that my expectations were unrealistic. It's hard to know what to expect when you're navigating the unknown, and although I had learned a lot about autism, Marc's case stood out in ways I didn't fully grasp at the time. His autism was different—more challenging—even for experts in the field.

Finding therapists experienced in behavioral therapy who had time for Marc was incredibly difficult. After months of searching, we finally found some good therapists, but none were available in Terrassa. We had to travel to Barcelona for therapy. Marc had been in behavioral therapy since he was six, and we never discontinued it.

Barcelona is only about thirty minutes from Terrassa by car, and at first, I'd drive Marc myself. But it quickly became impossible. He began having behaviors in the car—, he just released his seatbelt and laughed, and I would have to stop the car until he buckled back in. But, as always with Marc, things escalated. One day, he released his seatbelt and then grabbed my hair, pulling so hard that my tears burst in pain. He wouldn't let go, and I had to suppress my tears and pretend it didn't hurt so as not to give him attention. I pushed his hand toward my hair, but he still wouldn't stop. Desperate and in extreme pain, I decided to try a different tactic.

"Marc," I asked, "do you know how to be a chicken?"

Yes, that was my crazy idea… and you know what? It worked! He stopped pulling my hair and started acting like a chicken. He wouldn't stop clucking and flapping his arms. It was bizarre, but it got him to release me. That was the last time I drove Marc to therapy.

From then on, I decided we'd travel by train. Europe's train systems are amazing—punctual, widespread, and eco-friendly. I've always loved trains, but trains with Marc? That was another story.

There are reserved seats on trains for people with disabilities, pregnant women, or the elderly. Surely, Marc's autism qualified him for one of those seats, right? The reality, though, was that those seats were always taken. And since autism doesn't affect physical appearance, no one saw a reason to give up their seat for him. Marc, like many kids with autism, is adorable and looks completely typical to the untrained eye. So we'd sit wherever we could, but Marc's behaviors in public often made things difficult.

One day, an elegant older woman was sitting across from us. She had a prominent mole on her nose. Marc, in his blunt way, pointed at the mole and said in Catalan, *"Mama, té malet,"* which means, "Mom, she has a booboo." I could feel my face flush, but before I could say anything, Marc added, "She's going to die!" Loud enough for everyone to hear.

I was mortified. The woman looked at me with disgust as if I were some kind of monster for allowing my son to say such a thing. I immediately tried to explain, "He has autism," but back then, there was very little awareness of autism in Spain. The explanation didn't help.

"Your son is so rude!" she snapped.

I wanted to disappear right then and there.

It became more and more obvious that dealing with autism itself was less of a challenge for me than coping with the ignorance and arrogance of others. Ignorance, combined with a lack of kindness, is incredibly harmful. Once I recognized this as a key problem, I began working on solutions and developing strategies to manage difficult people.

On our next train ride, I decided we would sit in the reserved seats. As usual, the section was full, but it was clear that most people didn't need the seats. I stood there and said, "Could anyone please be kind enough to stand up and let my son sit?"

216

Someone responded, "He seems fine."

To which I replied, "My son needs this seat. Can someone please stand up? Also, if you sit in front of him, you might get kicked—he does that, and he can't control it."

Two young men stood up and let us sit down. I thanked them.

In front of us was a woman who rolled her eyes, clearly annoyed. She didn't have a mole like the woman on the previous ride, but she did have noticeably large breasts. Marc, with a look of wonder on his face, couldn't stop staring at them. I warned her, "Excuse me, I can tell from Marc's movements that he's about to start kicking, and I won't be able to stop him. If you don't have any impairment, it might be safer for you to stand. I'm really sorry—autism can be very complicated."

She didn't even acknowledge me. A few seconds later, the little kicks started.

At first, she pretended not to notice, but as the kicks grew in intensity, she snapped. "You're a bad mother! You need to educate your child! He's so rude!"

I was so exhausted from people judging me, from their refusal to cooperate or empathize with Marc's condition, that I had no patience left. So I calmly said, "You're right. I'm a bad mother. Why don't you keep my son for a week and teach him manners? I'll meet you here next week. Thank you!" Then I walked away. Marc was still laughing, his eyes were never leaving her chest, and his kicks continued.

At some point, she panicked and called after me, "Come back! Come back!" I returned, picked up Marc, and said nothing more.

I never stopped using the train, and over time, it became less difficult to ask people to stand up. It became routine for me to get Marc's seat and keep the one in front of him empty. I'm sure most people didn't fully understand the situation, but they could see how confident and determined I was, explaining everything in a calm, matter-of-fact tone. They simply followed my advice. Each time, I told myself, *"Another battle won!"* But it was still so exhausting.

I found documentation of Marc's behaviors when he was six—what triggered them, what his motivations were, and my planned responses. My goal was always to teach him how to behave, redirect him in the moment, and guide him toward more appropriate behaviors while giving him natural consequences when necessary. Implementing those strategies was key to managing Marc and was one of the most successful tools I've ever had. Still, Marc continued to be Marc, and the challenges never ceased.

Chapter Twelve
What a Refreshing Ocean Breeze! - My Sunshine, Gerard, is Born!

"The sea does not like to be restrained."

– Rick Riordan

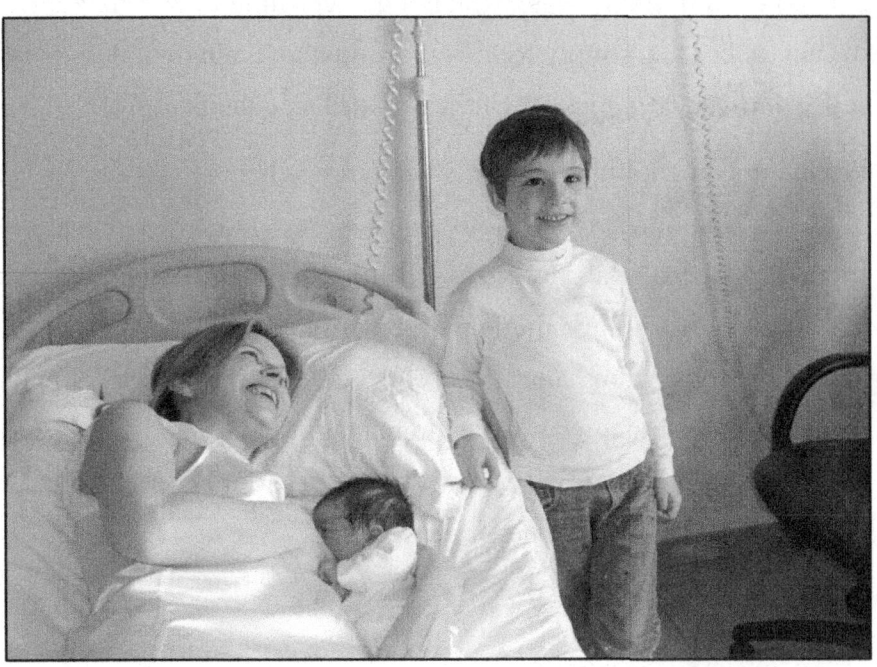

My heart pounded with excitement as I stepped into our usual Thursday restaurant. Titin was already seated, and as always, she could sense the thrill radiating from me.

"Hum," she chuckled, "What's going on? Spill it!"

I cleared my throat, barely able to contain my enthusiasm, as I slid into my seat. "I've decided to have another child!" I declared, grinning widely.

"Are you pregnant?" she asked, her eyes widening, eyebrows shooting up as they practically took over her forehead.

"Not yet, but I will be," I replied with a playful smile, biting my tongue in that goofy way I do. My eyes sparkled, and laughter bubbled out of me.

"What does Xavi think?" Titin inquired.

"He doesn't know yet, but I'll convince him. This child will change our lives, and I'll get to experience motherhood all over again," I said with calm certainty. I had thought long and hard about this, and now was the time to share it with my best friend. "It was never the plan to have only one child. It was never the plan to live my life as a bystander." I paused, then jokingly exclaimed, "SHOW MUST GO ON!" as I bursted into an impromptu impersonation of Freddie Mercury, my right hand dramatically swinging from the bottom left to the top right in a tennis backhand motion. In the process, I managed to knock over both of our beer glasses.

As the gentle waiter rushed over to clean up my mess, Titin mimicked my exaggerated performance, and we couldn't stop giggling like teenagers, tears streaming down our faces from sheer joy.

"I'm so proud of you!" she managed to say between snorts of laughter.

We hugged, grinning from ear to ear.

With her face flooded with emotion now, she said, "Imagine the connection there is going to be between these two brothers."

We kept hugging each other.

In truth, I was utterly drained. The battle with the school had taken every last ounce of my energy, and I had lost—Marc and I had suffered. It was in that lowest of lows that I saw a new light. *"Marc will always be Marc, no matter how hard I try to change him,"* I finally accepted. That realization was a turning point, a milestone. Since nursery school, I had been on a frantic mission to "fix" Marc, to recover the child I believed was trapped inside him, to close the gap between him and the other kids. But my perspective had shifted. I had evolved.

Acceptance was beginning to take root. "If I can't change Marc, I thought, then that can't be my goal anymore. I need to revise my strategy. This isn't a sprint—it's a marathon. And if I want to do anything meaningful with my life, it's now or never."

I had always wanted two children, but I kept telling myself I needed to work on Marc first, and once I'd managed to improve his behaviors, then I would think about another child. What I hadn't anticipated was that by the time Marc was six, he was essentially the same as he had always been. Every year, the gap between him and typical kids grew wider. He was developing on his own curve, and I realized this was Marc's curve, Marc's life.

The idea of comparing him to typical children—or hoping to "level him up"—started to feel grotesque. The reality was presenting itself to me in all its undeniable truth. I didn't doubt anymore. I didn't necessarily embrace that reality, but I knew it was ours to live with. And it wasn't as overwhelming as it used to be. I couldn't unsee the fact that Marc would always be Marc, and it was not within my power to change that.

I was learning to understand Marc better, and through that understanding, I started to help reduce some of his more maladaptive behaviors. That was huge. But still, our life wasn't less frantic. The "red code" was still in place, and we were living day by day in crisis mode, just as we always had. Marc was a work in progress, as we all are, but progress was measured on his terms—by Marc's own rule, not by the magical rule I had dreamed of for so many years.

He kept doing most of the things he had always done. The "progress" was that some of his more disruptive behaviors had decreased slightly. Instead of four races down the hallway each day, there were two. Instead of yelling for four minutes, he yelled for three. It was progress, yes, but on Marc's slow, steady rhythm.

I resolved, *"I accept Marc as he is. I will no longer try to change him. I will keep loving him unconditionally. It is my life's commitment to do everything I can to give Marc the best future possible in this world."* That became my guiding principle.

And it was then, in that moment of acceptance, that the idea of having another child was born—like a candle flickering in the darkness.

I knew there was a genetic component in autism, so my next step was to consult with a geneticist. While my heart was set on having another child, I wanted to approach everything with a clear head. I've always tried to keep my feet on the ground, even when my mind is soaring in the sky. To my surprise, the geneticist explained that as a couple, Xavi and I had a 3.4% chance of having another child with autism. What shocked us even more was that new parents have a 3%

chance, too—they just aren't usually aware of that risk. The difference between us and other couples wasn't significant, and that fact sealed our decision to move forward with trying for another baby.

That said, this is information I received from a geneticist more than a decade ago. I'm not a doctor, and I would never pretend to be one. Always consult with a geneticist when making decisions like these.

Everyone around me was scared that we could have another child with autism. But I wasn't. My gut reassured me, telling me this wouldn't happen. Still, I always like to have a backup plan, even for the worst-case scenarios. So, I had my response ready, *"Could a child with autism have a better family than ours? If I have another child with autism, I'll be so prepared to help him right away that I'm ready to take the risk."* The truth was, I wasn't afraid.

A few months later, the miracle happened. I was pregnant again. A boy—my sunshine, Gerard—was growing inside me.

My pregnancy felt like a fantasy. Gerard was already working his magic from within. Nuri, my mother-in-law, and Xavi were so generous, taking over many of my daily responsibilities with Marc so I could relax. I vividly remember a precious dream I had of Gerard before he was born. In the dream, I saw Gerard inside my womb. It was a close-up of his tiny face, and I studied every detail. His little nose curved gently upwards, giving his face an expression of pure gentleness. His long eyelashes mirrored Marc's—a testament to their brotherhood. His lips were full and thick, painted a rich hibiscus red, resembling those majestic flowers. These lips were from Xavi, a feature my mother had always pointed out with affection when she spoke of him. To her, they made him unique, and I adopted that belief.

In the dream, Gerard gently opened his eyes as if to see me. His eyes were perfectly round, the whites so pure they looked like freshly fallen snow. His pupils hadn't yet developed their color, but I wondered if they might resemble mine. Yet, Gerard's eyes looked more relaxed, as if they carried a refreshing breeze within—a promise of peace and kindness.

During my pregnancy, I continued to work because I felt privileged to do so. What surprised everyone, including me, was that my creativity and assertiveness skyrocketed. It was so apparent that I sparked a debate within the corporation: some leaders wanted to propose a higher bonus for my outstanding performance, while others opposed it because they knew I'd soon be working part-time again. I reveled in the conflict, feeling flattered by the attention. Everything around me was running smoothly, and I felt on top of the world.

I cherished the roundness of my body, especially in the eighth and ninth months. When I was pregnant with Marc, he was taken from me at the start of my eighth month, so I never got the chance to experience my body fully expanding, to feel the weight that made every step a challenge to my balance. This time, I embraced those moments and their uniqueness, treasuring them as one of the most precious gifts life had offered me. I was grounded and filled with confidence, and a permanent smile seemed to live within me.

Gerard was already bringing light into my life, even before he took his first breath.

Gerard is Born!

Marc, at Seven Years Old

The warmth was comforting, like being wrapped in the softest cashmere blanket, and I felt completely at peace. Then I noticed its wetness, and that woke me up. I was lying in a pool of warm water—my waters had broken. The bottom sheet of the bed had held it all in place, and my body weight kept it from spreading. I nudged Xavi. It was four a.m. "My waters broke," I whispered.

"Oh my God! What now?" he blurted out, panicked.

I took my time to respond, savoring the uniqueness of the moment. I let the warmth wash over me a bit longer, melting into the anticipation of my child about to enter the world. The saltiness of my tears lingered in my mouth, adding to the sweetness of it all. I turned to look at Xavi. He was frozen, waiting for my next move.

"Okay, we need to start counting contractions. If they happen every five minutes, last for at least one minute, and go on for an hour, then we head to the hospital."

Xavi looked at me in disbelief and boomed, "Silvia, get in the shower! We need to go now!"

I smiled, noticing how calm I felt in contrast to his urgency. I stood up, giggling as I made my way to the shower.

Hours later, I found myself sitting in a hospital chair, waiting. The midwife came in periodically to check my dilation.

"Not yet," she would say, in the same bored tone a plumber might use when talking about a clogged pipe. One of those times, she added, "The doctor asked me to remind you we'll be doing a cesarean today."

I immediately fired back, "No, no cesarean for me, thank you!"

The nurse explained, "Miss Prats, you know it's standard procedure to perform a cesarean when the first child is delivered that way. Your skin might not hold up under pressure during labor, and the previous scar could tear open, with all the associated risks."

I had heard this from my doctor many times before, and my response was always the same: "No." I looked her in the eyes and thundered,

"I will not allow it. This time, I will have my baby my way. My cesarean was seven years ago; my body can handle it."

She left, silent and stunned.

Gerard was born naturally, without the need to cut anything but his umbilical cord. Sometimes, I still wonder if they even cut that, considering how intertwined we are. The labor was beautiful and easy. Xavi was in the room the entire time. I wasn't sure if his presence helped or not—he's squeamish about blood—but he kept his cool, and I loved him even more for that.

Gerard's head appeared, and Xavi's face contorted. I worried for a second.

"He has a lot of hair!" Xavi snorted.

"How dare you!" I teased him, smiling with a playful glint in my eye.

The doctor chuckled. Moments later, Gerard was placed on my belly, and that warmth flooded over me again. I felt chills of joy. The sensation was like savoring a fresh cinnamon roll—the roundness of his body curled press to mine, the sweetness of the moment, and this life-full warmth transferring to my skin. I could even smell the comforting aroma of cinnamon. Gerard was here.

The doctor encouraged Xavi to hold him. With extreme caution, Xavi cradled Gerard in his arms, the towel wrapped snugly around him. It was a magical moment, a feeling of completeness as our family grew. Xavi held Gerard while the doctor finished preparations, and soon, our baby was brought to face me, his little body wrapped up and tidy.

As I gazed at Gerard, he was exactly as I had already seen him before in my dream. His dark, soft hair framed his tiny face, and I couldn't help but smile. He seemed to be looking at me, his little head lifting with effort, full of genuine curiosity and excitement to meet me. I took a deep breath, embracing the moment fully.

And then, with a sense of peace, I knew—it was confirmed: Gerard didn't have autism.

The midwife gently helped Gerard as he surprisingly began crawling toward my breast. Tears welled up in my eyes. She noticed and asked, "What's wrong?"

I whispered, "I'm not good at this. I couldn't breastfeed my eldest son. I don't produce milk."

She pretended not to hear and focused on her task. Gerard was nearing my nipple now, advancing with a determination that almost seemed impossible for a newborn. I felt a deep sorrow for him, my lips moving silently as I muttered, "I'm broken. I'm sorry."

The midwife clearly finished listening to what she likely saw as a wimpy mom and didn't respond. I stared up at the too-white ceiling, feeling disturbed by its brightness.

But then, I looked down and witnessed something that remains etched in my mind to this day. Gerard was nursing me graciously, and natural. He latched onto my nipple with an energy and confidence so foreign to me that I could only interpret it as a miracle. His movements were rhythmic and graceful, and I could feel the flow of milk nurturing him.

"All these years, I've blamed myself for not being good enough, for not being capable of that basic motherhood miracle. But now I know it was never about me." The realization hit me with the force of a wave. Marc hadn't been born with that ability to nurse; he had sort of learned it later, in his way, on his timeline. And that was okay. Tears of long-held remorse finally flowed as I celebrated this new-found understanding. I wasn't broken. I wasn't a failure. I had been a good enough mother all along. And now, here I was, nurturing Gerard right after his birth.

The midwife, though a bit bewildered by the emotional scene, didn't said anything. But I could imagine her thinking, *"Moms are getting stranger every day."*

From that moment on, Gerard became the sunshine of my life. His smile brought me everything I needed, and it wasn't just motherly love—there was something special about Gerard. Many others who encountered him felt the same warmth that radiated from him. It was undeniable: Gerard was unique in the most wonderful way.

Maternity leave was a precious gift. While Marc was at school, I dedicated all my time and energy to Gerard. It felt like an endless spring, with Gerard blossoming like the most beautiful flower, and I was there, watching him grow every day. His soft, chubby little arms, his rounded cheeks, and his cute cooing noises filled the house like a Sunbeam. Those first three months were overflowed with the cutest baby faces—some people said they were just reflexes, but they were adorable nonetheless. I remember how his lips would form a perfect "O," like a tiny, reddish cheerio crowning his little face. One day, those expressions disappeared, and I cried. I didn't want to let go of that precious time spent admiring my newborn.

But maternity leave eventually ended, and Gerard went to the same nursery school that Marc had attended. I can still see myself standing next to the little fence outside Gerard's classroom, my face wet with tears that spilled from my eyes now and then. I was torn. I shared my distress with Gerard's nursery teacher: "I want to be with Gerard, but I have to pick up Marc from school and be with him. No one is helping me with Marc. I'm stuck. Gerard needs my attention, too. I've hired a nanny to care for him when Xavi isn't home, but I feel awful. I want to be with Gerard."

Gerard's teacher was good at comforting me, saying, "You're doing the right thing. Marc needs you, and you're there for him. Gerard has you, too. Don't feel guilty—you're giving both of your children what they need. You're a great mom."

But it was still so painful to let go of Gerard each day. Every time I left him, I felt an intense ache in my chest, as if I physically needed to be with him. He was my everything.

When Gerard started preschool at El Pi School, Xavi and I attended our first parent-teacher meeting. We were sitting in his class on the ground floor, and my mind drifted to memories of Marc's first pre-school meeting, which had taken place just one floor above. I re-called the frustration of that meeting—the long list of things the teacher had explained that were entirely unattainable for Marc. But then, a commotion in the classroom brought me back to the present.

All the moms were talking at once, and Gerard's teacher asked them to quiet down. "Ladies, please," she said. "Basically, I want to tell you that all of your children are making a mess during lunch. It's not a big deal—they'll learn. But there is one child who stands out, and that's Gerard Feu Planas."

I was completely taken by surprise. All the other moms turned to look at me, and I could feel tears of joy rolling down my cheeks. *"Gerard is a role model for the other kids? What?"*

I remember those endless school meetings with Marc, where I would sit with my notebook and leave the pages empty because nothing ever seemed relevant to Marc. "Remember, handwriting is important," they would say, but Marc never wrote or read.

This moment was different. It was a gift from heaven, something so rare and special. Gerard had given me a glimpse of what it felt like to have a typical child, and I treasured that moment deeply.

***

Gerard turned one, and it was impossible not to fall in love with him. He was all kindness and joy, radiating pure happiness wherever he went. Gerard gave me energy when I had none left, and being near him was a guaranteed source of fun. We would lie in bed together, and I'd hold him tight, rolling to the right, then to the left, and each time, he'd let out the sweetest smile. I'd curl my legs toward my body, encircle his tiny frame with my arms, and suddenly stretch them both out, sending him into fits of laughter. His giggles were contagious, and I could have held him up for hours, feeling like I was holding a weightless piece of cotton candy. Dressed in his little blue outfit with cat ears, he looked even more adorable, and we'd laugh together endlessly. Time seemed to stop when we were together.

Gerard soon became the most important person in my life. During the week, I had to work and take care of Marc. Besides the times Nuri stepped in, no one else could replace me. Xavi's work didn't allow him the flexibility I needed, so I carried much of the burden myself. Xavi noticed how deeply I longed to spend more time with Gerard and how I cried when I couldn't be with him enough.

Seeing my struggle, Xavi made an incredibly generous decision: he would take Marc to the mountains every weekend. For the next year and a half, Xavi and Marc spent their Saturdays and Sundays hiking Sant Llorenç mountain, while Gerard and I stayed home or went out to parks around the city, meeting friends and family. This gesture gave me the space to heal, to breathe again, and allowed me the time to be with Gerard, who brought me so much peace and energy. When Xavi returned, I was ready to dive back into being Marc's dedicated mom, fully recharged by the magical, healing energy Gerard seemed to instill in me. I felt whole, embracing both of my children with love.

Around that time, after the disaster at El Romaní, Marc started attending a special education school for kids with disabilities, L'Espígol. He was there from ages seven to nine, from 2010 to 2012. The principal of L'Espígol was an incredible woman, immediately earning my respect with her care and experience in working with children with special needs. Our lives improved during those years because L'Espígol truly partnered with us. They struggled with Marc, but they didn't shy away from it. They rolled up their sleeves and did everything they could to help him and our family. Despite the limited resources, they made the most of what they had, and I will forever be grateful to that school.

Later in life, when Marc attended schools that were specifically prepared for autism, I realized just how much still needs to be done in our country. It all comes down to resources: teacher training, space adaptation, and everything in between. But in L'Espígol they knew who they were, worked with what they had, and stayed honest and committed throughout. They will always have a place in my heart for that.

Throughout my journey with Marc, I've been blessed with many angels—people who have helped me tremendously, often out of pure love, making the burden bearable in times of despair. One of those angels is Nuri Ricart, my mother-in-law. Nuri is unlike anyone I've ever met. I tease her, calling her *"The Bionic Woman,"* a reference to the science fiction series based on the novel *Cyborg* by Martin Caidin. Nuri is in her late seventies, but I've only ever heard her mention being tired once—just last summer. She and her late partner, Santi, who was tremendously loved by the whole family and who tragically is no longer with us, were adventurers. They were always hiking, skiing, traveling the world, and even parachuting. Nuri's boundless energy and strong personality made her the perfect person to handle Marc. Her energy was so contagious that Santi also took care of Marc as if he was his other grandpa.

With Nuri's confidence and unwavering tone, she could guide Marc and almost make his behaviors disappear. She was certainly equipped for the job. Nuri loved Marc deeply, and it took longer than Xavi and I did to realize his condition. When Marc was with her, he could accomplish the impossible.

I remember one afternoon when she picked Marc up from school, and as usual, they didn't return home until two hours later. "We went for our usual walk and had a croissant and hot chocolate at a coffee shop," she casually announced as she walked through the door, holding Marc's hand and guiding him down the hallway toward his room. Marc, relaxed and content, walked beside her. I was in shock.

"I can't believe it!" I exclaimed. The last time we had taken Marc to a coffee shop, he had broken three cups and two plates, and we hadn't dared eat out for three years. But Nuri had managed to do it, and she talked about it as if it were the most ordinary thing in the world.

Nuri truly was an angel, and her love and strength carried us through some of the most strenuous moments.

Marc was seven when Gerard was born. That day at the clinic, Gerard was resting in his crib when Nuri brought Marc to meet his little brother for the first time. Marc was dressed in an adorable white turtleneck sweater that made him look angelic, but inside, I was terrified. I didn't know how Marc would react to the baby, but I trusted Nuri, so I stayed quiet.

Marc walked over to the crib and peered down at Gerard. A sweet smile appeared on his face, and he just stood there, watching his brother with that smile for what felt like an eternity. Marc never held his attention on anyone or anything for more than a second, so this was different—he was captivated by Gerard's presence. The room was filled with silence, a magical stillness. Time seemed to stop. I was mesmerized by the moment, holding my breath.

Marc reached out, probably to touch Gerard, but Nuri, with her usual wisdom, gently redirected him, preventing anything from disrupting that beautiful moment. From then on, every time Marc was near Gerard, I felt that same intensity. It's hard to explain, but it's as if Gerard brings out a glow in Marc, a light in his face that shines whenever they're together. Marc seems captivated by his little brother. Marc has loved Gerard since forever. Nuri, who lives in Barcelona, has always been a huge help. Since Marc was two, she had seen how challenging it was for Xavi and me to care for him, so she committed to taking the train from Barcelona to Terrassa at least twice a week to spend the afternoons with him. She'd take Marc to all the city parks, giving me some much-needed respite. On the days I knew Nuri was coming, I woke up feeling relieved. In contrast, on the days I had to pick Marc up from school, I felt a deep disquiet that only worsened as the hours ticked closer to dismissal time.

Marc, at Eight Years Old

I felt incredibly privileged to spend time with Gerard. I would lay him down under his little rainbow tent, the same Marc had relished so much, with colorful animals and shiny objects hanging from the two rainbows that crossed above him, which held up the mat full of surprises. Watching him explore every tiny creature with such curiosity was a sublime experience. Then we'd sit in the rocking chair, and I'd feed him. Those moments felt like pure freedom and joy. Motherhood with Gerard was refreshing—a bright ray of sunshine, like splashing in cool water. Sometimes it felt as liberating as being at one of those heavy metal rock concerts I had been to in my life before Marc, where you can do whatever you want because nothing can go wrong. You just dance, sing as loudly as you want, and let your body groove. No one cares. Everything flows naturally.

It was the kind of normal that felt so special and unique to me. Hours would fly by during our playful, relaxed days with Gerard.

When you have a child with autism, you become an expert in evaluations. The people who perform them don't always understand your child, leading to experiences that are sometimes downright surreal. One evaluation stands out as the most absurd. A lady came to our home to assess Marc so he could officially be granted a disability designation, which would later allow our family to qualify as a *numerous family* (families with three or more children), granting us certain benefits in Spain. Ironically, this designation said that Marc counted for three typical children. If I'd had the energy, I would have argued that Marc was more like ten typical kids, but even families with ten children got the same benefits as those with three.

Despite the absurdity of that evaluation, it was just another part of the unpredictable world of navigating life with Marc. We carried on, holding on to the light that Gerard brought into our lives.

Returning to the story of the evaluator, she gave me all the instructions over the phone: "I want you, Mom, out of the scene. We will evaluate him, and only him. You moms spoil your kids with disabilities, and then they misbehave in your presence." I tried to explain to her that Marc's behaviors were quite intense and that leaving him alone could have consequences—for both my house and herself. But she didn't listen.

The day of the evaluation arrived. She walked into the house and, without much hesitation, told me she wanted to speak to Marc alone. They sat at the table, and I watched from a distance.

"What day is today?" she asked Marc.

Marc confidently answered, *"Wednesday."*

She gave me a look that screamed, "See? He's responding just fine. Not what you said at all!"

I couldn't believe her luck. Marc knew the days of the week but only in the sense that he could recite them in order. The concept of *today* being one day or another? He had never fully grasped that. Still, she felt victorious and said, "Now, Mom, please leave the room." So I did.

I hovered in the corridor, and soon enough, I began hearing all sorts of crashing sounds. I rushed back into the living room just in time to see the lamp hit the floor, the chairs scattered everywhere, and the evaluator panicked, sprinting toward the front door as Marc threw his sneakers.

As she reached the door, she said in a flustered voice, "I have enough information for the evaluation!" But before she could finish, Marc's second sneaker flew through the door and hit her on the head.

I couldn't believe what I was seeing, though I had known the interview wouldn't work. This? This was beyond what I could have imagined. It was a day I'll never forget.

In retrospect I remember that other day, it was time to pick up Marc from school. I kept repeating the instructions to myself: *"Today, we'll practice eating the doughnut. I have to stay calm. He'll throw it to the ground, but I'll ask him to pick it up. No facial expression. I'll just say, 'No, Marc, we don't throw food and then eat it from the floor."*

I can still see myself sitting on that bench on Las Ramblas in Terrassa. Marc came out of the school, and I greeted him with, "Hi, Marc! Are you hungry?"

He didn't look at me but exclaimed, "Yes!"

"What would you like for a snack?" I asked.

He looked around aimlessly and mumbled, "A doughnut."

We headed to the bakery, and, as usual, when it was time for Marc to order, the words didn't come out right. Instead of speaking to the patient baker who stood in front of us trying to decipher Marc's low, barely audible sounds, Marc directed his words toward the floor. The baker tried her best, but it was clear she was struggling to understand him. After a few moments, I could feel her eyes on me, politely asking for help.

Finally, I said, "He'd like a doughnut, please."

Now we were back on the bench. "Marc, do you want the doughnut?" I asked.

"Yes," he responded.

I handed him the doughnut, and, as expected, he immediately threw it onto the street. My energy dropped. "Pick it up, Marc," I instructed. He picked it up, ready to continue eating.

"No, Marc, we don't throw food and then eat it off the floor." Together, we threw the doughnut in the trash.

This scene repeated itself day after day. Looking back, I know I could have simply held onto the pastry and created a positive experience for Marc. But at the time, I was convinced he would learn. He didn't.

Today, I'd handle it differently, but back then, I didn't know better. It became our daily torture—one more trial in our endless battle with autism, always hoping for progress, even when it didn't come.

Nuri, Marc's grandma, taught him how to ride a bike without training wheels, something that seemed like "Mission Impossible X" to me. Marc had always loved riding his bike with those little wheels that kept him steady. But once we removed them and he felt the wobble of losing his balance, he completely rejected the bike, running away from it at every opportunity.

Then, one day, Nuri arrived, determined to make it happen. "Come on, Marc, get on the bike!" We were in front of our apartment in Calafat near l'Ametlla de Mar. "Just do it, Marc! Press one foot, and the other follows. One leg, then the other."

Marc hesitated, but the determined tone in his grandmother's voice left no room for doubt. He followed her lead, just like a duckling follows its mother. In front of my disbelieving eyes, Marc's feet started moving in a steady rhythm—left, right, left, right—while Super-Nuri held the back of the bike in an awkward position. Then, once Marc gained momentum, she let go.

Marc was riding a bike. I was speechless, completely in awe of my goddess-like mother-in-law, who made the impossible seem effortless.

One sunny day, I was walking around the city center with Marc. He loved dogs, and Carina had told me it was beneficial for him to interact with animals during our walks. I was not fond of the idea, but instead of following my instinct, I just believed that I'd follow the advice. So that's what we always did. Marc was particularly happy that day, moving with his usual athletic gait, occasionally making little jumps as if dancing and humming a tune as we strolled.

We spotted a young girl with a dog—a mix that looked somewhat like a German Shepherd. I asked her, as I always did if Marc could pet the dog, and she agreed, assuring me that the dog was gentle. Marc reached out and petted the dog, just like he had done so many times before. But this time, the dog jumped on him and bit him.

In an instant, panic consumed me. I watched in horror as Marc and the dog flew through the air, the dog throwing him twelve feet away. Blood covered Marc, and I feared the worst—it looked like it was coming from his neck. I rushed to him and saw that part of his ear was missing. As terrible as that was, it was oddly a relief that it wasn't his neck.

The girl and the dog quickly fled the scene, and soon, people gathered around us, searching for the missing part of Marc's ear. Suddenly, a man approached me, holding Marc's ear in his open hand. "I found it," he said. Someone had already called an ambulance, and we were rushed to the hospital.

Marc had always shown little reaction to pain. I'd heard that people with autism have a high tolerance for pain, but I've never fully believed that. I think it's more about their challenges in expressing emotions. But that day, he looked at me and said in Catalan, *"Mama, fa mal,"* which means, "It hurts, Mom."

I can still see myself running up the stairs at the hospital, heart pounding, with Marc in my arms. Suddenly, he stopped me and said, "I want a gown with those cute drawings." He had seen a child just out of surgery wearing a gown covered in cheerful little designs. I promised him he would have one too. It made me cry—not because of the gown, but because Marc was using his words for something beyond his immediate needs. That was rare, and every time it happened, it filled me with the deepest happiness. In the middle of all the chaos and fear, Marc had gifted me with a precious moment of joy.

Soon after, Marc was dressed in his cheerful gown and wheeled into surgery. I was allowed to stay by his side, holding his hand, and he kept eye contact with me the entire time—another small miracle—until the anesthesia took over.

The next few months were a test of endurance as we tried to keep the bandages on his head without him ripping them off. The doctor had warned us that due to the lack of capillaries in the outer ear, the chances of a successful reattachment were slim, but of course, we tried. Every parent would, no matter how remote the possibility.

Unfortunately, the process didn't work, and Marc had to undergo a second surgery to reconstruct his ear. The surgeon did an excellent job, and although it took me a while to accept that Marc's right ear would always be smaller than his left, I eventually did. It was just one more thing to receive in the long list of things I had already come to terms with in my journey with Marc.

When Gerard turned one, we started taking family trips to the mountains on weekends. These were unique experiences, filled with beauty but not without risks. My attention was always on Marc. Xavi couldn't run because he had Gerard on his back, so I was in charge of keeping up with Marc, who was constantly on the move. From time to time, I would glance at Gerard, who looked so adorable in his seat, taking in the world around him.

"Looks like he needed a nap," I thought, seeing Gerard's little head resting comfortably on the pillow built into his seat. I sighed. *"I need to stay focused and not get lost in Gerard's cuteness."* But it was hard not to. He was discovering nature, and at one point, a monarch butterfly landed on his tiny arm. His eyes were glued to the butterfly, his lips in a pout, not blinking as he watched the insect with deep concentration.

When he finally waved his arm to shoo it away, I could almost hear him saying, "Go away, weird beast!" He was so solid and so cute at the same time.

Suddenly, I heard Xavi shouting, "Maaaaaarc!" I snapped out of my daze and charged after Marc, who had taken off his clothes and was running naked down the hill, laughing loudly. His laughter echoed off the mountains, making him laugh even more.

"Thank God I caught him!" I thought as I finally grabbed his arm and helped him stand. "Let's go back up to Dad and Gerard, buddy! We've got a steep climb ahead, but I know that's no challenge for you." We made it back, and I was exhausted. Xavi had already gathered Marc's clothes and was quietly dressing him. I knew it was my fault for getting distracted, but Xavi didn't said a word.

242

For a while, we walked in silence. Then Marc started singing a song, and soon we were all singing along. Even Gerard made little noises, and we laughed.

"Look, Marc, do you see this long mushroom?" I pointed out. Marc's face lit up. He was fascinated by mushrooms, just like me when I was a child.

We took a break, and Marc got closer to the mushroom. "We don't touch it—it's poisonous!" I warned, and he didn't touch it. Xavi unbuckled Gerard, who walked in his adorably awkward way, his baby steps a little shaky on the uneven ground. He, too, was captivated by the mushroom, and from his perspective, it must have looked huge.

Gerard watched his brother, the mushroom, and me. "No touch!" he repeated, mimicking me. He was such an angel. Marc grinned at him. Moments later, Xavi was chasing Marc around the mountain for fun, and Marc's infectious laughter filled the air. I laughed, too, sitting cross-legged on the ground, feeling tired but happy.

Gerard, surrounded by wildflowers in shades of yellow, orange, and red, was learning how to navigate the rocky terrain. He looked confident. Another butterfly appeared, and I watched with curiosity to see how he would react. This time, he seemed thrilled by the butterfly's presence, having learned that they didn't hurt him. As he sat down on his diapered bottom, he burst into laughter, just as Marc's laughter echoed through the mountains.

When Gerard was eighteen months old, Marc's behavior took a challenging turn. Despite all the attention I was giving to Marc, it became clear that he felt jealous of the attention I was giving to Gerard. After all, before Gerard, Marc had me all to himself. Now,

243

he had to share my attention, and his way of coping with those new feelings was by becoming aggressive—towards me.

This was one of the hardest periods of my life. What's worse for a mother, ready to do the impossible to make her child happy, than to be abused by that same child? I recall situations where I was terrified, but the worst part was the sense that I was losing my dignity and my self-respect because I couldn't control the situation or change the course of action.

I set myself in the backseat of the car, sitting between Marc and Gerard. Gerard was in his little red seat for a baby, unaware of the turmoil around him. Marc looked at me and spit in my face. "Marc, no!" I said, but he did it again. And again. His face turned aggressive as he built up more saliva.

I gave up, enduring the humiliation, until Marc escalated further. He lunged at me, grabbing my hair with both hands and pulling it with all his strength. The pain was unbearable, each hair adding to the torment. I tried to escape, but it was impossible. Xavi pulled the car over on the highway and peeled Marc's fingers off my head one by one. It took him five long minutes to do it, with Marc resisting the entire time.

I was broken, physically and emotionally, abused by my child. It was one of the most painful experiences of my life. From that day on, we never traveled alone in the car without a nanny. We asked Gerard's nanny to accompany us wherever we went. She sat between the two kids in the backseat while I sat in the front with Xavi, my hair tied up and covered with a cap, just in case.

It's a pattern in my life that I grow through challenges, and that time was no different. On one side, I couldn't have been more beaten down, quite literally, by my son. On a scale of one to ten, my crisis with Marc was an undeniable ten. His school was barely managing to keep him afloat, but with their limited resources, there wasn't much more they could do. Marc was growing, and their classes were designed for younger children; they simply didn't have the space or capacity to accommodate his needs. The director knew this, and the constraint added more stress to a child who was already suffering and to a family that had been hurting for too long.

With no availability in any programs that suited Marc, I finally surrendered. *"There's nothing here worth fighting for anymore,"* I told myself. The more I fought, the more I got hurt. This was taking us nowhere.

This realization was another milestone, one that would once again change our lives. Sometimes, you might not yet know what you want, but you are certain of what you don't want—and that in itself is a winning position. I had something solid to hold onto all the energy from Gerard. That energy, combined with my unwavering commitment to never give up on helping Marc, was like a rock—immovable. These feelings were grounded in my deepest values and beliefs, and they empowered me. I became a fighter again, focused entirely on Marc's improvement. My frustration, low self-esteem, exhaustion, and even Xavi's long silences—all of that became secondary. My will to help Marc came first and drowned out everything else.

It was time to reinvent ourselves and chart a new course, though I hadn't yet decided on the next move.

Throughout my career, I'd been offered opportunities to relocate to other countries—once to Austria, another time to Wilmington in the U.S. I had always rejected those opportunities, believing that they wouldn't benefit Marc. His old therapist, Carina Robles, had told me to stop exposing him to multiple languages, warning that it would confuse him further. As a result, as a family, we always turned down those chances.

But I later learned that this wasn't true.

Children with autism have communication challenges that are entirely separate from their ability to learn or speak multiple languages. These two functions occur in different parts of the brain. I read about this much later, and it felt like a door had been unnecessarily closed for us.

One day, I was scheduled to host a major conference call with attendees from Asia to the U.S. The meeting was supposed to start at eight a.m. But that day, Marc woke up on the wrong side of the bed. He refused to go to school and ended up lying on the ground in front of the entrance, kicking me with all the force of nature. Finally, the school psychologist came and literally dragged him into his class, reassuring me that it was the right thing to do.

By the time I made it home, it was already 8:10 a.m. I started the call sweating and feeling awful—unable to process what had just happened and embarrassed for being late to such a critical meeting. It was the first time in my career that I'd ever been late to open a conference call, and I was ashamed. It felt so unprofessional. Right at the start, in a moment of vulnerability, I decided to be honest.

Timidly, I said, "I'm sorry for being late. I have a son with autism, and this morning, he had a tantrum and didn't want to go to school. I beg your pardon."

As I was about to proceed with the usual business, someone on the other end of the line spoke up. "Silvia, I want to talk to you at the end of the call."

I had no idea who that person was, but I stayed on the line after the meeting as requested.

"I'm ready to talk now," I said.

"My son has autism, too," the voice began.

There was a pause, and then, in a quiet tone, almost whispering, he said something I'll never forget. "I'm very embarrassed to admit this, but for years, when my son went to school like yours does now, I used to think that he was the most useless person in the world."

"I must admit it," he continued, "if it hadn't been for my wife, his mother, who enrolled him in every autism program available in Wilmington, Delaware, I don't know where we'd be today."

"She believed in his potential, and she was right!" His tone now sounded triumphant. I was hanging on every word, my ear practically glued to the phone. Back then, it was all audio—no video calls yet—and I didn't want to miss a single thing. "Through effort and training, he's now twenty years old and a proud employee at one of the nation's biggest banks."

Tears welled up in my eyes and spilled down to my lips, and my whole body was shivering. It was the first time I'd ever considered the possibility of Marc being able to work. My entire being was suddenly filled with hope, and I was just contemplating that new reality.

He was euphoric. "Look for an opportunity to move to the U.S.! Do it! Do it for your family!"

When I put the phone down, I knew—*this* was the card I needed to play, the next move for our family.

"I have a good reputation at my company," I thought, *"It shouldn't be that difficult to find an opportunity to move to the U.S."*

That evening, when Xavi came home from work, I didn't even wait for him to settle in before blurting out, "We're moving to the U.S.!"

He looked at me, puzzled, and asked, "Did you get a transfer from DuPont?"

"No," I replied, "but I'll figure it out. We're moving there, no matter what."

The very next day, Marc was scheduled to go on a field trip with the wonderful Esplai El Timbal. Xavi and I went to the bus stop to say goodbye. Every time we said goodbye to Marc, it felt monumental. We would hug him, and he'd march onto the bus with determination, and, without fail, he'd sit down and never once look back. Yet, I'd stand there, waving and shouting, "Marc! Marc!" hoping for just a glance that never came.

I shared my desire to move to Wilmington, DE, with my DuPont direct supervisor in the U.S. He passed the news on to the global operations leader, and they were all excited to help make it happen.

248

But just as quickly as the door had opened, it slammed shut. My supervisor called back to inform me that DuPont was beginning a divestiture of the business unit I worked in, and there was an immediate personnel freeze. My options evaporated in an instant.

That same day, Marc was away on his first-ever overnight field trip, so Xavi and I treated ourselves to a quiet breakfast together—a rare moment of reflection. We sat there, savoring the buttery French croissants, and I asked him, "Through the bank, would you have the opportunity to work in the U.S.?"

Xavi, who was working for a leading Spanish bank as a private banker in Barcelona, looked at me thoughtfully and replied, "I know the U.S. headquarters are in Miami, but that's all I know. I suppose I could look into it."

Later that evening, I saw him in the living room, deep in conversation on his phone. He was speaking with the CEO of the Miami office about the possibility of transferring. Just like that, he got the job.

All the dedication and passion I'd poured into my career at DuPont and all my dreams of advancing further suddenly felt secondary. I quit DuPont. It wasn't even a difficult decision. By that point, I understood how much I cared about Marc and that his needs would dictate the course of our lives. There was no other option.

Marc had been expelled from two schools. The doctors had done all they could, and the therapies—though helpful—were limited and far too expensive. Marc was only receiving a few hours of behavioral therapy each week when I knew he needed at least three hours a day.

His future as a teenager, let alone as an adult, looked so bleak that it was clear he needed a radical change.

That move to the U.S. felt like the only possible solution. A lifeline.

Around the same time, I received a call from my cousin Elena, who had become a doctor and was living in Germany with her husband and family. Although we didn't call each other often, hearing her voice always felt comforting; she was more like a sister to me than a cousin.

"Hi, Elena! What a surprise," I said warmly.

Her voice trembled as she replied, "My mom has pancreatic cancer."

Before I could fully absorb the news, she continued, "There's nothing to be done. She's dying." The words came out abruptly, as though she was pushing them past the pain, her breath heavy with grief. I could practically hear her tears and feel her anguish over the phone. It took everything in me to hold back my tears, trying to be strong for my "little sister."

Just like that, Maite—sweet, gentle Maite—was gone, taken from us far too soon in her fifties. A part of me dimmed. In many ways, I felt like I had lost my mother all over again.

The time had come for my family to leave Catalonia and move to Miami, FL. We gathered with family and friends at the top of Sant Llorenç mountain, at a place called La Mola, and then had lunch together. Rosa—yes, Rosa, the same dear friend who encouraged me to write my biography—surprised us all with a large cake decorated with the American flag. It was a touching gesture, a nod to the new chapter of our lives that was about to unfold.

I also sent an American flag cake to Gerard's nursery. He was only eighteen months old at the time, and his teachers played the American anthem while the little ones made airplane motions with their tiny hands. The video they sent me was beyond adorable. As a keepsake, they created a handprint board with all the children's painted hands. It was such a thoughtful gesture.

Marc also had a farewell party at his school. I brought a cake, and the class prepared a beautiful collage filled with pictures of his friends and heartfelt messages. It was incredibly touching.

The following week, I researched everything I could find about autism services in Miami. One name kept popping up above the rest: Michael Alessandri. Before we even set foot in Miami, I had three conference calls and exchanged numerous emails with "the man," and he seemed so knowledgeable and kind that I was eager to meet him in person.

The bank offered us a "watch and see" trip to Miami to ensure we were certain about the move. My reaction was immediate: "It's Miami—who hasn't seen *Miami Vice?* We don't need a visit; we need to move there ASAP!"

Leaving Nuri behind was one of the toughest decisions we faced. Her unconditional support had been a cornerstone of our lives. But even the thought of missing her didn't sway us from stepping toward new horizons.

We were ready for the next chapter, and there was no turning back.

Part III
By the Atlantic

"Every time I slip into the ocean, it's
like going home."
– Sylvia Earle.

Chapter Thirteen
The beginnings of our American Dream! - Sun, Beaches, and the Untold Kindness of Miami

"Sometimes we are lucky enough to know that our lives have been changed, to discard the old, embrace the new, and run headlong down an immutable course."

−Jacques Yves Cousteau

Two months after Xavi's job opportunity call, we found ourselves living in Miami, FL, where we stayed for seven years.

The family flight to Miami was, simply put, an ordeal. We had booked first-class—not because we were frequent first-class travelers, but to give Marc more space, hoping it would make the long flight more manageable. We even got some medication to help him sleep. Well, let's just say things didn't go exactly as planned.

As soon as boarding was over and the plane taxied toward the runway for the nine-hour international flight, Marc turned to Xavi and asked, "Are we there yet?" Then he added, "I want to get off the plane."

Xavi was in charge of managing Marc since we had anticipated a rough journey, and he was definitely the stronger of the two of us. I sat with Gerard, who was only eighteen months old but completely cool with everything. All our strategies seemed to work perfectly for him. Marc, however, was standing in his seat, yelling loudly and persistently.

Thankfully, I had informed the airline in advance that Marc had autism, so the flight crew was understanding and supportive. "Is there anything we can do for the young man?" one flight attendant kindly asked.

I smiled appreciatively but replied, "No, thank you. It's his first time on a plane. My apologies!"

Meanwhile, Xavi had managed to pull Marc down into his seat and buckle him in, though it was clearly a struggle. "Oh no, you're fine, sir," the flight attendant reassured us, but the stares from the other passengers were unavoidable.

Marc wasn't calming down. First-class passengers began to glance over at Xavi and Marc, whispering among themselves. Xavi sighed, then sighed again. Marc, now fixated on trying to undo his seatbelt, repeatedly peeled Xavi's hands away, determined to stand up and leave the plane. The extra space and luxury of the first class did nothing to soothe Marc's anxiety.

He screamed at the top of his lungs, then burst into laughter, finding amusement in the disapproving faces around him. The more he yelled, the more animated the passengers' expressions became—raised eyebrows, pursed lips—and Marc thrived on their reactions. Xavi was visibly exhausted, his shirt damp with sweat, as he tried to maintain control. I could feel the sweat on my skin, too. *"How are we going to endure this for nine hours?"* I wondered.

I forced a smile at a woman who had finally pieced together that I was Marc's mom. My smile tried to communicate what words couldn't: *"Believe me, we're good parents. We're doing our best, but it's not working right now. I'm sorry this flight isn't as peaceful as you hoped for in first class. I feel terrible."* Of course, a smile can't convey all that, but I didn't dare to say it aloud.

I clung to the hope that the medication would kick in and Marc would fall asleep, but reality had other plans. His eyes remained wide open for the entire flight, his anxiety too powerful for the medication to overcome. Xavi's face showed the strain. His arm must have been hurting from holding Marc, who hadn't stopped trying to break free from his grasp. Marc seemed to think the cabin was some kind of inescapable fortress.

"I need to go to the bathroom," Marc said, almost as a plea. Xavi knew it was a stall tactic but still took him to the restroom, over and over—maybe twenty times in total.

"I know he doesn't need to go," Xavi confided to me during one of the bathroom trips, "but at least we both get to stretch."

When the meal was served, I momentarily marveled at the luxury of it—some smoked salmon, foie de canard, and champagne. I watched as Xavi swiftly declined the champagne. *"Smart move,"* I thought, imagining the chaos that could ensue if bubbly liquid spilled on both of them.

Marc gets served some pasta, and for a moment, he looks pleased. Xavi and I both breathe a sigh of relief while Gerard happily puts away his crayons and smiles at his pasta, content as ever, just as he's been throughout the entire flight. But in the blink of an eye, I see a food tray flying across first class. I know it's Marc. My eyes try to follow the various pieces of the meal, now airborne like missiles aimed at passengers. The salmon lands on the neckline of a woman adorned in shiny diamonds. The foie gras splatters across the gentleman engrossed in *The Times*. The bread, brie cheese, and utensils scatter, with bits of Marc's gourmet chaos finding new homes with other unsuspecting passengers. It was as though "Chef Marc" had prepared a complementary order for everyone aboard.

I wanted to stand up and apologize, but all I could do was putting my hands together in a prayer gesture, shrugging my shoulders in shame. I glance over at Gerard, my little sunshine in the middle of this storm, and I pulled him into a hug. He hugged me back, completely unfazed, his calm demeanor grounding me in that moment.

Finally, we landed in Miami; the nightmare was over. A determined American woman walks up to me and snaps, "This is unacceptable."

I chuckled nervously and immediately responded, "I'm so sorry that you had to endure this. My son has autism. It's his first time on a plane, and these nine long hours have been really tough for him."

Her response took me by surprise. "I can tell he has autism," she said as if stating the obvious. "You should know that those behaviors improve with therapy. You should take your son to therapy."

Her condescending tone was the last thing I need at that moment. I snort slightly and reply, "Yes, I'm well aware. Do you know why we're on this airplane? My whole family is moving to Miami to get my son the therapy he needs for his future."

She looked at me, still with that self-assured attitude, but then quickly replaced it with a wide smile and a hint of surprise. "Well done!" she exclaimed, giving me a thumbs-up. "That's a very good idea indeed."

Upon arriving at the airport, I found myself sitting in a highchair with a phone number I had saved for a parent support organization that helps families of children with disabilities: Parent to Parent of Miami. Gerard was sitting next to me in his stroller, as easygoing as ever. I took out some draft paper from my purse and called the number. Within minutes, I realized I'd found another angel: Nicolette. She patiently answered every question I threw at her, one after the other, while I jot down notes furiously. Five double-sided pages later, I have my first plan of action for the years ahead.

After the airport, we headed to our hotel in Brickell, where the bank had arranged for us to stay for a couple of months until we could find a house, rent a car, and receive our belongings from Spain, which was currently making their way across the Atlantic in a container.

The next day, we took a taxi to the University of Miami to meet the man I had been in contact with from Spain—Michael Alessandri.

He turned out to be everything I hoped for and more. As Executive Director of UM-NSU CARD, a powerhouse autism organization in South Florida, he was truly an autism champion. Little did I know then that he would become a steady presence in our lives from that day forward. Michael was like a lighthouse for autism in South Florida, his light visible all the way from Barcelona, and it never dimmed. With his guidance, we mapped out plans for Marc right from the start.

Our arrival at the hotel in Brickell was a statement on its own. The moment Marc entered the apartment, the first thing he noticed was the TV screen. In a flash, he pushed it to the floor, shattering it instantly. Xavi and I were stunned, standing there in shock. My heart was pounding so loudly I could hear it in my ears. We hadn't even fully stepped inside when Marc darted into another room. We dashed after him, but it was too late again—the loud crash of a second TV hitting the floor echoed through the suite. Yes, that was life with Marc—no cease-fire just because of our move. In fact, the move didn't ease things; it only heightened Marc's already sensitive nature. As we tried to settle into a new country, it felt like we were walking on eggshells around him.

A testament to how chaotic things were: when we finally got a moment to explore the apartment, I realized we had forgotten to order a toddler bed for Gerard. It became a family joke later how Gerard spent his first night in the U.S. sleeping on a pillow on the floor, like a baby Jesus in Bethlehem, while Xavi and I kept to our usual "night shift," staying on guard.

But Miami itself was love at first sight. Those towering banyan trees, with their aerial roots hanging down like natural chandeliers, took my breath away. They seemed to create endless pockets of shade, offering relief from the city's persistent heat and humidity. As we drove through Coral Way, I was captivated by the majestic oaks lining the street; their branches were arching over the road to form a natural tunnel of love. Each tree's limbs seemed to intertwine with its neighbor, like passionate lovers embracing in the heat of Miami's tropical air. The vibrant green foliage was unlike anything I had ever seen, so lush, so exuberant—it was as if nature had been magnified.

And then there was the Royal Poincianas, their deep red flowers ablaze like fiery exclamation points against the blue sky, a final testament to Miami's intensity. For someone who had grown up surrounded by the more muted tones of Mediterranean woods, with their pines and earthier hues, Miami's tropical plants, with their gigantic, almost cartoonish leaves, were mesmerizing. I even joked to myself that there must be a mad scientist hidden in the Everglades, working some nighttime magic to turn every plant into a green giant.

Being a mango lover, the abundance of mango trees everywhere felt like a personal welcome.

Our first 4th of July celebration was on a crowded beach in Miami Beach. It took us a while to discover the more serene beaches, like the paradise-like shores of Naples, but we made do. We were amused by the overabundance of silicone and muscles strutting around—it was exactly what we'd expected from "Miami Vice." Gerard, in his little American flag t-shirt, looked adorable as we walked along Ocean Drive, soaking in the atmosphere. When night fell, we watched the fireworks explode over the ocean. It wasn't the most spectacular 4th of July, but we did it—we were officially in the U.S., and that was a way to start.

The heat and humidity took a toll on our bodies at first. It felt unbearable, excruciating even, but eventually, we adapted. Living with air conditioning 24/7 was another shock, but that, too, became part of our routine. Miami was full of contradictions to my Catalan eyes. Rain would come out of nowhere, fall in heavy sheets, and then disappear just as quickly, with no logical pattern. It was as if the weather had a personality all its own, just as passionate and unpredictable as the city itself. I remember driving in a torrential downpour, only to hit a patch of dry sunshine a minute later, and then, at the next traffic light, the rain was back again. It was so bizarre. The automatic windshield wiper must have been invented by someone living in Miami!

At first, we found it difficult to make plans around the unpredictable weather, but soon, we learned to go with the flow. "Let's go to the beach!" we'd say, only to be stopped by sudden rain. Eventually, we realized we just had to head out anyway, rain or shine—it always seemed to work out somehow.

One of the most incredible things about moving to Miami was the immediate support we found for Marc, thanks to Michael Alessandri. Within a week, we had enrolled Marc in a summer camp specifically designed to work on behaviors for children with autism at Florida International University. I remember thinking, *"Wait, what? This exists?"* After all the struggles we had faced in Spain just to get

Marc accepted into any kind of summer program, it felt like stepping into a dream. I couldn't believe it—I was like Alice in Wonderland, stumbling into this unexpected paradise for autism.

On the rooftop of that hotel in Brickell, there was a beautiful pool that Gerard absolutely loved. We would spend hours there, splashing around to escape Miami's humidity. One day, we decided to bring Marc along. Since he enjoyed water, we thought he might have fun in the pool. He looked so handsome in his trunks, and everything seemed to be going well. Xavi stayed close to Marc while I played with Gerard. Suddenly, I noticed Xavi's face tense with worry. In a rush, he pulled Marc out of the pool and hurried away. At first, I didn't understand what was happening, but Gerard was still cheerfully floating, so I stayed with him. Then I heard it: "No, noooo! Everyone out of the pool!"

I looked around and, at first, saw nothing unusual. Then it hit me: *"Oh no, he did it—Marc pooped."* Embarrassed and disarmed, I left the pool without saying a word. The hotel staff took over the situation, and that was Marc's last day at the pool.

A few days later, I started interviewing nannies for Gerard in the hotel's business center. It was time to establish some routine amidst all the chaos.

After a short stay in Brickell, we moved to Kendall, living in two different houses before finally buying a home in Palmetto Bay. The Royal Poincianas so enchanted me that when it came time to choose a house, I picked the one with three stunning trees in the front yard. I thought that being close to these trees would bring beauty and passion into our family's life. Our house was perfect—huge, with beautiful walk-in closets that I loved since such spaces hardly existed in Europe. It had a spacious playroom and a large pool with a shallow end ideal for Gerard, and both the pool and the house were completely gated, making it safe for Marc to wander. The house backed onto one of Miami's many canals, and from time to time, we were visited by an iguana who became like a family pet. We'd watch her while having lunch, her back legs on the pavement and front legs on an iron ring surrounding a palm tree. "Look at her, so fit, doing her morning push-ups," we'd joke.

A political event during the midterm elections reaffirmed for me that we were in the right place at the right time. One of our first days in the new rental house in Kendall, I was watching President Obama debate Mitt Romney when I heard Obama say, "...if we're talking about a family who's got an autistic kid and is depending on Medicaid, that's a big problem." Tears ran down my cheeks. It was the first time I had ever heard a politician acknowledge families like mine. It felt like a confirmation that I was now living in a country where the president not only knew I existed but understood the challenges I faced with Marc.

Not only was President Obama aware of autism, but he was also fiercely defending Medicaid, a lifeline for many American families dealing with autism—something that didn't even exist in Spain. He wasn't just speaking about autism at a small event; he was doing it on national TV during one of the most-watched political events in the country, the presidential debate.

With tears still in my eyes, I listened as Mitt Romney responded, "... the revenue I get is by more people working, getting higher pay, paying more taxes. That's how we get growth and how we balance the budget." For a moment, I found myself agreeing with Romney, too. In Spain, even though 42% of the economy is spent on government spending (as of 2023), autism therapies are not covered by the government or private insurance. Families are left to pay for everything out of pocket, making it nearly impossible for 99% of Spanish families to afford the recommended forty hours a week of behavioral therapy. Most can barely afford three hours a week, and back when I lived there, it wasn't easy to find experienced behavioral therapists at all.

Despite its challenges, the U.S. was offering Marc something Spain never could: a chance to truly grow and develop with the right resources.

It was during our early days in the U.S. that I began to understand why the woman on our turbulent flight from Barcelona could recognize Marc's diagnosis so immediately. Since we arrived in 2012, autism awareness in the U.S. has grown immensely. Ads about autism aired on TV, cartoons featured characters with autism, and news stories about children with autism regularly appeared in the media. Autism was becoming normalized, and though there was still plenty of work to be done, the first crucial step—awareness—had already reached a large portion of the population.

At nine years old, Marc was intensely curious, but he also had little sense of danger, and his movements were often rushed and less precise than those of a typical child his age. One day, while I was pre-paring chicken soup for dinner, he smelled the aroma and, eager to explore the science behind the delicious treat, tried to peer into the pot. In his haste, the pot fell, and the boiling soup poured onto his legs and feet, with some splashing onto little Gerard, who, as tod-dlers do, was following his older brother and me everywhere we went. We rushed them both to urgent care. Gerard cried with all his might—understandably so, as burns are excruciating—but Marc, ever stoic, only complained a little, even though his red, raw flesh would have made me faint had I not needed to focus on handling the situation.

Marc was diagnosed with second-degree burns. The hospital imme-diately sent a therapist specializing in autism, and she was incredible at her job. Thanks to her support, the doctors and nurses were able to treat Marc's legs and feet while he cooperated, something that wouldn't have been possible without her help. Gerard, who had a minor third-degree burn on his foot, healed quickly in a few days. Marc, however, started his first day of school in the U.S. in a typical class with a cast on his right leg.

When Marc started attending the summer camp, we finally started to breathe a little easier. Not only was he in a structured environ-ment, but it also helped him behave better at home. It was at this camp that Marc began learning his first English words, and despite his short attention span, he picked them up surprisingly quickly.

We also repeated all the doctors' appointments we had gone through in Spain, this time in Miami. This body of work allowed me to pre-sent Marc's case thoroughly to the school system. However, even in

Miami, no system is perfect. Despite the obvious signs, Marc was placed in a typical class setting, which was a recipe for failure. Infuriated, I picked up the fight. For two grueling months, I went back and forth with different parties in the school system, sometimes engaging in tense arguments, but I never stopped pushing forward. Eventually, Marc was placed in the right setting, with a one-on-one aide in class.

At first, I thought everyone in the school system would resent me for being such a demanding mother. However, much to my surprise, I started receiving tokens of appreciation from many people. What struck me most about Miami was that the more I pushed the boundaries, the more I got back from the community. This became a pattern for me—I was winning battles for Marc, but others were winning too because my determination was breaking down barriers that the autism community needed to overcome. I felt an overwhelming sense of gratitude toward Miami and the U.S. for empowering me to pursue what made sense for my son. This loop of advocacy and positive feedback never stopped during our entire seven years in Miami.

The parent organization that had supported me nominated me as a kind of "change agent" for the community for our triumph in placing Marc so fast and with all the resources he needed in the school system. Soon after, they invited me to join their board, and later, I became the Treasurer. Michael Alessandri, during one of my visits, congratulated me for getting Marc placed in the right school in just two months, explaining that, in his experience, such placement processes could take up to nine months. His words filled me with pride and relief, knowing that my relentless advocacy had paid off not only for Marc but for other children in Miami.

One of the most touching moments came from Marc's special education teacher, Darlene. After an IEP (Individualized Education Plan) meeting where I had recommended revising many of Marc's goals, I left feeling uneasy. I worried that I had been too harsh or suggested too much change too quickly. But later, I found a small silver medal on a thin chain in Marc's backpack. It was engraved with the words, "We are all touched by autism." Darlene, Marc's teacher then, later told me that she had appreciated my suggestions so much that she not only changed Marc's IEP goals but also reviewed and revised the goals of all the other special education students she worked with. Her humility and openness to new ideas touched me deeply. Throughout my time in Miami, I encountered many people like her—individuals who weren't concerned with defending their own ideas but were solely focused on making things better.

Individualized Education Plan (IEP) meetings became an invaluable tool for our family as we navigated the U.S. special education system. With the guidance of Parent to Parent of Miami, this wonderful Parent Organization so dear to my heart, I studied the laws and processes thoroughly. Once I knew it, I found myself surrounded by the best team. Marc's IEP team was extraordinary: his behavioral analyst, Nicolette, the education specialist I'd connected with upon our arrival in the U.S., and Dr. Michael Alessandri. Each of these individuals played a vital role in advocating for Marc. In every meeting, we ensured he received all the support he needed—an accomplishment that made me feel deeply grateful. Within just three months of arriving in Miami, Marc had everything in place, and I couldn't have been more relieved. Although life would undoubtedly throw more challenges our way, this felt like a monumental achievement and a solid foundation for the future.

While we worked on Marc's education, Gerard was blossoming in his way. He attended a summer camp at a Montessori school, and I immediately fell in love with the environment and teaching philosophy. It seemed perfectly tailored to Gerard. Everything was so organized, tidy, and peaceful. At just two years old, he was preparing food in a miniature kitchen, petting the class mascot (a cute rabbit), growing vegetables in the garden, and building colorful block towers. Parents were invited to join in on activities from time to time, and it felt like a dream. I had never experienced such peace and calm with my first child. The garden at the school was like paradise, complete with mango trees full of ripe fruit that the toddlers brought home. Gerard was acquiring language at lightning speed, and every little thing about him fascinated me.

One day, near the end of the school year, Gerard's teacher asked to speak with me. "You see," she began, "Gerard is too kind." I couldn't believe my ears. She explained, "There are a couple of new students who only speak Spanish; their families just moved here from Argentina and Chile. They sit in the back, and sometimes, in the middle of class, Gerard stands up and goes to them. You know we're flexible in Montessori, but when this happened repeatedly, I asked Gerard why.

He said, "They sit in the back because they're scared. When I see that they don't understand what you're saying, I go to them and translate it into Spanish."

The teacher had been taken aback by his kindness and had told him, "Gerard, that's very kind of you, but that's my job. I'll do better so that you don't have to translate for them anymore, okay?" Gerard nodded, understanding, but his kindness left me speechless.

Meanwhile, Xavi was hitting his stride in his new job, although the long commutes and Miami traffic were challenging. His work frequently took him to South America, especially to Venezuela, which was tough for all of us, but every new adventure comes with risks.

Seeing my two children and Xavi so well-adjusted to their new lives gave me the peace I needed to start working as a business consultant. While balancing work, I remained Marc's powerhouse mom and still found time to exchange butterfly kisses and share playful moments with both kids. Sometimes, I managed to get Marc and Gerard to play together, which felt like magic. One of my favorite games was the "mummies game." I'd put both boys in the children's room closet and instruct them to stay inside until I called them out as mummies. "Mummies stay in the closet!" I'd say in my most dramatic, scary voice. Then, I'd call out, "Gerard, you can come out now!" and Gerard would emerge, trying his best to be a spooky mummy, which was absolutely adorable. Then I'd say, "Marc, your turn!" and Marc would come out with such enthusiasm and intention, his face lighting up with a huge smile. That smile was pure happiness, a moment I treasured deeply.

I felt empowered by a system that worked far more efficiently than the one in my home country, and I'd never looked back not a single day. I was proud to be a mother to a child with autism with high support needs, another child who was so kind, and a husband who loved me. Together, we were strong, and Miami had given us exactly what we had been searching for: a brighter future for Marc and our entire family. We were winning, our dreams were becoming true.

Chapter Fourteen
Choose Your Dreams Well because Dreams Do Come True

"The pessimist complains about the wind; the optimist expects it to change; the realist adjusts the sails."

– William Arthur Ward

As a child, I didn't know exactly what life had in store for me, but I knew one thing: I didn't want a boring life. That became my driving force, my motivation throughout all the years leading up to Marc. I sought fun and joy, and the values my family instilled in me from a very young age served as my guiding star. These values illuminated my path and shaped the choices I made.

However, I learned early on that no matter what you plan, life throws unexpected challenges your way. I couldn't control the fact that my brother, Toni, became an addict. His choices were his own, but I still had the power to decide how I would respond. I chose to help him, but in the end, I couldn't save him. That failure ignited a deep anger in me, an anger I carried for years. If I could go back, I'd choose differently. Life has taught me that anger only harms the one who harbors it. Anger breeds more anger. True peace, both within yourself and with others, comes from calm and thoughtful action.

As a teenager, I didn't know that. I carried the trauma of Toni's addiction with me, and it took years to realize that sometimes the best thing you can do is let go. Some things are simply beyond our control, and not every problem is meant for us to solve. Learning to detach from negative emotions has been a struggle for me—my feelings are intense, and I feel deeply. But holding on to anger and shame for not being able to save my brother didn't change the outcome. These emotions trapped me in a cycle of negative thinking that lived in my mind for years. I'm still learning to release these feelings and focus on what truly matters—my purpose and my motivation in life. We all have one but the challenge we all face is to find what it is.

Life is like the ocean. We all experience moments when we effortlessly ride the crest of a wave, moving toward our goals with the wind at our back and the sun lighting the way. During those golden times, feeling appreciated and loved comes as easily as a summer breeze. But it's easy to forget, when the waters are calm, that storms are always lurking on the horizon.

When I was twenty-six, life carried me to a small island—a place that felt safe and happy, just like the one I'd often dreamed of. If I had stumbled across a genie, I would have wished to stay there forever.

Today, though, I think safety is overrated. Safety, while important, can also keep us from taking the risks we need to grow. I have always been someone who thrives on challenges. During my career at DuPont, I had the privilege of taking on tasks far beyond my role, stretching my abilities, and forming connections with incredible people around the world. Their challenges became my own, and I grew because of them. Yet, as stimulating as my career was, I've come to realize that a job doesn't define a person. I used to think it did, but now I know that true growth comes from within, from the entirety of who we are—not just what we do in a job.

Marc, and only Marc, helped me answer what is probably life's most critical question: "What is your purpose?" All my previous purposes and beliefs seemed not to belong anymore in my life after Marc. Before Marc, I had a list of absolute truths that, one after the other, proved to be wrong. I believe that all human beings are free to shape their destiny. But Marc showed me that some people need others to help them find their path. I also believed that my career was the essence of my identity. The day I chose Marc's future in the U.S. over my career, I was following my instincts, but my mind hadn't fully grasped the magnitude of that choice.

Purpose, values, and ethics help us stay true to ourselves. They give us the inner strength to persevere, allowing us to navigate even the stormiest seas without losing our way. My journey with Marc has taught me that our purpose is the compass that keeps our ship steady, no matter what the ocean throws at us.

In my life after Marc, my dream was simple yet profound: to give him a future. For many years, I believed that helping Marc meant changing him. I was wrong. It took me years to realize that Marc, like everyone else, is who he is—and that's just reality. I had to learn the hard way, often through difficult people and situations, that in order to help Marc, I needed help from others. I found the winning team to bring Marc forward in Miami.

Discovering that despite all my efforts, I couldn't force my dream into reality was devastating and infuriating at first. But today, I see it as humbling. It taught me that sometimes, I can't influence or convince others that there are ways to help Marc grow. People like that school director are who they are and might not be ready to learn. Another learning is that if someone isn't adding something positive to your life, it's okay to let them go. Sometimes, fighting has to give way to acceptance. Acceptance doesn't mean you approve of their ways, but that you learn some lessons from that person and move on.

Acceptance of Marc's autism was not a straight line; it was a process that had many different stages, and I knew I wasn't at the end yet. It was also a process of letting go of false expectations while letting in some enigmatic discoveries and new experiences.

It was also an uphill battle to admit that my own country didn't provide the healthcare systems my family needed. But again, that was our reality. Accepting these truths was a key step in persevering toward my dream by finding new horizons.

Miami and the U.S. became the door to Marc's future of opportunity. When you're moving in the right direction, you can feel it—the same way that when you're met with constant resistance, it's often a sign that you're stuck and need to change course. In Miami, I found the village we needed to help raise Marc, and yes, my dream became a reality. Marc had a future, and so did our family.

Letting go of my city, my country, my friends, my family, and my career was challenging, but in a way, it was not. My dream was clear and my priority, so I never doubted for a second.

Moving to Miami, U.S., was the best decision I ever made. I didn't understand it fully then, but today, I know that what we did was adapt to Marc's environment. To do that means recognizing that it is often the typical person's responsibility to adapt to the person with autism and not the other way around. Why? Because the typical person usually has this ability, but it's generally more challenging for the person with autism.

My dream came true; Marc had a future. It was not achieved by fixing Marc the way I had tried so hard for so many years. Marc had a future because we chose the right environment, the right people to support Marc, and because our family adapted.

A dream came true: Marc and his family were awaiting a future filled with opportunity, happiness, and growth.

But Marc was only ten years old. As I looked ahead, I often wondered what the future would hold for him and our family over the next decade as Marc grew into adulthood.

Where would my acceptance process take me next?

What would my next actions be to adapt to Marc's environment?

How would Marc be as a teenager? Would he overcome his behaviors? Would he develop new abilities?

What would be our family's biggest achievements? And our biggest disappointments?

What new angels would we meet along the way? Who would help shape Marc's and our family's future?

How many more deep crises would we still have to endure?

Would I ever be able to give back to Miami and the U.S. for all they had given us?

Would the sacrifices we made for Marc impact our family as time passed?

And what would become of us all when Marc reached adulthood?

According to the Milestones tracker CDC, in 2023, one in thirty-six children in the US had autism where, whereas in 2002, when Marc was born, around one in one hundred fifty children had autism.

As I put the finishing touches on this memoir, Marc is twenty-one. This next chapter of our lives is filled with all these questions—about his future, the choices we will make, the paths that lie ahead and also some very unexpected turns. The answers are woven into the fabric of our ongoing journey, waiting to unfold in the next part of our story.

While uncertainty often accompanies this life, I choose to embrace it with hope. I know that each new day brings us closer to understanding and connection, both as a family and within ourselves. Our journey is far from over, and I invite you to walk with us into whatever comes next: **From Struggle to Strength – Part – II/**

Meet Silvia Planas Prats

Autism Coach | Consultant | Speaker | Author

As the founder of the KINDNESS IN SPECTRUM Foundation and the MIAMI IS KIND Program, Silvia's mission is to bring understanding, support, and kindness to the autism community. Inspired by her eldest son, Marc, who has Autism, Silvia's journey is fueled by his light and spirit. Join us in creating a world where every individual with Autism is celebrated and empowered.

Did you connect with the story? Want to know more about the author?

Follow this QR code to learn more about Silvia Planas Prats.

Would you like to support families touched by Autism, especially those with high support needs (often referred to as severe autism)?

Or, would you like to contribute to the reopening of the MIAMI IS KIND program, which creates employment opportunities for individuals with Autism, including Marc's first job?

Follow this QR code to donate to the KINDNESS IN SPECTRUM Foundation.

Do you have a loved one with Autism? Are you struggling?

Are you looking for new ideas to become stronger or gain a fresh perspective? Would you benefit from advice on improving your life and the life of your loved one with Autism?

Follow this QR code to learn about Silvia Planas Prats as your Autism Coach. Silvia will meet you where you are and assess how she can best support you.

Follow this QR code to book Silvia Planas Prats as your Autism Coach.

Interested in starting a business to employ individuals with Autism?

Follow this QR code to learn about Autism Consultant.

Are you considering hiring someone with Autism? Follow this QR code to book Silvia Planas Prats as your Autism Consultant.

Looking for an Autism speaker for your event?

Follow this QR code to book Silvia Planas Prats as your Autism Speaker.

"Through Autism Coaching, Consulting, and Speaking, I want to share the light that my son and the employees with autism at MIAMI IS KIND have shown me. I call it the 'Spectrum Light.' My goal is to empower every stakeholder in the autism community to transform their challenges into strengths."

— Silvia Planas Prats

About the Author

Silvia Planas Prats is a co-founder of the Miami EmployABILITY Movement and an ardent supporter of families with children with disabilities. Silvia, who is originally from Terrassa, Catalonia, relocated to Miami in 2012 with her husband, Xavier, and their two kids. She brought with her the desire to support her son Marc, an 11-year-old boy with autism who is happy, intelligent, and energetic as he navigates the world in his unique, special manner.

In 2013, Silvia started her lobbying career as the Treasurer of Parent to Parent of Miami. Later on, she rose to the position of Vice Chair of this outstanding organization, where she dedicated her life to helping families that have children with disabilities. Silvia is the founder and CEO of the MIAMI IS KIND Foundation, which Silvia founded in 2015 and that has evolved to KINDNESS IN SPEC-TRUM to support persons with autism and their families wherever they are. She sees a time when persons with autism and other challenges can succeed in the workforce if they have the proper training and assistance and when families get the needed support to provide their children a future.

Her outlook on life has been profoundly influenced by her personal experience as a mother, especially parenting Marc, who has a unique perspective on the world. The difficulties and rewards of raising a kid with developmental disabilities have inspired Silvia to address the issues of acceptance, identity, and the subdued strength that comes from accepting life as it comes. In addition to advocating for change through her profession, she draws inspiration from Marc's unwavering joy and honesty, which always pushes her in the direction of a more compassionate, open-hearted worldview.

Silvia enjoys writing and advocating, but she also enjoys dancing to the Barça anthem with Marc and cherishing the little things that give their lives purpose. Her narration stems from her experiences, both personal and professional, particularly influenced by her leadership positions at DuPont Corporation, as she works to make the world a more accepting and compassionate place for everyone.

Glossary

ABA therapy: Applied Behavior Analysis (ABA) is an approach to understanding and changing behavior in autistic children and children with developmental disabilities.

Autism Spectrum Disorder: Autism spectrum disorder (ASD) is a neurological and developmental disorder that affects how people interact with others, communicate, learn, and behave. Every time the word Autism appears in this memoir, it can be read as ASD.

Asperger's Syndrome: Asperger's Syndrome is a form of Autism Spectrum Disorder. It is a developmental disorder. Young people with Asperger's Syndrome may have a hard time relating to others socially, exhibit repetitive behavior patterns, and have a narrow range of interests.

ADHD: Attention-deficit/hyperactivity disorder (ADHD) is one of the most common mental disorders affecting children. Symptoms of ADHD include inattention (not being able to keep focus), hyperactivity (excess movement that is not fitting to the setting), and impulsivity (hasty acts that occur at the moment without thought).

Developmental disabilities: A group of conditions due to an impairment in physical, learning, language, or behavior areas.

Intellectual disabilities: A term used when there are limits to a person's ability to learn at an expected level and function in daily life. Levels of intellectual disability vary greatly in children.

Condition: This refers to the physical or mental state of an individual.

Disability: A physical or mental condition that limits a person's movements, senses, or activities.

Special Needs: Refers to individuals who require additional support due to physical, learning, language, or behavioral challenges.

Mental Health: A person's condition regarding their psychological and emotional well-being.

Acceptance: The process of recognizing and coming to terms with the reality of a situation, especially regarding one's child's condition.

Communication cards: Tools used to aid individuals with communication difficulties, providing visual prompts to express needs or feelings.

Developmental milestones: Key skills or behaviors that children typically achieve by certain ages, used as indicators of a child's growth and development.

Emotional regulation: The ability to manage and respond to emotional experiences in a socially acceptable manner.

Executive functioning: A set of mental processes that help with planning, focusing attention, remembering instructions, and juggling multiple tasks.

Individualized Education Program (IEP): A plan developed for U.S. public school children who need special education, outlining specific educational goals and the services the child will receive.

Inclusion: The practice of educating children with special needs alongside their typically developing peers.

Meltdown: An intense emotional response, often resulting in uncontrollable crying, yelling, or other forms of distress, typically seen in children with autism when they are overwhelmed.

Neurodiversity: The concept that neurological differences, such as autism, should be recognized and respected as a social category, akin to diversity in ethnicity, sexual orientation, gender, or ability.

Sensory integration: The process by which the brain organizes and interprets sensory information from the environment, which can be challenging for individuals with autism.

Made in the USA
Las Vegas, NV
23 April 2025

21237847R00194